The handbook of environmental education

The 1990s have seen a tremendous increase in environmental concern in all sections of the population. Young people in particular want to know more about how they can contribute to the conservation of the planet, and formal education is beginning to reflect this. The National Curriculum in England and Wales, for instance, includes environmental education as a compulsory cross-curricular theme and in Australia and the USA there are similar moves to ensure that all students are given an opportunity to learn in this area. Joy Palmer and Philip Neal, experienced teachers and teacher educators in primary and secondary classrooms, here explain what environmental education is and how it can best be implemented at school and classroom level. In this handbook, school heads and curriculum coordinators will find advice on establishing a whole-school policy and motivating the staff who need to implement it. Class teachers will find practical ideas for planning and assessing environmental education in the whole curriculum context. Throughout the book, case studies drawn from a variety of settings allow teachers to see how environmental education can work for them, while the final section directs teachers who want to explore certain issues further with annotated lists of organizations in the UK, USA, Canada, Australia and New Zealand which can provide information, class materials and further help.

Joy Palmer is Senior Lecturer in Education at the University of Durham and a past chairman of the National Association for Environmental Education. Recent publications include *Environmental Education in the Primary School* (also with Philip Neal). **Philip Neal** is a former secondary school head, and until the recent past General Secretary of the National Association for Environmental Education. He is editor of the journal *Environmental Education* and has published widely in the area of environmental education and environmental issues.

The handbook of environmental education

Joy Palmer and Philip Neal

Education Library

London and New York

First published 1994
by Routledge
11 New Fetter Lane, London EC4P 4EE

Simultaneously published in the USA and Canada
by Routledge
29 West 35th Street, New York, NY 10001

© 1994 Joy Palmer and Philip Neal

Typeset in Palatino by
Florencetype Ltd, Kewstoke, Avon

Printed and bound in Great Britain by
Mackays of Chatham PLC, Chatham, Kent

British Library Cataloguing in Publication Data
A catalogue record for this book is available from the
British Library

Library of Congress Cataloging in Publication Data
A catalog record for this book has been requested

ISBN 0-415-09313-9 (hbk)
ISBN 0-415-09314-7 (pbk)

Contents

Appendices

Foreword

Environmental education is now well recognized in schools and colleges world wide and firmly established in some of them. Many national and international exchanges of views have taken place. During 1992 each of us was privileged to attend a world conference where environmental education was highlighted. Joy Palmer was at Rio de Janeiro for the Earth Summit in June of that year, attending the Global Forum. Philip Neal represented the National Association for Environmental Education (NAEE) at the World Congress for Environment and Development (Eco-Ed) in Toronto in October, a follow-up to the Earth Summit. Both were able to present papers to international delegates and to listen to other opinions. Although different views on, and approaches to, environmental education are apparent, it is evident that global views have much in common.

Colleagues, both local and overseas, are eager to find out more about environmental education and to develop worthwhile curricula. Surprisingly, few texts exist where an attempt has been made to encompass just what is meant by environmental education in the school system and what needs to be done to implement it in the whole curriculum. It is against this background that this handbook has been written.

We have drawn on our long experience in English schools and colleges and on our involvement with the UK's NAEE and the Council for Environmental Education. At the same time we have tried to use our contacts with other parts of the UK and overseas to exemplify and further the debate. *Any readers outside the English system are asked to transpose the implications of any part of the text which is English orientated to their own situation.*

One of the conclusions drawn from global meetings is how similar are the aims, objectives and methods of approaching environmental education in various countries. Only the specifics of organization for learning and opportunity are different. The handbook has tried to cover as much ground as is possible within the limitations of reasonable size. It follows that some readers may not find any comment on the particular aspect in which their interest lies. For instance one problem throughout the world is lack of coherent programmes in teacher training for environmental education. It has not been possible to concentrate on this here and reference to initial teacher training and in-service training are only made in passing. Providers of resources for environmental education are numerous and any that have been omitted are the victims of restricted space; no other implication is intended.

Whatever the stage of development of environmental education in any school, wherever located, we hope that this handbook will be of some use to its teachers in furthering this vital area of the curriculum.

Acknowledgements

We wish to thank all who have helped with the publication of this handbook. Special thanks are due to Professor John Kirk (USA), Delyse Springett (New Zealand), Steve Malcolm (Australia), Ralph Ingleton (Canada) and Kate Sankey (Scotland) for their assistance with details of environmental education in their respective countries. We are most grateful to Kate Arnold, Stephanie Taylor, Gail Stocker and Mary Seaman for their ideas for teaching about rainforests and population. Many others have been generous enough to allow their ideas and environmental work to be quoted: these include Richard Moseley, Krysia Baczala, Nigel Vaughan, John McGuiness, Don Passey, Ruth Adams, D.W. Walters and Heather Goodson. Jackie Donnelly, the administrator of the NAEE office, has been a great help. Our thanks to them all.

Joy Palmer
Philip Neal

Part I

Setting the scene

The purpose of this Part is twofold: firstly to provide an overview of the development of the cross-curricular theme of environmental education – its aims, definition and content; and secondly to focus on the implementation of the subject in the formal education service today – its objectives, place in the curriculum, student entitlement, and key issues which arise from these. In short, it will be concerned with national and international policy developments in environmental education and what these mean in practice for teaching and learning in schools. Key issues arising will be outlined, and will be carried forward for illumination and discussion in subsequent pages.

Chapter 1

Concern for the environment

A reflection on the conjunction of the two words 'environment' and 'education' raises the key questions of why, when and for what purpose they have been linked. Presumably answers to these questions range from the feelings and concerns of individuals through to events of international and global significance. In the belief that no educational programme of work in this area can be successful without individual commitment and personal concern, we begin with a glimpse at the preliminary findings of a research study in progress at the University of Durham (Palmer 1992) on the development of personal concern for the environment.[1] The first phase of this research is an investigation into formative life experiences of environmental educators who presumably are persons already environmentally aware. They are not to be classed as the general public in this context, with whom it is likely that any increase in environmental concern has been triggered in the main by TV programmes and international disasters such as Bhopal and Chernobyl. The research is based on the assumption that if the ultimate aim of environmental education is to sustain our planet and its resources for future generations, then a related aim must be to provide an education which encourages people to strive towards that goal. Presumably, if environmental education is about producing well informed and environmentally active adults, then those responsible for it should have some idea of the kinds of learning experiences which help to influence the development of environmental care and concern.

The research technique involves retrospective analysis of the experiences of environmental educators who currently demonstrate their personal care and concern for the world in their everyday lives. Participants in the study were invited to supply details of their approximate age, gender and of their present activities which demonstrate an informed and responsible approach to environmental matters (e.g. practical conservation, recycling, belonging to organizations active in environmental affairs, enjoyment of the outdoors, living a 'green' lifestyle and reading books and journals about environmental issues). The purpose of seeking this latter information was to ensure a sample of subjects who demonstrate genuine and practical concern for the world, rather than paying lip service to the essence of environmental education. Participants were then asked to provide an autobiographical statement of life experiences and formative influences which have contributed to their present concern for the environment and interest in environmental education, indicating if they consider there to be any single most important influence or life stage. Details sent to participants included the purposes and requirements of the study, but did not give any examples of suggested experiences or influences. Thus the responses were original and free from bias.

A total of 232 usable responses was received, comprising 102 from males and 130 from females. Full details of the breakdown of ages of subjects and analysis of data are provided elsewhere (Palmer 1992), but an overview of the findings raises some key issues relevant to subsequent discussion in this present volume. The autobiographical statements were subject to content analysis, and all experiences/influences mentioned explicitly or prominently by subjects were coded into one of 30 preliminary categories of response. These were then refined and results expressed in 13 final categories, which included a number of subcategories from the original list of 30. The response frequency for the final categories is shown in Table 1.1.

Table 1.1 Number of subjects responding in each category
$N = 232$

Outdoors	211
Education/Courses	136
Parents/Close relatives	88
Organizations	83
TV/Media	53
Friends/Other individuals	49
Travel abroad	44
Disasters/Negative issues	41
Books	35
Becoming a parent	20
Keeping pets/Animals	14
Religion	13
Others	35

The category 'Outdoors' comprised three subcategories: 'Childhood outdoors' (97 responses), 'Outdoor activities' (90 responses) and 'Solitude/Wilderness' (24 responses). A large number of people make explicit and detailed reference to memorable experiences outdoors as a child, perhaps as a result of being brought up in the countryside, going on holidays or being encouraged to play in the open air:

From an early age I was taken to watch fish in the stream and to see the different flowers as the seasons passed. My walks to school took me along country roads where scabious and orchids grew. I was encouraged to appreciate the beauty of the common flowers . . . to marvel at the swallows as they flew at speed through narrow gaps to their nests. . . .

Very strong images persist – swinging on farm gates, rolling down steep fields until dizzy, the smell of new mown hay and the cattle byre, the shade of a huge sycamore, lots of walks to 'secret' places, sitting on large boulders in fast flowing rivers, laughter and sunshine . . . the greyness of the city on return.

I particularly remember feeling the beauty and wonder of nature, bathing in a freshwater pool, walking in woodlands and hills.

For many, such experiences developed into a great enjoyment of the outdoors later in life and numerous outdoor activities are mentioned which have contributed to environmental care and concern: walking, hostelling, canoeing, camping, sailing, mountaineering, backpacking and birdwatching to name but a small selection. Twenty-four subjects specifically mention the significance of solitude and feeling 'at one' with nature through remote or wilderness experiences.

The category 'Education courses' (136 responses) comprised two sub-categories, 'School courses' (51 responses) and 'Higher education/Adult courses' (85 responses). Many subjects talk enthusiastically about experiences at school, particularly relating to 'A' Level courses:

My concern for the environment stems from my increased knowledge about global issues four years ago, when I started my 'A' Levels.

The single most important influence was my 'A' Level ecology field course, which was the only part of my 'A' Levels I enjoyed.

For others, environmental concern was most strongly influenced by courses in higher education:

I believe the single most important influence has been my education. Having degree level input in geography . . . studying developing countries . . . this has heightened my concerns for the future of the planet.

The influence of other people on the development of young people's attitudes, knowledge and concern cannot be overestimated as the research data shows. 'Parents and close relatives' are cited by 88 individuals as a major influence, and another 49 are in the category 'Friends and other individuals'. Many nostalgic accounts detail happy memories of the influence of others:

My granny was a herbalist and taught me in-depth understanding of the countryside, how animals and plants react together; and respect for the environment.

I was brought up by intelligent, caring lovers of the countryside (my parents) who believed that the greatest and longest lasting influences were to be found outside.

Probably the most important influence was my mother, who has brought me up in the belief that any unnecessary waste is wrong.

My parents loved the country. Uncles and aunts were bright green before green existed, growing vegetables and tobacco, making elderberry and cowslip wine, eating all sorts of wild plants and loving birds. My grandparents grew tomatoes, kept pigeons, taught me to milk cows and tickle trout.

My interest and concern was born from the enthusiasm of one particular teacher.

The category 'Organizations' includes subcategories of 'Childhood/ Youth organizations' (28 responses) including Brownies, Guides, Cubs, Scouts and Duke of Edinburgh Award programmes, and 'Adult organizations' (55 responses) ranging from natural history clubs and environmental education associations, through to 'green' political parties and active campaigning bodies. The Scout and Guide organizations can take credit for a great deal of influence on the youth of yesterday and citizens of today:

One of the earliest influences on my environmentalism was my scout training. We were taught how to live in and off the environment without damaging it. . . . When we left a site, all trace of our visit would soon disappear.

Subjects speak very positively of the TV and Media influence (53 responses):

I have always enjoyed watching nature and scientific programmes on television, and I think that David Attenborough's 'Life on Earth' series, which I followed avidly with my family in my early teens, was vastly responsible for my interest and enjoyment in the environment from an early age.

I suppose that my concern was born primarily of intellectual stimulation by the media.

and another 35 speak of the great influence that reading books has had on their lives. By far the most commonly mentioned book is Rachel

Carson's *Silent Spring*, which clearly made a huge impact on individual thinking.

For some, it was 'Travel abroad' (44 responses) that made a major impact:

> There is no question of what influenced me, and that was travel, going to new environments that gave me a 'buzz', a wanting to learn as much about the world around me as possible. The outstanding event was at 16 when we went to the Sahara Desert. The beauty of this desert contrasted with the stereotype wasteland that I had been taught about.

and for others, 'Keeping pets/Animals' (14 responses), 'Religion' and the presence of God the Creator in the natural world (13 responses) and 'Becoming a parent' (20 responses):

> When my daughter was born was the most influential factor, I want her to see and remember green countrysides. Most of all, I want her to see 'a safe planet', not a nuclear desert or a war-torn world.

> I think having my first child made me first question the environment around me. It was the fear that my son might be harmed by atmospheric pollution from lead emissions from cars that brought out a certain anger in me.

While the majority of subjects write extensively of positive influences, a gloomy shadow is cast by 41 who refer to environmental 'Disasters/Negative issues' including catastrophes, nuclear dangers, pollution, planning issues, animal cruelty, and factors particularly affecting developing nations:

> The single most important influence to me was the famine in Africa. It made me realize that our climate is changing not just because of natural change but because of pollution and deforestation. What we do in our own back yard affects us all.

> . . . soot-covered buildings, polluted rivers, traffic. . . .

> I was surrounded by whole, dead, bloody pigs hanging from hooks.

> I grew up in Teesside and saw pollution pumped into the air from industry.

> A real shock to me was seeing my childhood village transformed to suburban dormitory . . . characterless . . . shaved lawns, cars, design-accommodating patios and pavement.

The final category of 'Others' (35 responses) includes 9 responses from subjects who describe their bad experiences of living in a town/concrete jungle; 7 who have a particular awareness of health issues as a result of being ill or witnessing ill health in others as a result of environmental factors; 5 who have been inspired to concern by music/poetry; 4 who claim that working with the disabled or homeless has been influential; 3 who cite death of another individual (2 tell the tragic tale of death of a close relative as a result of environmentally related diseases); 2 who have been influenced by living in an 'environmentally aware' community; 2 who cite modern technology as a major impact on thinking; one who is influenced by an awareness of a lack of environmental education in her own life; one who describes the influence of personal heritage, and one who claims that personal networking, 'being' with others, has been a major source of inspiration for concern.

A second phase of data analysis involved coding of references to single most significant life experiences. As shown in Table 1.2, 80 individuals identify a single most important influence. The same 13 final categories are used to record the analysis.

Table 1.2 Single most important life influences
N = 80

Outdoors	23[a]
Education/Courses	7[b]
Parents/Close relatives	21
Organizations	5
TV/Media	2
Friends/Other individuals	4
Travel abroad	5
Disasters/Negative issues	4
Books	3
Becoming a parent	1
Keeping pets/Animals	0
Religion	1
Others	4

Notes
[a] Childhood outdoors (16), Outdoor activities (4), Solitude/Wilderness (3)
[b] School courses (2), Higher education (5)

While present space does not allow for a lengthy discussion of the results of this autobiographical data analysis, a number of trends may be identified and issues raised which are of great significance to anyone who is concerned with the development of environmental education programmes in the formal education service. As mentioned at the outset, if environmental education is about 'producing' informed and environmentally active citizens of tomorrow, then presumably those

responsible for it should have some idea of the kinds of learning exp
ences which help to influence the development of environmental care
and concern.

Without doubt, the single most important category of response at all
levels of data analysis in the present project is experience outdoors, and
particularly at a young age. The influence of parents, other close relatives, individual teachers and adults is also of paramount importance.
For many readers, this will no doubt seem a statement of common sense
alone, for which elaborate data analysis is hardly necessary, yet it
should be stressed that all subjects' statements are of original, unbiased
thought, and so represent a remarkable affirmation of these influences.
Furthermore, they have far-reaching implications for schools and
teachers. If the data achieve nothing but a little persuasion of those who
are responsible for budgets for field centres and environmental programmes to the effect that outdoor activities are essential at all levels of
schooling, then the project will have achieved a tremendous amount for
the planet. Responses concerned with education courses per se also lead
to some interesting, if worrying conclusions. At a positive level, readers
can be pleased at the apparent impact of higher education, hopefully a
reflection of the proliferation of degree level courses in environmental
matters in recent years. Of the 7 respondents who single out education
as the most important influence on their lives, 5 refer to higher education courses and 2 to 'A' Level courses. But what of schools? Those
who speak enthusiastically of school as an influence refer in the main to
'A' Levels and related field work. Not one subject singles out a school
course below sixth form level as single most important influence, and
few refer at all to lessons or activities in primary education (including the
55 subjects under 30 years of age and thus educated in the fairly recent
past).

For some, the development of concern for the environment was
'sparked' by a single memorable person or event. For many, it was a
process of gradually becoming aware:

> There wasn't a single important influence, but rather a gradual dawn-
> ing of the mess the world was in. I cannot pinpoint an experience
> similar to St Paul's, just a spark that grew into a fire.

One common trend seems to be for individuals to have a childhood rich
in outdoor experiences and sensory awareness of the natural world,
followed by more 'latent' teenage years, and then a reawakening of
enthusiasm for the quality of the environment in early adult life. This
may be fuelled by higher education courses, reading, the media, or
becoming a parent. The role of organizations, books and the media has
been crucial to many in channelling this enthusiasm into positive action.
Surely it is essential for environmental educators to consider all of these

possible influences, including disasters and negative issues, and take account of them when planning school programmes? Further key issues arising from this research which have relevance for forthcoming sections are of course the tremendous significance of the impact of outdoor experiences, and the apparent need to make far more impact in general on the lives of the young with school based environmental education programmes. Hopefully ideas and discussion in subsequent pages will go some way towards preventing adults of the future sharing a view of a number of research respondents expressed along the following lines:

> I cannot remember any school experiences that fostered an interest in the environment. . . . School most certainly was NOT an influence.

It is hoped that reference to this research will encourage readers to reflect upon their own lives and experiences, and that the more positive words of another respondent will be echoed by many:

> Constant interaction with the outdoors has facilitated a monitoring of the inexorable dominance of human impacts upon this countryside. . . . Often a feeling of helplessness at the march of this ecological dominance, leading to a belief in the 'stewardship' role. Feedback from reflection and concern has led me to the conviction that the best way I can make any effective contribution is through my teaching skills to highlight the issues and possible strategies for young people.

NOTE

This chapter relates to Phase 1 of the Durham study. Further phases use autobiographical methodology to investigate the acquisition of pre-school children's environmental subject knowledge and concern, and the development of children's environmental knowledge and concern during the first three years in school. The overall project is funded by the ESRC.

Chapter 2

Environmental education: international development and progress

The 232 individuals referred to in Chapter 1 are all enthusiasts for the environment, and for the provision of 'environmental education', whatever that might mean. If we were to write again to the members of the research sample, this time requesting a description of what the movement of 'environmental education' means in practice, we predict the responses would entail widely differing interpretations of its key ideas and principles, and of how its aims are perceived and understood. For some its essence lies in aesthetic awareness, 'being at one' with nature, appreciating the beauties and fascination of natural life on our planet. For others, it has close association with key events which have raised awareness and the need to take action to preserve our Earth and its resources: perhaps the publication of Rachel Carson's *Silent Spring* in 1962, of Paul Ehrlich's *The Population Bomb* in 1968 or Schumacher's *Small is Beautiful* in 1973 . . . perhaps the near-meltdown of Three Mile Island Nuclear Power Plant in Pennsylvania, USA in 1979; the catastrophic failure of a Soviet nuclear power plant at Chernobyl in 1986 which contaminated large areas of northern Europe; the tales of the Mobro, a Long Island 'garbage barge' that travelled 6000 miles in 1987 to dump its load, becoming a symbol of the USA's waste problems; the running aground of the oil tanker *Exxon Valdez* in Prince William Sound, Alaska in 1989, spilling millions of gallons of oil into ecosystems; or the 1991 war in Kuwait, drawing world attention to the environmental damage of war . . . the origins of the need for environmental education, and the nature of its aims, are interpreted in many and various ways by individuals around the globe.

For some, the name of Sir Patrick Geddes, a Scottish botanist (1854–1933) is associated with the earliest links between education and the quality of the environment. His pioneer work included the extensive use of the outdoors as a resource for active learning. Also, the thinking of some of the world's 'great' educationists undoubtedly made a substantial contribution to philosophical deliberations on the interaction between people and their environment: 'The difference between the aesthetic and the intellectual is thus one of the place where emphasis falls in the constant rhythm that marks the interaction of the live creature with his surroundings' (Dewey 1934).

The first recorded use of the term 'environmental education' in Britain may be traced to a conference held in 1965 at Keele University, Staffordshire, with the purpose of investigating conservation of the countryside and its implications for education. At an international level, it is claimed that the term 'environmental education' was first used in Paris in 1948, at a meeting of the International Union for Conservation of Nature and Natural Resources (Disinger 1983).

Many attempts have been made to define the term, particularly during the past 25 years when many critical problems facing our planet have been acknowledged and publicized. Worldwide concern after the publication of Carson's *Silent Spring* (1962) intensified and in 1970 the International Union for the Conservation of Nature and Natural Resources (IUCN) held a working meeting on 'Environmental Education in the School Curriculum' in Nevada, USA. The deliberations of that conference continue to be a major influence on the development of environmental education. The definition drawn up at the conference is accepted by Britain's National Association for Environmental Education and by many other organizations both in the UK and elsewhere:

> Environmental education is the process of recognising values and clarifying concepts in order to develop skills and attitudes necessary to understand and appreciate the interrelatedness among man, his culture and his biophysical surroundings. Environmental education also entails practice in decision making and self-formulation of a code of behaviour about issues concerning environmental quality.
>
> (IUCN 1970)

The support of key international institutions continued to raise the profile of environmental education during the 1970s, leading to a great deal of common understanding of the aims, objectives and approaches to the subject. Principle 19 enunciated at the United Nations Conference on the Human Environment, held in Stockholm in 1972, stated:

> Education in environmental matters for the younger generation as well as adults, giving due consideration to the underprivileged, is essential. . . .

Subsequently the United Nations Environment Program (UNEP) was established, which together with UNESCO founded the UNESCO/ UNEP International Environmental Education Programme (IEEP) in 1975.

THE INTERNATIONAL ENVIRONMENTAL EDUCATI
PROGRAMME

The IEEP was launched in 1975 at an International Works
Environmental Education held in Belgrade. This produced t
intergovernmental statement on environmental education. It listed the
aims, objectives, key concepts and guiding principles of the programme,
in a document prepared at the meeting known as 'The Belgrade Charter
– a Global Framework for Environmental Education'. The brief, but
comprehensive set of objectives for environmental education prepared
at Belgrade are summarized as follows (UNESCO 1975):

1 To foster clear awareness of and concern about economic, social,
   political and ecological interdependence in urban and rural areas.
2 To provide every person with opportunities to acquire the knowledge,
   values, attitudes, commitment and skills needed to protect and
   improve the environment.
3 To create new patterns of behaviour of individuals, groups and
   society as a whole towards the environment.

Belgrade was followed in 1977 by the first intergovernmental
Conference on Environmental Education, held in Tbilisi, USSR, organized by UNESCO and attended by 66 member states. The conference
prepared recommendations for the wider application of environmental
education in formal and non-formal education. This significant event,
and subsequent publications based on it, continue to provide the framework for the development of environmental education in the world
today.

THE WORLD CONSERVATION STRATEGY

In 1980, the World Conservation Strategy was launched (IUCN 1980),
one of the most significant documents concerning conservation and
environmental education at a global level ever to be published. This key
document stressed the importance of resource conservation through
'sustainable development', and the idea that conservation and development are mutually interdependent. The World Conservation Strategy
included a chapter on environmental education, containing the
message:

> Ultimately the behaviour of entire societies towards the biosphere
> must be transformed if the achievement of conservation objectives is
> to be assured . . . the long term task of environmental education [is]
> to foster or reinforce attitudes and behaviour, compatible with a new
> ethic.
>
> (IUCN 1980)

Since 1986 work at an international level has continued on preparing supplements to the World Conservation Strategy, dealing with issues such as environmental education, ethics and culture.

TBILISI

1987 marked the tenth anniversary of the first Tbilisi conference and a 'Tbilisi Plus Ten' conference, jointly organized by UNESCO and UNEP, was held in Moscow. A number of major themes emerged from the deliberations of this event, including the vital importance of environmental education, as summed up in the opening address:

> In the long run nothing significant will happen to reduce local and international threats to the environment unless widespread public awareness is aroused concerning the essential links between environmental quality and the continued satisfaction of human needs. Human action depends upon motivation, which depends upon widespread understanding. This is why we feel it is so important that everyone becomes environmentally conscious through proper environmental education.
>
> (UNESCO 1987)

OUR COMMON FUTURE

In that same year, 1987, the World Commission on Environment and Development produced the report *Our Common Future* (WCED 1987). This presented a major statement on a 'global agenda' to reconcile environment with development, thus reinforcing and extending the essence of the 1980 World Conservation Strategy. Education was seen as a focal point in this agenda: 'The changes in human attitude that we call for depend on a vast campaign of education, debate and public participation' (WCED 1987). Debate arising from this report led to the second major conference of the United Nations, two decades after Stockolm: the United Nations Conference on Environment and Development – the Earth Summit, Brazil, 1992.

THE EARTH SUMMIT

The Earth Summit (UNCED) Conference took place in Rio de Janeiro, 3–4 June 1992. It was attended by some 120 heads of state and government, together with delegates from over 170 countries. Parallel to this was the Global Forum, involving representatives from several hundred special interest groups and non-governmental organizations in a series of presentations, displays, seminars and workshops on a wide range of environmental issues and topics. Several important documents were signed at the summit, representing the beginning of a long process of interpreting, responding to and implementing recommendations and agreements designed to change the future of planet Earth. The centre-piece of the Rio agreements is known as Agenda 21, a major action programme setting out what nations should do to achieve sustainable development in the 21st century. The 40 chapters of Agenda 21 cover topics ranging from poverty, toxic waste and desertification to youth, education and free trade. There are implications for environmental education throughout this document, but of particular significance are Chapters 25 (Children and Youth in Sustainable Development) and 36 (Promoting Education, Public Awareness and Training). Further details of these are provided in Appendix A, page 217. A second crucial document produced and signed at the Summit is the Rio Declaration, a statement of 27 principles for sustainability which provide the basis for the programmes of international cooperation in Agenda 21. In other words, the Rio Declaration sets out a blueprint for a sustainable future, while Agenda 21 provides a guiding programme for its interpretation. The UNCED also agreed: The Climatic Change Convention, the first international treaty to acknowledge the threat of global warming; The Biodiversity Convention, the first treaty to deal with ownership of genetic resources (signed by 153 governments excluding the US) and Forest Principles, a non-legally binding text on principles for sustainable forest management. One of the key outcomes of the conference for educators is the recommendation that environmental and development education should be incorporated as an essential part of learning, within both formal and non-formal education sectors. A proposal is made that 'Governments should strive to update or prepare strategies aimed at integrating environment and development as a cross-cutting issue into education at all levels within the next three years' (Agenda 21, Ch. 36).

THE EUROPEAN COMMUNITY

The European Community has also been active in the environmental education debate. A most important motivation to a more positive attitude of the UK government to the topic was the May 1988 meeting of the Council of the European Community when they agreed on 'The need to take concrete steps for the promotion of environmental education so that this can be intensified in a comprehensive way throughout the Community'. A Resolution on Environmental Education was adopted to that end with the following objective and guiding principles:

The objective of environmental education is to increase the public awareness of the problems in this field, as well as possible solutions, and to lay the foundations for a fully informed and active participation of the individual in the protection of the environment and the prudent and rational use of natural resources. For the achievement of the objectives environmental education should take into account particularly the following guiding principles:

• the environment as a common heritage of mankind
• the common duty of maintaining, protecting and improving the quality of the environment, as a contribution to the protection of human health and the safeguarding of the ecological balance
• the need for a prudent and rational utilization of natural resources
• the way in which each individual can, by his own behaviour, particularly as a consumer, contribute to the protection of the environment.

(Journal of the European Communities, 6 July 1988)

It was resolved that member states would make every effort to implement certain measures, including:

The promotion of environmental education in all sectors of education . . . giving consideration to the basic aims of environmental education when drawing up curricula . . . taking appropriate measures to develop teachers' knowledge of environmental matters in the context of their initial and in-service training. . . .

(Journal of the European Communities, 6 July 1988)

ENVIRONMENTAL EDUCATION IN THE UK

This significant international endorsement of environmental education over the past 20 years or so has inevitably helped shape the aims, objectives and planning of this curriculum area within schools and local education authorities in the United Kingdom. Environmental education has been well established on the curriculum map of schools for some three decades. Local authorities, national organizations and individual schools and teachers have done a tremendous amount to promote its importance and to develop effective teaching and learning strategies. In 1967 the Plowden Report confirmed the value of using the environment for learning. During the following years, 'environment' became a widely discussed word in education, and environmental education evolved rapidly as a curriculum area. In 1968 the Council for Environmental Education (CEE) was established as a focus for organizations concerned with the environment, having three broad goals:

Development: CEE aims to facilitate the development of the theory and practice of environmental education.

Promotion: CEE aims to promote the concept of environmental education and facilitate its application in all spheres of education.

Review: CEE aims to monitor the progress of environmental education and assess its effectiveness.

The National Association for Environmental Education, the UK professional association for all educationists interested and involved in this area, has been influential through its meetings, journals and publications, including its *Statement of Aims* (NAEE 1975, 1982, 1992).

Undoubtedly the May 1988 Resolution of the Council of Ministers of the European Community played a significant role in the inclusion of environmental education as an officially recognized cross-curricular theme of the National Curriculum for schools (see pp. 23–33) and government individuals and initiatives have continued to reinforce its importance:

Good environmental education, like any good education, must lead pupils and students out and on from their immediate perceptions and experience to a wider understanding. It must develop their capacity to go beyond the anecdotal and the particular. None of that happens by chance. A number of subjects and aspects of the school curriculum deal with matters to do with the interplay between man and his environment. . . . I am convinced that pupils must first learn about natural phenomena in order to understand complex environmental matters. . . . The importance of environmental education is that it sensitises us to the causes and effects of problems of which, for too long, we have been only dimly aware. The environment is our children's future and many already know that we must encourage them to think positively about it . . . what needs to be done to reduce the damage we do to it, what opportunities there are for improving the quality of our surroundings – and to come up with practical solutions. *They should draw on what they learn at school.*

(Speech by Angela Rumbold, UK Minister of State
for Education and Science, 27 July 1989,
London International Science Fortnight [emphasis added])

Chapter 3

Threads of a theme: principles and structure

As a result of international initiatives, a broad consensus has emerged on the principles and objectives of environmental education. These largely reflect the outcome of the Tbilisi Conference of 1977, whose Final Report sets out three 'goals of environmental education':

1 To foster clear awareness of, and concern about, economic, social, political and ecological interdependence in urban and rural areas.
2 To provide every person with opportunities to acquire the knowledge, values, attitudes, commitment and skills needed to protect and improve the environment.
3 To create new patterns of behaviour of individuals, groups and society as a whole towards the environment.

(UNESCO 1977)

Defining the content of environmental education is problematic. Since the environment is all embracing then it must, to some extent at least, be considered in its totality to include aspects which are urban and rural, technological and social, aesthetic and ethical: 'Throughout primary and secondary education, the human environment, both rural and urban, should be regarded as a continuum from the wilderness, through the productive countryside, small settlements and suburbs, to the heart of the inner city' (NAEE 1975). The eclectic nature of the content may be regarded as a strength, but also as a weakness – either environmental education becomes equated with the whole of education, thus essentially losing its identity, or else selected features must be singled out for a focus of teaching and learning tasks. At either of these extremes, fundamental elements of environmental education may fall by the wayside. A way to overcome this problem is to recognize that *an environmental dimension can be found in most aspects of education* – thus *environmental education may be considered to be an approach to education which incorporates considerations of the environment*, rather than being a separate part of education. It does, however, have a discrete 'content' which must be incorporated into teaching and learning situations.

It is generally accepted that education related to the environment includes three 'threads'. This threefold structure was first formalized in the Schools Council's *Project Environment* (1974):

There are three threads which have contributed to our present ideas and it has become almost commonplace nowadays to characterise these as education either ABOUT, FROM or FOR the environment. . . .

Education ABOUT the environment seeks to discover the nature of the area under study often through investigatory and discovery approaches; the objectives are chiefly cognitive ones in that the aim is to amass information. . . .

In educating FROM the environment, teachers must have sought to forward the general education of the child by using the environment as a resource in two main ways: firstly as a medium for enquiry and discovery which may lead to the enhancement of the learning process, the most important aspect being learning how to learn; secondly, as a source of material for realistic activities in language, mathematics, science and craft. . . .

To be educated FOR the environment . . . is education which is environmental in style with emphasis on developing an informed concern for the environment. The objectives go beyond the acquisition of skills and knowledge and require the development of involvement to the extent that values are formed which affect behaviour. . . . Thus the aim is to develop attitudes and levels of understanding which lead to a personal environmental ethic; that is, to educate pupils so that their actions and influences on collective action will be positively for the benefit of the earthly environment.

(Schools Council 1974)

The three threads may be set alongside four 'elements' of the curriculum area – *empirical, synoptic, aesthetic* and *ethical*. These have been referred to and expressed in slightly different ways in a number of curriculum statements, including the 1974 report by HM Inspectors of Schools in Scotland (Scottish Education Department 1974) which states that a programme of environmental education should disseminate the views of *Project Environment*:

It contains empirical, synoptic, aesthetic and ethical elements, none of which can be studied in isolation:

a) The Empirical element. This is concerned with those aspects of the environment which lend themselves to objective observation, measurement and analysis . . . the main priority is to ensure that all pupils have as many opportunities as possible of making direct contact with the environment through observation and by measuring, recording, interpreting and discussing what has been observed.

b) The Synoptic element . . . pupils need to be made aware of the complex nature of the environment. The aim of synoptic studies is to help pupils to realise the complexity of such issues and to introduce them to the inseparable nature of the various components of an environment and to the interrelations of these. Method is as important as content in achieving this.

c) The Aesthetic element. Of the many aspects of the environment, perhaps the most important are qualitative rather than quantitative. . . . The aesthetic elements . . . can help a pupil to realise that there is no right or wrong answer in absolute terms to aesthetic questions and that the answer to environmental issues is frequently a compromise.

d) The Ethical element. A programme of environmental education aims at introducing pupils to the idea of personal responsibility for the environment and to the concept of stewardship. It trains pupils to ask if the criteria of proposed actions are based on morally justifiable values.

(Scottish Education Department 1974)

THE THREE DIMENSIONS OF LEARNING

Inextricably interwoven with these various threads and elements are the three dimensions of the learning process: *knowledge and understanding*, *skills* and *attitudes*. Once again, these are referred to and articulated in a variety of documents which attempt to define the aims and content of environmental education. For example:

Knowledge and skills

i)   To develop a coherent body of knowledge about the environment, both built and rural, sufficient to recognise actual and potential problems,

ii) To be able to gather information from or about the environment independently or as part of co-operative activity,

iii) To be able to consider different opinions related to environmental issues and to arrive at a balanced judgement,

iv) To appreciate the ways in which environmental issues are interrelated so that one factor affects others,

v)   To be able to evaluate information about the environment from different sources and to try to resolve environmental problems,

vi) To understand and to know how to use the mechanisms available in society for bringing about environmental change.

Attitudes and behaviour

i) To develop an appreciation of the environment and critical awareness of the natural and built environment,
ii) To develop an attitude of concern for environmental matters and a wish to improve environmental understanding,
iii) To be critical of one's own environmental attitudes and to take steps to change one's own behaviour and actions,
iv) To have a desire to participate in initiatives to care for or improve the environment,
v) To wish to participate in environmental decision making and to make opinions known publicly.

(CEE 1987)

General aims for environmental education include: The need to develop attitudes of care, curiosity and concern for the environment in such a way as to develop a sense of responsibility towards home, school and community; to demonstrate to children the complex interrelationships between humanity and the environment, and to give pupils the necessary skills to do these things.

(DES 1986)

In summary, the general consensus which has emerged on the nature of environmental education reflects the goals and principles set out at Tbilisi in 1977. The following set of statements, taken from Sterling (1992) is based upon the Tbilisi Report Recommendation 2 (1978).

Tbilisi Recommendations

Environment education:

• is a lifelong process;
• is interdisciplinary and holistic in nature and application;
• is an approach to education as a whole, rather than a subject;
• concerns the interrelationship and interconnectedness between human and natural systems;
• views the environment in its entirety including social, political, economic, technological, moral, aesthetic and spiritual aspects;
• recognizes that energy and material resources both present and limit possibilities;
• encourages participation in the learning experience;
• emphasizes active responsibility;

- uses a broad range of teaching and learning techniques, with stress on practical activities and first-hand experience;
- is concerned with local to global dimensions, and past/present/future dimensions;
- should be enhanced and supported by the organization and structure of the learning situation and institution as a whole;
- encourages the development of sensitivity, awareness, understanding, critical thinking and problem-solving skills;
- encourages the clarification of values and the development of values sensitive to the environment;
- is concerned with building an environment ethic.

These goals and principles have been carried forward into and underpin the content of preliminary papers and final documentation for environmental education in the National Curriculum for schools in England.

Chapter 4

The National Curriculum

Although this chapter is based on the National Curriculum in England, the principles enunciated which led environmental education to be recognized as a cross-curricular theme, are applicable to curriculum development anywhere. We hope readers outside England will gain benefit from it, for however it is described, environmental education is inter-disciplinary and spreads influence across the whole-school curriculum.

Discussion at UK government level at present focuses on whether environmental education should have a statutory place in the National Curriculum rather than as a 'voluntary' cross-curricular theme. Any decision in no way alters our thinking behind this chapter.

Environmental education is an officially recognized and documented cross-curricular theme of the National Curriculum for schools. It is one of the first five themes to be documented, alongside health education, education for citizenship, careers education and guidance, and economic and industrial understanding. Themes are regarded not as an appendage to be 'tacked on' to the core and foundation subjects, but as a central element of the curriculum as a whole, having progression and continuity like all subject areas. By definition, they are cross-curricular, and thus can feature in or arise out of a number of other areas of the curriculum. The themes share the ability to promote thinking and discussion on questions of values and belief; they add to knowledge and understanding; and they rely on practical, experiential learning and decision making. Schools have freedom to interpret the guidelines for the various themes and to decide how best to incorporate them into the curriculum as a whole.

In primary schools they can be adapted either to the theme or topic approach, a common method of organising the curriculum, or to more formal subject teaching . . . they will often be identified as threads running through topics and through subjects. . . . In secondary schools again there is more than one way of tackling the themes. At one extreme they can be separately timetabled, at the other they can be completely subsumed within the subjects of the curriculum. Environmental education, for example, could well be covered in science, geography, technology, English and mathematics. What is important, is that they appear in a coherent and planned manner throughout the secondary curriculum in a form which ensures continuity and progression.

(NCC 1990a)

Thus the National Curriculum recommends no single approach to organization of the curriculum or teaching methodology for environmental education. It is suggested that a variety of approaches is best. Five possible timetabling arrangements are identified for the inclusion of cross-curricular themes (NCC 1990a), namely:

1 taught through National Curriculum and other subjects
2 whole-curriculum planning leading to blocks of activities (e.g. a series of subject-based topics lasting for varying periods of time)
3 separately timetabled themes
4 taught through separately timetabled personal and social education
5 long-block timetabling (e.g. activity week).

Documentation for the cross-curricular theme of environmental education (NCC 1990b) sets out objectives for it which reflect the three key dimensions of learning, namely, knowledge, skills and attitudes:

Knowledge

As a basis for making informed judgements about the environment pupils should develop knowledge and understanding of:

- the natural processes which take place in the environment
- the impact of human activities on the environment
- different environments, both past and present
- environmental issues such as the greenhouse effect, acid rain, air pollution
- local, national and international legislative controls to protect and manage the environment; how policies and decisions are made about the environment
- the environmental interdependence of individuals, groups, communities and nations
- how human lives and livelihoods are dependent on the environment
- the conflicts which can arise about environmental issues
- how the environment has been affected by past decisions and actions
- the importance of planning, design and aesthetic considerations

- the importance of effective action to protect and manage the environment.

Skills

- communication skills
- numeracy skills
- study skills
- problem-solving skills
- personal and social skills
- information technology skills

Attitudes

Promoting positive attitudes to the environment is essential if pupils are to value it and understand their role in safeguarding it for the future. Encouraging the development of the attitudes and personal qualities below will contribute to this process:

- appreciation of, and care and concern for the environment and for other living things
- independence of thought on environmental issues
- a respect for the beliefs and the opinions of others
- a respect for evidence and rational argument
- tolerance and open-mindedness.

Seven areas of knowledge and understanding are identified which may form the basis for the development of worthwhile topics or subject-based interpretation. These are:

- climate
- soils, rocks and minerals
- water
- materials and resources, including energy
- plants and animals
- people and their communities
- buildings, industrialization and waste

Clearly there are extensive possibilities for classroom interpretation of these and subtopics deriving from them. Many coincide with common topics of a general nature frequently undertaken in primary school classrooms, and they also have obvious links with other curriculum areas, notably science, geography, history and technology.

National Curriculum documentation reflects the three threads of environmental education reinforced in the Tbilisi conference papers (UNESCO 1977):

- education *about* the environment (that is, basic knowledge and understanding of the environment)
- education *for* the environment (concerned with values, attitudes and positive action for the environment)
- education *in* or *through* the environment (that is, using the environment as a resource with emphasis on enquiry and investigation and pupils' first-hand experiences).

An integral part of planning for the inclusion of environmental education in school curricula, as discussed below, must be the need to develop an understanding of the interrelationship between these three components.

ENTITLEMENT

A statement of proposed entitlement of pupils in environmental education was prepared in England by the working group convened by the NCC in 1989 to examine this theme and prepare documentation for *Curriculum Guidance 7*. This entitlement formed part of a collection of key papers (unpublished) circulated widely for consultation and response. It suggests that a pupil's learning should be founded on knowledge, understanding and skills. A summary follows.

Summary of entitlement

By the age of 16 all pupils should have had educational experiences, which range from local to global in scale, and which enable them to:

1 Understand the natural processes that take place in the environment, including the ecological principles and relationships that exist.
2 Understand that human lives and livelihoods are totally dependent on the processes, relationships and resources that exist in the environment.
3 Be aware of the impact of human activities on the environment including planning and design, to understand the process by which communities organize themselves, initiate and cope with change; to appreciate that these are affected by personal, economic, technological, social, aesthetic, political, cultural, ethical and spiritual considerations.
4 Be competent in a range of skills which help them to appreciate and enjoy, communicate ideas and participate in the decision-making processes which shape the environment.
5 View, evaluate, interpret and experience their surroundings critically so that a balanced appreciation can be reached.
6 Have insights into a range of environments and cultures, both past

and present, to include an understanding of the ways in which different cultural groups perceive and interact with their environment.

7 Understand the conflicts that may arise over environmental issues, particularly in relation to the use of resources, and to consider alternative ways to resolve such conflicts.

8 Be aware of the interdependence of communities and nations and some of the environmental consequences and opportunities of those relationships.

9 Be aware that the current state of the environment has resulted from past decisions and actions and that the future of the environment depends on contemporary actions and decisions to which they make a contribution.

10 Identify their own level of commitment towards the care of the environment.

Underpinning this entitlement is a clear emphasis on values and attitudes. Indeed a critical component of cross-curricular issues in general is surely their ability to promote discussion or questions of values, belief and personal decision making as a response to interaction with the environment.

LEARNING

Further to the above statement of entitlement, a broad outline structure for every child's learning in environmental education was articulated (unpublished NCC Task Group papers, 1989). This is based on two broad dimensions which relate to other subject areas of the curriculum. Each of these areas is further divided into three subsections as follows:

1 *Knowledge and understanding*
(a) Knowledge about the environment at a variety of levels, ranging from local to global.
(b) Knowledge and understanding of environmental issues at a variety of levels, ranging from local to global; to include understanding of different influences, both natural and human, on the issues.
(c) Knowledge of alternative attitudes and approaches to environmental issues and the value systems underlying such attitudes and approaches.

2 *Skills*
(a) Finding out about the environment, either directly through the environment or by using secondary sources.
(b) Communicating:
   (i) knowledge about the environment;

    (ii) both the pupil's own and alternative attitudes to environmental issues, to include justification for the attitudes or approaches advanced.

(c) Participation:

    (i) as part of group decision making;

    (ii) as part of making a personal response.

The National Curriculum clearly regards environmental education as an essential part of every pupil's curriculum. It considers the threefold aims of this entitlement as:

- to provide opportunities to acquire the knowledge, values, attitudes, commitment and skills needed to protect and improve the environment
- to encourage pupils to examine and interpret the environment from a variety of perspectives – physical, geographical, biological, sociological, economic, political, technological, historical, aesthetic, ethical and spiritual
- to arouse pupils' awareness and curiosity about the environment and encourage active participation in resolving environmental problems.

In so doing, it promotes the long-term aims of improving management of the environment and promoting satisfactory solutions to environmental issues.

    So what does all this rather academic-sounding guidance mean for schools?

PLANNING

The key to successful implementation and achievement of these worthy aims and objectives undoubtedly rests on the skills of *planning*, at all levels. Environmental education must never be left to chance. As an essential part of every pupil's curriculum, it must be planned for with as much care and attention to detail as any other aspect of teaching and learning.

    The final part of this chapter now examines some of the key principles of planning and implementation and considers the key question of what this actually means for schools. Issues highlighted will then be the subject of further discussion in the context of practical examples and case studies of good practice.

PRINCIPLES INTO PRACTICE

Environmental education should provide experience of problem solving, decision making and participation, with considerations based on ecological, political, economic, social, aesthetic and ethical aspects. It is also about promoting changes in behaviour that will help to solve existing problems relating to the environment and to avoid the creation of new ones. A restatement of its ultimate aim, already discussed, is for each school leaver to have formulated a responsible attitude towards the sustainable development of Planet Earth, an appreciation of its beauty and an assumption of an environmental ethic. To fulfil this aim, every school needs adequate arrangements for planning and implementing successful programmes of work, and teaching and learning tasks.

Planning for the inclusion of environmental education in the curriculum needs to take account of the three interlinked components which comprise the theme:

- education about the environment
- education for the environment
- education in or through the environment.

These elements are interrelated and are essential components of planning at every level, ranging from whole-school and year-group curriculum planning to the more specific plans for topics, programmes of study and tasks applicable to a class, group of learners or an individual. An integral part of the planning process must take account of the need to develop an understanding of the interrelationship between the three components. This is likely to be achieved through elaboration of content of the seven areas of knowledge and understanding, and the development of related skills, concepts and attitudes. Figure 4.1 represents these components of environmental education in diagrammatic form. The dimensions of skills, concepts and attitudes are inextricably bound into the core content of the three structural elements:

- Education *about* the environment has the purpose of developing knowledge and understanding about *values* and *attitudes*.
- Education *for* the environment encourages pupils to explore their personal response to and relationship with the environment and environmental *issues*. This is linked to the development of *attitudes* and *values*, including elements of human understanding and behaviour necessary for the development of sustainable and caring use of the environment.
- Education *in* or *through* the environment uses the environment as a resource for learning. It is a resource which enables the development of a great deal of knowledge and understanding as well as *skills* of investigation and communication.

Anyone responsible for planning the curriculum and learning tasks concerned with environmental education needs to take account of all of these interrelated elements.

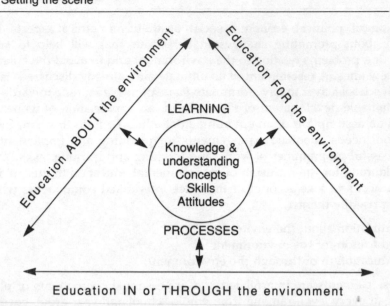

Figure 4.1 Interrelated components of environmental education

The inclusion of the development of skills is, of course, vital, not only to planning for progressive schemes of work in environmental education, but also to planning for incorporating skills of a cross-curricular nature into the curriculum as a whole. Environmental education has a critical role to play in skill development.

As a cross-curricular theme, environmental education allows children the opportunity to understand the many and varied environmental issues that surround them, how decisions are made about the environment and how people can have the opportunity of participating in the decision making process. Work in environmental education represents a good opportunity for children to use a whole range of skills in a way which is both relevant to their lives as well as useful to their future as citizens. By stretching children intellectually and creatively, by asking them to communicate ideas and work in a cooperative manner on environmental issues that face them, it is hoped to produce adults provoked and challenged into making a positive and constructive contribution to the future and well-being of the world.

(NCC Task Group 1989, unpublished)

Any sound model for planning the incorporation of environmental education in the school curriculum will clearly need to take account of both content and skills, and also the overall entitlement of pupils, including emphasis on attitudes and value-laden issues.

In sections which follow, examples of good practice will be described and discussed, which take account of these elements of planning and the successful organization of appropriate classroom tasks.

Other related issues which will be elaborated include the need for a whole-school policy, coordination of environmental work within a school, and arrangements for record keeping, assessment and evaluation. At this stage, brief reference to the importance of these is in the context of this section's emphasis on the nature and structure of environmental education and implementation of 'holistic' programmes of environmentally related work.

Every school which aims to develop and implement an entitlement of good quality teaching and learning in this curriculum area will require successful coordination of the whole curriculum framework within the school. This will be linked to carefully structured policies for environmental education. Arrangements for the inclusion of cross-curricular issues as a whole cannot be left to the particular enthusiasm of individual members of staff. Whole-school planning and coordination is necessary to ensure consistency, adequate coverage, progression and evaluation. Critical to the satisfactory implementation of the whole policy is recognition of the central importance of progression and assessment procedures. Progression must be achieved through planned programmes of study which are devised to allow for the fact that environmental education will be included in progressive schemes of work of other subject areas. In the case of the National Curriculum for schools in England, this may be interpreted to mean cross referencing with the attainment targets and statements of attainment of the core and foundation subjects. It is necessary to identify and construct levels of achievement for the relevant knowledge and understanding so that pupils at the main reporting stages can demonstrate the appropriate assessment objectives. It is recognized that skills progression may not follow a similar sequential pattern of development to that of knowledge and understanding, yet it is essential that skills progression is also included in the design of topics or programmes of work. As far as assessment is concerned, this should relate to the three central teaching objectives for environmental education, i.e. knowledge and understanding; skills; and attitudes. The national framework for assessment will of course be an essential baseline since a great deal of environmental learning will occur through the teaching of core and foundation subjects. Nevertheless, innovatory methods of environmental assessment will need to be developed in relation to certain skills and to the formation of values and attitudes.

Pupils' records need to be maintained which provide a profile of experiences and attainments. Documentation may comprise a wide range of written material including pupil profile sheets, class and individual records and samples of children's work. Record keeping schemes will need of course to reflect the individual needs and circumstances of a school.

Holism

Chapter 1 opened with an account of a research project which is investigating aspects of the lives of environmental educators, and it is to this topic that we now return. If a school's coordinated approach to the inclusion of environmental education is to be successful, then it depends as much upon the attitudes of those designing and implementing it, as on the content of that which is being taught and learnt. The critical importance of the attitudes of educators has so far escaped with scant attention in the worlds of research and publication. Central to environmental education itself is the importance of attitudes and values, and if a fundamental aim is to change the attitudes in people from ones of exploitation and dominance to ones of protection and care for the world, then a teacher's role cannot be overemphasized. In the research sample described, 137 out of 232 respondents cited the influence of other adults as a major factor in shaping their own environmental concern. If a real impact is to be made then environmental awareness in the school as a whole is surely essential. In part this would involve the successful implementation of programmes of work and progressive topics of an environmental nature, incorporating those components which this section has highlighted. This in turn depends upon teacher subject knowledge, awareness, and enthusiasm for the task. It would take account of the *whole* school environment, its ethos, its approach to caring for people and other living things, and of course of the overall personal development of each child within this holistic world. This is not the place for a lengthy discussion of philosophical foundations for environmental education – the attention of interested readers is drawn to authors who focus on alternative views and paradigms relating to environmental interpretation (Cooper and Palmer 1992, Engel and Engel 1990, Sterling 1990, Cooper and Sterling 1992); nevertheless no overview of the structure and interpretation of environmental education would be adequate without reinforcing the fundamental importance of holism. The Tbilisi conference talked of the 'holistic approach' in its acknowledgement that environmental education focuses on an overall perspective of the world, and the interdependence of natural and man-made environments. In educational terms, a holistic orientation concerns itself with education for the whole person, a concern with values, practical, experiential learning situations, and personal responses to issues at both local and global levels.

In more practical terms, holistic education has implications for educational objectives and curricula (which should reflect the whole school/whole institution approach), for learning style and methodology (which should be participative), and for the learning environment and for institutional organisation and structure.

(Sterling 1992)

Building upon first-hand experiences, practical investigations and interactions with the natural and built environments, helping pupils to begin to appreciate the complex interrelationships that exist among 'people culture and biophysical surroundings' are essential starting points for teaching and learning in this area. Pupils in school, perhaps at primary level in particular, are fascinated by their surroundings and have tremendous capacity to build upon natural learning experiences that take place within them. Aside from academic debate and jargon, the 'real world' experiences of a wide sample of educators show the vital importance of education *in* the environment as a prerequisite to a concern *for* it. The most valuable and readily available resource to all schools is the environment itself.

Part II

Environmental education in schools

This Part of the book is concerned with approaches to the planning, organization and implementation of environmental education in the school classroom. Details of coordination, management and school policy are debated in Part III.

Environmental education
in schools

Chapter 5

Planning and practice at the primary level

OVERALL MODEL FOR TEACHING AND LEARNING

We believe that there is no single 'right or wrong' way to approach the teaching and learning of environmental education in the primary phase. Case studies which follow will show that the theme can be a highly successful starting point for formal, subject-based learning or a unifying element in topic work. Whichever approach or combination of approaches is utilized, it is, however, essential that *first-hand experiences of the environment are at the forefront of teaching and learning*. The knowledge, understanding and processes of related curriculum areas such as science, mathematics and geography should be developed through environmental experiences in the context of each pupil's individual potential and natural curiosity.

A helpful framework to be borne in mind when planning topics might well be one that consists of two mutually dependent components. This can be expressed as a matrix in which the vertical component corresponds to the core and foundation subjects and the horizontal component corresponds to the cross-curricular theme of environmental education. Both components should show the relevant range of knowledge, understanding and skills, and will demonstrate a great deal of common ground. A useful place to start when building up more complex plans is by a simpler analysis of components of environmental topics, key issues involved, and knowledge and skills to be developed.

These aspects of structured planning will be exemplified through case studies of good practice from primary school classrooms. First however, we introduce a comprehensive model for teaching and learning in environmental education which underpins effective work in this area.

Part I provided an overview and diagrammatic summary of the interrelated components of environmental education (Fig. 4.1, p. 30). This identified the importance of educating for, in and about the environment, while planning teaching and learning tasks across a range of environmental knowledge, understandings, concepts, skills and attitudes. We now expand upon this framework to suggest an overall model for planning teaching and learning, which is represented diagrammatically in Figure 5.1. The various components of this model are those to be borne in mind when undertaking the planning task. It expands upon the threefold framework which underpins planning: tasks should be planned that educate about the environment, for the environment, and that are accomplished in the environment. Within this framework, we identify the three crucial elements of personal *experience* in the environment, the development of personal *concern* for the environment, and the taking of personal *action* in and on behalf of the environment. Sound programmes of environmental education in the primary school (and at later stages) need to take account of the inclusion of all of these elements, by providing appropriate tasks and experiences.

Using this model as a basis, a more elaborate statement of skills, concepts, and areas of knowledge and understanding to be covered can be made, perhaps in table form. Columns can indicate precise learning objectives in relation to learning for and about the environment in any particular topic, links with attainment targets of core and foundation subjects, experiences in the environment, and attitudes that it is planned to develop with the aim of promoting the development of environmental concern and action.

We note that this schema cannot, of course, be separated from assessment procedures, and it is discussed further in Part III.

As a whole, the model forms a basis for topic development and, most importantly, for linking a specific topic or environmental starting point into a coherent and progressive overall curriculum plan for the key stage as a whole.

We turn then to some practical examples which will illustrate this, and begin with two case studies particularly chosen to illustrate how primary age pupils may interact with the natural environment, engaging in direct experiences, and developing a sense of enjoyment of and motivation for learning about the world around them. After descriptive accounts of these two educational settings, the programmes will be discussed and analysed in a more systematic way. The descriptions are written in the style of 'connoisseurship and criticism', a descriptive and qualitative approach to looking at classrooms (after Eisner 1979, 1991). It is intended that the inclusion of two case studies employing this methodology will in itself add a useful dimension to the book as a whole, providing examples of a particular way of appreciating and communicating activities in classrooms. Interesting as it might be in its own right as a methodology, it may also be of assistance to those readers concerned with developing skills of observation of children and learning situations for the purposes of assessment and future planning. If a key to providing schemes for inclusion of cross-curricular themes lies in the

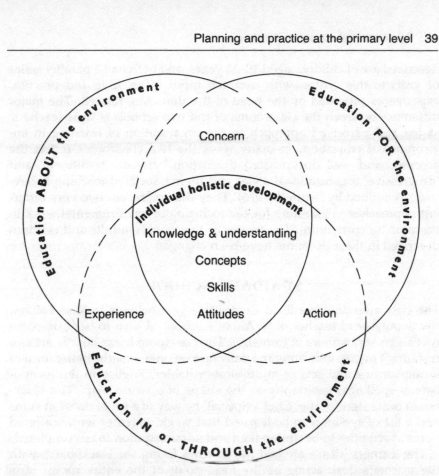

Concern

Education ABOUT the environment

Education FOR the environment

Individual holistic development

Knowledge & understanding

Concepts

Skills

Experience   Attitudes   Action

Education IN or THROUGH the environment

Figure 5.1 Model for teaching and learning in environmental education

ability to 'see' and interpret the curriculum as a whole, to know or to diagnose what is happening in classroom situations, then emphasis must be placed on the skills of observing, describing and interpreting classroom life in an informed manner. Space does not allow for a detailed account of the philosophy underpinning the development of the Eisner model or for a critique of its validity. Readers' attention is drawn to the key works which set the approach in philosophical and practical context (Eisner 1979, 1982, 1985, 1991).

Both of the situations illuminated below have a common starting point. Their schemes of work and topics are based on a series of visits to an environmental studies centre in the heart of a large city. The centre comprises a classroom surrounded by nine acres of land within which are demonstration gardens, a nature reserve, a pond, woodland, green-houses, an animal unit, a poultry unit, and facilities for studying bee-keeping, weather, outdoor birds and conservation. The classes described are of children aged 10–11 years, and both had a parallel series of visits to this centre, with common input of teaching and practical experiences provided by the head of the unit, Mrs Russell. The major difference between the classrooms of the two schools is their teachers' stated and perceived approach to the organization of learning in environmental education. In many ways the two classrooms reflect the accepted and well documented distinction between 'traditional' and 'progressive' organizational styles and their associated teaching behaviour, as defined by Bennett (1976). They thus represent two very different approaches to planning for the inclusion of environmental work in the primary curriculum. The names of the schools, adults and children described in these accounts have been changed.

ST AIDAN'S SCHOOL

The class attending the Field Centre this year belongs to Miss Fairfax, the deputy head teacher of St Aidan's School. A visit to her classroom reveals an atmosphere of formality. The classroom frieze boards act as a restaurant menu, indicating the daily fare on offer – maths in the form of a number line and sets of multiplication tables, English in the form of lists of spellings, geography in the shape of a world map. The blackboard bears signs of the 'Chef's Special' by way of a set of division sums and a list of spellings to be learned that week, together with scattered notes of activities to be undertaken and administration to be completed.

The learners' desks are laid out in rows facing the blackboard, with the teacher's desk acting as the focal point of the entire room. Miss Fairfax's no-nonsense attitude might be mistaken for sternness or even severity, but a happy, purposeful classroom atmosphere prevails. For much of the day, it is business as usual with Miss Fairfax, the classroom chef, mixing the main ingredients of the three Rs with the recommended amounts of instruction, information and invocations to 'listen', 'remember' and 'concentrate'.

On my first visit, last autumn, the children were identifying and studying the many leaves they had brought back after their recent Field Centre experience. As is the pattern with Miss Fairfax's lessons, she began by reviewing the work that had been done during the previous lesson as she handed out the children's folders of work. These folders were kept as records of the class's Field Centre lessons, and added to throughout the year; at this early stage in the term each folder already contained numerous work sheets, diagrams to label and pictures to colour, all on the theme of trees and leaves. The majority of folders were commented upon while her audience waited with bated breath. The written work had all been marked in great detail, and notes of corrections to be made had been left on each page.

During this process Miss Fairfax was not slow to praise well presented work, showing it to the rest of the class for their discussion:

'That's a nice oak leaf sketch, Robert . . . ' or

'Neat handwriting here, Jennifer . . . well done!'

Miss Fairfax proceeded briskly onward to the business of the day, producing and distributing the follow-up work sheet she had devised for this lesson. She then reviewed the learning which had taken place during the class's recent visit to the Field Centre, and which had been incorporated into the design of the work sheet. This was done by means of a question and answer session, aimed at factual accuracy:

'What do we call some of the foods that trees get from the soil?'
'Minerals, miss.'
'That's right, Akeel. Well remembered.'

As she went on to work through the work sheet line by line and answer by answer, Miss Fairfax was at pains to employ the correct scientific vocabulary and constantly encouraged her pupils to do likewise. Her revision of the work sheet included mentioning every missing word needed for an answer, writing them on the blackboard and pronouncing them phonetically to help the less able children. A number of other children, considered able to do this, were given the option of producing their own piece of writing rather than including the facts in work sheet form.

Before setting the children to work, Miss Fairfax was careful to emphasize the importance of correct spelling and vocabulary:

'What's the word we use to describe a leaf which is drying up?'
'Dead, miss.'
'No, Pauline. Think again.'
'It's a bit like a potato crisp, miss.'
'That's not the word I'm looking for. Come on, somebody. . . . It starts with a letter B.'
'Breaking up?'
'That's two words, Ka-Kit. I'm looking for one. It's got something to do with breaking up, but it's an adjective not a verb. It's a describing word. It means easily broken.'
'Brittle, miss.'
'Well done, Patrick. You can have a house point for that. Do you remember? Mrs Russell used it at the Field Centre. And how do you spell it – with one "t" or two?'
'Two ts, miss. It's like "little".'
'Good, Melanie. You were listening well yesterday.'

The lesson continued in much the same vein, with teacher-directed questions and answers, based on the facts of the subject in hand. Miss Fairfax answered any questions the children had about the tasks they were set and once the introduction was over, the children were set to work on filling in the answers to the sheet.

The children clearly enjoyed the tasks they were engaged in. On this occasion, they settled down quickly to the task of completing the work sheet, pleased to demonstrate all that they had remembered from their out-of-classroom tasks. The peaceful atmosphere of the classroom was broken only by the clatter of the occasional shifting chair; the task was carried out painstakingly, and with success. A number of other assignments including identifying and sketching the collected leaves, using squared paper to help measure their areas and calculating the amount of deterioration (i.e. loss of chlorophyll) within each leaf were organized for pupils to move on to when the work sheet was finished. The children were expected to complete all these in due course, but were allowed to choose the order in which the activities were attempted. The leaves available included hawthorn, oak, horse chestnut, eucalyptus, laurel and sycamore. In case of doubt detailed tree charts of Britain and Northern Europe were pinned up on a frieze board, and there was a plentiful supply of reference books to aid identification and sketching; samples of each leaf had also been dried, mounted on card, labelled and covered with clear film by Miss Fairfax as further teaching aids.

The topic under consideration in the spring term was a study of the various bird species in the grounds of the Field Centre. The children spent their time at the centre identifying the birds and learning about their colours, characteristics, habitats and diet, making notes which they could write up on their return to school.

Back at St Aidan's, the children continued to work on Miss Fairfax's planned recording sheets, as well as colouring and labelling various line drawings of birds. As before, the atmosphere remained purposeful and industrious. One lesson I visited generated a lively discussion; the children remembered much of what they had been told at the Field Centre. Higher order questions of 'how' and 'why' intermingled with Miss Fairfax's ideas of what the class needed to know. Sketching and painting took place from objects brought back to the classroom and from reference books, and the more able children engaged in valuable research work using the classroom library books. As a result, a number of colourful and accurate bird pictures were displayed on frieze boards and in the corridor, alongside neatly written captions describing their colour, dimensions, habitats, diet and so on.

In the summer term, the class engaged in pond-dipping at the Field Centre. The children were placed in mixed ability groups, and challenged to see how many different invertebrates they could gather from the pond, and identify successfully.

'Who can tell me what different small creatures we might find in or around the pond?'
'Insects, miss.'
'Good . . . '
'And arachnids.'
'Well done, Tammy.'
'How many legs do insects have, Lisa?'
'Six.'
'And arachnids?'
'Eight, Miss.'
'Well done, Lisa. Now children, what about creatures with shells. What do we call them?'
'Crustaceans.'
'Molluscs.'
'Which is it? Do you know the difference? That's something we can find out at school. What other creatures might we find, Islam?'
'Um . . . centipedes, miss.'
'Yes.'
'And millipedes as well.'
'Good boy. Do centipedes really have a hundred legs?'
'No, miss. Just quite a lot.'
'Any other creatures you can think of? Carl?'
'Plurals, miss?'
'No, Carl. Plurals are what we do in English, remember? Plural means more than one.'
'What about leeches, miss? There might be some in the pond.'
'Yes, there might, Nadia. Good girl.'

With help from a number of ready reference charts at the centre, the children soon began to learn how to use keys and identify each species. Miss Fairfax continued to direct operations, maintaining concentration and enthusiasm:

'When you find something in your net and you want to know what it is, these four Key Cards will help you. They have lists on them of all the pond dwellers you might find this morning. Key A has the names and pictures of all creatures with a shell and no legs. On Key B you'll find creatures with no legs and no shells. Key C has creatures with three pairs of legs on it. . . . '
'They're insects, miss.'
'That's right, Abdul. And on Key D you'll find creatures with more than three pairs of legs. Now before we start, I want you to look at the

Key Cards and find out which one has centipedes and millipedes on it.'

The children looked slowly and carefully through all the cards in turn.

'They're not on any of the cards, miss. Why not?'
'Because centipedes and millipedes don't live in water. They're not pond dwellers, you see. Right, off you go. . . . '

Upon returning to school, the children launched themselves on further sketching, work sheets and fact-finding about the characteristics and life styles of the various pond dwellers they had seen. The great majority of the class soon became adept at identification and description of each species, producing numerous drawings and paintings for the classroom walls and corridor; the emphasis in both prose and picture was firmly upon factual accuracy. Close observation of both Miss Fairfax and her approach, the considerable effort put into the preparation of lesson material beforehand and its delivery in the classroom, reveals a genuine concern for the progress of the pupils in her care. The children themselves reminded me forcibly of rows of empty bottles edging slowly along on Miss Fairfax's conveyor belt of knowledge. There was no doubt in my mind that the bottles would be filled to a greater or lesser extent, and that the children would know what Miss Fairfax wanted them to know by the end of it. Furthermore, they would have much fun and enjoyment on the way.

STONEBRIDGE SCHOOL

The class selected to visit the Field Centre this year was the year 6 class of the deputy head teacher, Mr Bailey. The children at Stonebridge also had an extra resource available in the shape of Mrs Castle, the environmental studies coordinator at the school. Mr Bailey and Mrs Castle worked together as a teaching team.

The classroom is bright and cheerful, with displays of mathematical and language work competing with a striking pantheon of the gods from Greek mythology, all freely interpreted by the children themselves, gazing down rather intimidatingly from Olympian heights upon the classroom below. Well stocked bookshelves and neat piles of assignment cards guarantee work for idle hands. The window ledges are crammed with models and pot plants, carefully labelled with the names of their owners. The children are seated in ability groups of between four and six pupils, the desks arranged informally around the room. Mr Bailey plans and organizes visits and equipment. Mrs Castle takes the responsibility for much of the follow-up work to each Field Centre visit.

When the children visited the Field Centre in the autumn term, they began by studying the invertebrates in the pond. Various groups of children took up positions around the edge of the pond and, nets in hand, began gently to skim the surface of the water. Using Mrs Russell's charts, the children had little difficulty in applying their newly acquired knowledge of insects, crustaceans, arachnids *et al.* and classifying their catches according to number of body parts, legs, etc.

'Look what we've got – a water boatman and a pond skater!'
'What's this one, John?'
'Well, if it's got six legs it's an insect. Any more than that and it might be an arachnid or a crustacean. You'd better count 'em and see.'
'Can we swop you a water scorpion for a snail?'

Having accounted for all the creatures they had caught and replaced them in the water, the children returned to school and began to record the results of their activity. With the help of Mr Bailey, the school's computer studies leader, the children began to refer to library books and set up their own database on 'Mini-Beasts'. Group and individual contributions were composed, edited by a committee of the children, typed in on the computer and the results printed out neatly in extra-large letters, ready for display. Creative writing in the form of poems and stories was drafted in longhand, however laboriously, and then transferred to the keyboard. Even the captions for the many paintings and drawings around the classroom were produced by the computer, operated by young typists with casual ease. The children chose the creatures they wished to write about; Hafiz's is a typical example of how even the less academic children in the class felt able to make a contribution:

'My animal is called a newt. A newt lives in water and it eats insects. It is a vertebrate and it has four legs. It can be brown or green. It has a head, a body and a tail. It has a backbone too.'

This in ten minutes from a pupil who normally dawdled for anything up to an hour in constructing even a couple of simple sentences.

It did not take the children very long to set up a database which had detailed references to the habits and lifestyles of ladybirds, dragonflies, water scorpions, butterflies, newts, bees, leeches, snails, pond beetles, spiders, caterpillars, water boatmen, frogs, water beetles, pond skaters and various other creatures. Information could be (and often was) called up at the touch of a button, and the entire database was made available to the rest of the school as a reference source.

Other visits to the Field Centre included a similar search to find and classify invertebrates on land, carried out with such painstaking attention to detail that the entire nature reserve, woodland, field and garden seemed to be plagued by grazing swarms of locust-like children, rummaging through the undergrowth. Once more, the catches were identified, observed and recorded.

The children soon became expert in identifying the various species they found. They took particular pleasure in observing some of the more unusual invertebrates kept at the centre.

'That Giant Snail was fantastic, miss.'
'I liked the Hissing Cockroach best.'
'I wonder why it's hissing – perhaps it doesn't like people.'
'What noises do you think Giant Millipedes might make, children?'
'A lot if they all had boots on, miss.'
'How did the Red Rumped Spider get its name, miss?'
'I don't know, Basmin. What do you think?'
'I think the King of the Jungle smacked him for being naughty. Perhaps he trapped someone he shouldn't have in his web. I'm going to write a story about him when we get back to school.'

As time went by, the children became more and more absorbed in the new worlds they had seen at the Field Centre. They had no difficulty in separating fact from fiction, and yet were not at all afraid to fantasize or speculate about how or why these tiny creatures came to be. Indeed many were the Kiplingesque tales of 'How The Red Rumped Spider Became' or 'Why The Cockroach Came To Hiss'.

Later in the year, their interest in the more curious or bizarre forms of animal life developed into a study of reptiles and amphibians, ranging from the snake and the axolotl to the fire salamander and the wall lizard. Once again, speculation ran riot, alongside attention to scientific detail.

'What a strange name – axolotls. Where do they come from?'
'What do they feed on?'
'I'm going to look these places up in an atlas, and draw a big map of where their real homes are.'

Throughout these visits, Mr Bailey and Mrs Castle remained discreetly in the background, setting and steering tasks and complex questions, making themselves available for consultation but allowing the imaginations of the children to guide progress alongside formal knowledge and skills. The nature database on the Stonebridge computer was expanded week by week to include detailed biographies of new creatures from anolis lizards to xenopus toads.

Some of the boys developed a curious, almost ghoulish interest in 'skellingtons', and they were intrigued by those of lizard, frog, rabbit, fish, fox cub and snake which could be seen at the centre. One of Mrs Castle's contacts worked at a local hospital, and was able to borrow X-rays of human bones for the children to inspect. They were amazed at the variety of skeleton 'designs', and took great interest in comparing animal with human. Higher order skills of comparison, prediction and using evidence were actively promoted:

'I thought all skellingtons were the same – just bigger or smaller. But they're not . . . compare these two. . . . '
'Watch how this leg moves, miss.'
'How do our knees and elbows work, miss?'
'I bet elephants have big skeletons – not as big as a dinosaur, though!'
'If we didn't have no bones we'd be all floppy, wouldn't we, sir?'
'Go on . . . suggest what it would be like to be an invertebrate. . . . '

And perhaps the ultimate question:

'Who decided skeletons should be made this way?' [followed by a discussion on the Creation story and evolution]

Towards the end of their year's work, the children progressed from reptiles and amphibians to mammals and fish. The differences between species were analysed and discussed.

'Mammals have hair or fur on their bodies . . . '
'. . . and they're warm-blooded, sir.'
'Fish live in water, they're cold-blooded.'
'Sir – if tropical means hot, how come tropical fish are cold-blooded?'

The children considered which creature they would like to be if they had the choice.

'I'd be a lion, 'cos they're king of the jungle.'
'I'd be a sloth – you can do nothing all day and nobody grumbles at you.'
'Bet you'd be bored in no time, Abbas.'
'I'd be a cheetah, 'cos they can run ever so fast.'
'I wouldn't like to be an elephant, 'cos you get killed for your tusks.'

This latter statement reveals evidence of the pupils' increasing aware-ness of current conservation issues. At various times of the year, often spontaneously, they touched on issues such as pollution, acid rain and nuclear waste; even though these considerations were incidental to the task in hand, both Mr Bailey and Mrs Castle were flexible enough to realize that the children were genuinely interested and to give time to discussions of the matter. To those who value a lesson by the amount of written work and formal statements of attainment springing from it, no doubt these sessions may have been considered 'a waste of time'. However, I feel that this was far from the case – the children were addressing issues on which they had genuine concerns, and were applying higher order thinking skills to a range of subject matter.

The learners applied their newly gained science knowledge to the school grounds at Stonebridge. Various habitats were designed and constructed to encourage wildlife. They also built a small wormery in the classroom, drew diagrams (top and cross-section) and experimented by leaving various foods on the surface of the soil.

'Look, sir – the cheese is still on top.'
'The small leaf has been pulled down under the soil . . . '
'. . . but the two big leaves are still there.'
'Worms don't seem to go for cauliflower.'
'I'm not surprised, sir. I can't stand it either!'
'Have the worms taken any of the food we left, children?'
'Yes, miss. The onion . . . and the small bits of crisp.'
'What flavour crisps do worms like, then?'
'Ready salted, I think.'
'Not a lot of people know that!'

The children also kept weather charts, carried out traffic and litter surveys, and observed and listed the number of wild birds visiting the playground. They sorted and decorated pebbles, and tried some simple woodcarving from broken branches and tree roots. They used fir cones and other natural materials to make models of hedgehogs and spiders, collected and classified leaves from the playground, and set up a nature trail around the neighbourhood encompassing a number of new discoveries they had made.

Parents were closely involved in this aspect of the learning process:

'My dad was surprised when I told him all about the wildlife around our streets. He said he must have been walking about with his eyes closed for years. I'm taking him round our trail next Saturday.'

Throughout the year, the pupils wrote – often before being asked, and with increasing confidence:

The owl listens carefully,
Unblinking,
Silent in the too-peaceful night.
He waits, still as a feathered statue,
Dappled in moonlight,
Menacing,
Awaiting his timid and unwary prey.
Suddenly his eyes flash red with fire,
Back go his wings
And he dives from his perch. . . .
The owl is wise
Because he looks
Before he leaps –
Not like we do!

There is no doubt that the partnership of Mr Bailey and Mrs Castle harnessed the interests and talents of their pupils to the full throughout the year.

Before pursuing an elaboration of the differences in these settings, we provide further details of the 'common ground' shared by the two schools.

Both demonstrate meticulous levels of planning and organization applicable to both whole-school policies and individual class topics/programmes of work in environmental education. While it is not possible for reasons of space to give precise details of curriculum plans and a task analysis for both schools, an overview of the key features involved will serve to illustrate points taken up in further discussion about how they organize the curriculum for learning.

Both schools have a well thought out and discussed policy document for the teaching of environmental education. This policy is applicable to the school as a whole, taking account of progression and a variety of approaches to learning. It includes:

- aims
- objectives
- methods of teaching
- statements on timetabling/time available
- content (knowledge, understanding, skills, concepts, attitudes)
- resources and organization of materials for teaching and learning
- assessment, record keeping and evaluation
- policy for developing and maintaining the school and its grounds as an environmental resource
- policy for field work (including visits to the environmental studies centre discussed above).

The policy and plans of both schools take full account of the National Curriculum guidelines for Environmental Education, *Curriculum Guidance 7* (NCC 1990b) which describe the three essential and inter-related components of the theme, as discussed in Chapter 1:

- education *about* the environment (that is, basic knowledge and understanding of the environment)
- education *for* the environment (concerned with values, attitudes and positive action for the environment)
- education *in* or *through* the environment (that is, using the environment as a resource with emphasis on enquiry and investigation, and pupils' first-hand experiences).

Plans also take account of the nature and scope of environmental education and how this subject area might be delivered through the attainment targets of the core and foundation subjects of the National Curriculum. This scope consists of the two broad areas which relate to these core and foundation subjects:

1 *Knowledge and understanding*
(a) Knowledge about the environment at a variety of levels.
(b) Knowledge and understanding of environmental issues at a variety of levels.
(c) Knowledge of alternative attitudes and approaches to environmental issues.

2 *Skills*
(a) Finding out about the environment, either directly through the environment or by using secondary sources.
(b) Communicating:
   (i) knowledge about the environment;
   (ii) both the pupils' own and alternative attitudes to environmental issues.
(c) Participation (as part of the class group and personally).

Skill development also takes account of the inclusion and progressive development of cross-curricular skills in the curriculum as a whole, including:

• communication
• numeracy
• study
• problem solving
• personal and social
• information technology.

National guidance for environmental education identifies areas of knowledge and understanding of the environment which are suitable starting points for learning. We have previously identified the named topics as:

• climate
• soils, rocks and minerals
• water
• materials and resources including energy
• plants and animals
• people and their communities
• buildings, industrialization and waste.

The topics of both Stonebridge and St Aidan's School were firmly rooted in these suggested areas of learning, and took account of cross-curricular implications. Each school had topic work plans or matrices, indicating the range and extent of knowledge about the environment to be addressed, key issues involved, links with attainment targets and statements of attainment of core and foundation subjects, details of skills to be developed relating to education in and for the environment, and details of more general cross-curricular skills to be included.

Plans were linked to assessment procedures. Because of the cross-curricular nature of the theme of environmental education, these procedures were linked to the whole curriculum and the broad national framework for assessment. Records were kept of tasks set, attainment targets covered, and of specific environmental content covered – including knowledge, understanding, skills and concepts.

In summary, it must be emphasized that both schools had full documentation of intended learning, its relevance to the National Curriculum framework and related assessment and record keeping procedures. Yet the two approaches to implementation of these plans differed considerably, as the classroom descriptions show.

As already made clear, no single approach to the organization of the curriculum or teaching methodology for environmental education or any other theme is recommended. The schools in our case studies illuminate two very different approaches, which are both successful in practice.

At St Aidan's School, environmental matters are addressed through National Curriculum and other subjects, and to a certain extent the approach incorporates elements of separate timetabling of the theme. At Stonebridge, study of the environment results from whole-curriculum planning and a series of integrated yet subject-based topics. Both arrangements are in line with national Orders. Thus it is interesting to have the benefit of the written criticisms and their illumination of the learning processes taking place in each setting.

Five criteria were established to look more closely at organizational issues at Stonebridge and St Aidan's, i.e. the way in which the classes and classrooms are structured to facilitate teaching and learning in environmental education. These were:

- the way in which the children are organized in the classroom
- the way in which adults are organized in the classroom
- the use of classroom space
- the use of time
- the approach to curriculum organization/integration.

At Stonebridge School, the following characteristics were observed. There is a high level of individualization of learning. The head teacher and teacher concerned believe that this is important for developing children's ability to work independently and autonomously. A large amount of group work also takes place, encouraging collaborative work where children listen to and learn from each other. Because of this approach to child organization, the class teacher inevitably seems to have a limited amount of time to spend with an individual child or with a small group. The classroom space is organized in 'seating groups', where a number of children sit around adjoining desks. This is a flexible arrangement in so far as it allows children to work individually and to join in group discussions as and when appropriate.

The seating groups are formed by the teacher and are based on pupil achievement. The stated reasoning behind this is that when children of similar academic ability are seated together, this is helpful for setting up tasks and activities that are well matched to the needs and abilities of the learners. The school favours an integrated topic work approach to learning from field experiences, involving the integration of subject areas in teaching sessions and the minimal use of timetabling. Arguments put forward in favour of this method of organization of time and curriculum include the fact that there is flexibility for the pupils to choose how much time is to be spent on an activity, thus encouraging a significant level of responsibility for their own work. Also, there should be an increase in the pupils' intrinsic motivation to address tasks, resulting from the fact that to a large extent they have control over and involvement in their own learning and can follow up individual interests arising from visits. Subject areas of the curriculum tend to be integrated throughout the teaching day, rather than the more traditional approach of teaching core subjects or 'basics' in the morning and topics in the afternoon. A multidisciplinary focus is followed, rather than a single and separate subject focus, though it must be emphasized that environmental education is clearly linked to core subjects, and planning takes due account of the need for inclusion of and balance between all National Curriculum subject areas. An array of evidence is found in this school to demonstrate explicit planning for integration of work based on the Field Centre visits. The visits are regarded as the beginning of integrated investigation and enquiry, rather than as a subject-related end product in themselves.

In contrast, little emphasis is placed on individualization of learning tasks in St Aidan's School. The class works together on a common activity deriving from field visits for the majority of time. Staff justify this whole-class organizational procedure with arguments stemming from the ever-increasing time constraints imposed by the National Curriculum, and the need to cover so much material. It is claimed that the teacher can spend much more time in discussion with the class, giving opportunities for encouraging collaborative learning, exploring ideas, demonstrating objects and experiments, sharing problem solving and encouraging all pupils to participate in finding solutions. Where group work does occur, the organization tends to be for teaching purposes, where the teacher instructs a group of children who are at the same stage and ability level and are undertaking the same task at the same moment in time. Otherwise, groups are for convenience and serve organizational purposes such as sharing resources and equipment. Reasons articulated for this more formal approach to organization and timetabling include the fact that there can be difficulty over monitoring 'who is doing what' in a large class: so many resources would be required that the teacher would spend more time on resource allocation and management than on teaching, and be able to devote very little time to individual children and their needs. It is considered that more effective follow-up work is done as a result of visits to the Field Centre if the class as a whole undertakes structured follow-up lessons arising out of first-hand field experiences. Follow-up sessions are generally timetabled as science or environmental education, and take place as separate sessions from the other core areas of the National Curriculum, mathematics and language. The whole class does similar work which is usually teacher directed, often following a single subject focus. The term 'direct instruction' applies to the organization of this learning environment, referring to an academically focused (National Curriculum specified), teacher-directed classroom using sequenced and structured materials. Goals are clear to the pupils and coverage of content, including National Curriculum attainment targets, is extensive. Rather than viewing the field experiences as the beginning of integrated investigation and enquiry, there is a tendency to perceive them as an (important) end product in themselves. The field visits 'provide answers' to be reinforced in subject-specific, timetabled slots rather than 'raise questions' for negotiated enquiry.

The classroom observations described above suggest that integrated topic work as a result of direct contact with the environment involves children in thinking for themselves, in personalized and meaningful learning, and in expressing facts and ideas in an original and interesting way, without regard for subject barriers and formalized, rigid 'right or wrong' answers. Children in the Stonebridge classroom working in this way readily developed great fluency and speed in their writing and recording. The sheer volume and speed of their work was impressive throughout the periods of observations; so too was the range and scope of their ideas, their willingness to tolerate uncertainty, to try things out and to improvise. The criticism shows that they could cope with the unusual, perhaps the bizarre and certainly with situations which had no obvious or 'right' answer ('How did the Red Rumped Spider get its name? 'Who decided skeletons should be made this way?'). These children were encouraged to and were willing to investigate and to seek out answers and solutions They also demonstrated a good sense of humour, and very obvious enjoyment of their investigations. Many thoughts and ideas clearly derived from active imaginations.

Children in the St Aidan's classroom also enjoyed their studies enormously – a fact without doubt, though a far more formal atmosphere prevailed. Focus of attention was almost always on that which was 'right', the obvious and the factually accurate. Facts were to be learned (and indeed they were) and recorded in an appropriate format. Work on the whole appeared to be far less fluent but a great deal of ground was covered. Much recording was done by way of work sheets – in class-based lessons, usually requiring correct answers to be filled in. While a great emphasis on factual knowledge was documented, there was perhaps a lack of personal enquiry in the children's work. Data support the description of direct instruction provided by Rosenshine:

> Direct instruction refers to academically focused, teacher-directed classrooms using sequenced and structured materials.
>
> Questions are at a low cognitive level so that students can produce many correct responses and feedback to students is immediate and academically oriented. . . . Interaction is characterised as structured, but not authoritarian. The goal is to move students through a sequenced set of materials or tasks.
>
> (Rosenshine, in Stodolsky 1988)

Nevertheless, it was apparent that after a year of working in this way, the children showed understanding of issues and a personal involvement in environmental matters. Beyond the knowledge lay a genuine concern, born out of first-hand experiences and understanding of facts. The criticisms also reveal interesting insights into teaching styles and teacher–learner interaction. In the Stonebridge classroom, an atmosphere of 'freedom' prevailed. Pupils were at liberty to explore and develop their own interests, enthusiasms and original ideas and the teachers also recognized freedom in so far as they were not constrained within the limits of pre-planned and rigid organization of activities. Mr Bailey's children were free to choose the creatures they wished to write about and include on their database. They side-tracked into investigation of various conservation issues and composed creative writing, often without being asked. The teachers supported this spontaneous expression and self-initiated learning, actively encouraging the pupils to hypothesize, to explore ideas and problems and to engage in practical investigations and experimentation.

Whether consciously or unconsciously, it would also seem apparent from the observations of Stonebridge classroom life that these teachers actually encourage higher order thought processes in so far as they support and facilitate the development of ideas in new directions, the

making of connections that are not immediately obvious, and the building on to the novel ideas of others. They do not readily supply solutions
or give away outcomes.

'Why don't you ask Mrs Castle? She'll know the answer.'
'I've tried doing that, but she told me to find out on my own.'

Furthermore, Mrs Castle and Mr Bailey recognize that factual errors
occur and are indeed expected and inevitable. The whole notion of
uncertainty and ambiguity is handled in a positive and purposeful way.
Questions discussed with the children are meaningful yet open-ended,
perhaps having no predetermined answers – certainly having no
answers that are speedily arrived at by recall to rote learning of facts: this
is, of course, in such contrast to the teaching style of Miss Fairfax which
has little space for error and ambiguity, and emphasizes rote learning.

Thus another component to be taken into account when approaching
environmental work is individual preferred styles of teaching and learning. Personality differences and preferences cannot be ignored. Some
children may prefer (and learn far more readily in) a highly structured,
didactic approach as demonstrated in Miss Fairfax's classroom. Others
may find the experiential, problem solving style as displayed by Mrs
Castle and Mr Bailey more suitable.

Whether one is more inclined to the style of Miss Fairfax or of Mrs
Castle and Mr Bailey, clear criteria need to be established when grouping children or undertaking whole-class instruction, so that the best
possible match is made between task, learner and situation. Planning for
teaching in environmental education, as in all subject areas, needs to
take account of:

- size of groups (individuals, groups, whole classes)
- composition of groups (personality, ability, friendships, interests,
  ability to cooperate, level of task)
- monitoring of outcomes.

Furthermore, aspects of the teacher's own role are a vital consideration:

- style of interaction
- use of questioning, clarifying, intervening, prompting, imparting
  information
- balance between consistency and flexibility.

The case studies reported above demonstrate very adequate coverage of
certain elements of the planning model articulated at the beginning
of this chapter (Fig. 5.1). In particular, they address the critical areas of
learning about the environment and learning in or through the environment, with a focus on the natural world and first-hand experiences in
the locality. The learners developed knowledge and understanding,

concepts, skills and attitudes through their out-of-school experiences, and no doubt developed an enhanced awareness of and concern for living things in the world around them.

What is missing from these case studies is a predetermined and obvious focus on environmental issues and a global perspective (considering education *for* the environment). This should not be interpreted as a criticism. No one topic or programme of study can adequately address all aspects of the planning model and two similar case studies were selected for inclusion so that differences in approach to organization could be illuminated and discussed.

To redress the balance, we conclude this chapter by emphasizing the need to incorporate issue-based themes and topics in environmental education curriculum plans throughout the primary phase.

ISSUE-BASED THEMES AND TOPICS

The scope for choice of themes is almost limitless; common topics for which a great deal of published resource material is available include tropical rainforests, population increase, acid rain, the greenhouse effect, Antarctica, food production, waste materials, pollution, and endangered species. Planning for topics of this kind should take account of what the learners already know, bearing in mind that knowledge derived from the media, films, books and talking with other adults may well be incomplete, incorrect, biased or stereotypical. A useful starting point for planning could be to list the key concepts that will be addressed throughout the topic in order for the children's knowledge and understanding to be developed. For example, concepts relating to a study of population growth might include:

● Many regions of the world are overpopulated.
● World population is increasing.
● Migration into cities is causing overpopulation.
● Overpopulation causes a wide range of problems including lack of water, health problems, insanitary conditions, unemployment, pollution, squalor, lack of amenities and basic services, and increased crime.

Key concepts relating to a topic on acid rain would include:

● Acid rain affects buildings, human health, and the life of animals, plants and all organisms.
● It crosses national boundaries, and is thus a problem not confined to single countries.
● There are laws designed to prevent and reduce acid rain.

- Acid rain is caused by pollution and gases produced by industry, power stations and some vehicles.
- Such pollution enters the atmosphere, forms acid in clouds and is then deposited as acid rain, snow or dry deposition.

The above are not intended to be comprehensive lists, merely examples. They are written in 'adult' language. The teacher's task is to consider the key ideas to be addressed in a topic, design a range of activities which will help pupils learn or develop their knowledge of these ideas at an appropriate level, and provide the necessary background resource material (films, video, posters, books, etc.) for these activities to be successfully pursued. It is highly likely that in practice, such environmental topics will be incorporated into or linked with planning for learning in geography and/or science. Related aims of practical tasks and activities designed for the children, irrespective of the precise content, should be to:

- develop existing knowledge and understanding
- eliminate misconceptions/false knowledge brought to the learning situation from other sources
- counteract biased and stereotypical ideas that may be held by the pupils.

Activities which are successful in meeting these aims will no doubt share common characteristics: they will provide accurate, up-to-date and unbiased information, well matched to the abilities and existing knowledge of the learner; they will be interactive in the sense that they will engage the learner in thought-provoking and stimulating tasks; and they will encourage reflection, debate and decision making rather than merely providing 'the right answer'. After all, environmental issues are predominantly controversial; few are straightforward enough to be presented as matters of fact.

In these days of ever-increasing public awareness about environmental matters, a proliferation of reference and illustrative materials is available for teachers to adapt and use to support learning activities. It is hoped that tasks based on such resources will be a judicious mix of acquiring background information, interpretation and debate. Task design is an exciting challenge – an almost limitless range of possibilities exists including comprehension exercises, research studies, games, role play situations, art and craft work, debate, quizzes and dramatic representations. The following examples are intended to 'give a flavour' of possible classroom tasks that could be developed on a range of environmental issues:

On the subject of tropical rainforests

Tropical rainforest comprehension

Read the passage carefully and then answer the questions.
Rainforests grow in tropical parts of the world where the climate never changes. There are four different layers of plants in a rainforest – the emergent layer, the canopy, the under-storey and the forest floor. Many special flowers like orchids grow in rainforests. Some very unusual animals can also be found there – like monkeys, gorillas, sloths, snakes and toucans. Special people live in the forests and know them well. Some tribes are called Pygmies and others Amerindians. They use all the natural resources from the forest to live on. However, today, rainforests are being destroyed as so many of the trees are being cut down. The land is needed for growing crops and the timber is sold to other countries. This has made many plants and animals die and floods have occurred during rainstorms. Cutting down the trees makes the world's weather change and we have to make sure that we help the conservation groups to save the special rainforests.

1 Where are rainforests found?
2 What can be found in the forests?
3 Who lives in the forests?
4 Why are rainforests being destroyed?
5 Can you think of what can be made from the timber?
6 What happens when the trees are cut down?
7 Who helps to save our rainforests?
8 See how many words you can make from TROPICAL RAINFORESTS.

Use with Key Stage 2

This comprehension is suitable for Key Stage 2 pupils. Some work on rainforests would need to have been covered prior to this work sheet. Each pupil must answer in full sentences to ensure that they have understood the comprehension passage. This work sheet may be followed up by some class discussion and by elaborating the key concepts, perhaps by further writing or art and craft work.

Tropical rainforests role play

Characters:
Indigenous people   Tourists
Commercial foresters   Forest clearers, e.g. bulldozer
Government officials   drivers, tractor drivers, road
Environmentalists   makers and lumberjacks

Rubber tappers	Trees
Mine companies	Flowers
Migrants looking for land	Animals
Cattle ranchers	Birds
Farmers	

Use in primary schools

A play can be written through discussion and input from the whole class or groups. A script can be devised using some or all of the characters. The play can then be performed for class members or the whole school, or maybe even performed for parents and the money raised can be used to support a registered conservation group. It is important that the teacher works at the right level for the pupils and that the interests of each character are put forward in the script. This is a fun way for children to learn about the various issues raised in rainforest topic work.

On the subject of population growth (for Key Stage 1)

These activities have been designed within National Curriculum guidelines for geography, AT4 Human Geography, levels 1 to 4.

Activity 1

Aims and objectives: to help the children understand that population growth causes overcrowding in some countries. That this overcrowding can in turn cause problems.

Equipment: a rope and two cones; a playground.

Strategy:
1 Rope off a small corner of the playground using the rope and cones.
2 Ask half the class to fit within the roped area.
3 Now ask the other half of the class to fit within the roped area – this should result in the children being squashed.
4 Encourage the children to think about what it would be like to live so closely. Introduce ideas such as: 'What might happen if Susan had a cold?' (Disease would spread quickly, etc.)

Activity 2

Aims and objectives: to help the children understand the water pollution and food contamination problems in shanty towns.

Equipment: a glass of dirty water and a stale bread bun.

Strategy:

1 Introduce the children to the water and bread bun and ask them if they would like to eat and drink the bread and water. Ask them why not.

2 Explain that this is what some people have to eat and drink. Ask them what they think might happen if someone drinks dirty water and eats bad food. (Bad health and illness occur.)

[Note: ensure that they do not sample the visual aids!]

Activity 3

Aims and objectives: to introduce the children to shanty towns and the problems that can occur there.

Equipment: photographs of shanty towns in cities such as Rio de Janeiro.

Strategy:

1 Introduce the photos to the children and ask them to tell you about what they see.

2 Follow what they observe and expand on this/ask questions about the problems that can occur from the shanty towns.

3 Compare it with the children's home neighbourhoods.

Activity 4

Aims and objectives: to introduce the ideas of population growth and overcrowding to the children.

Equipment: clear plastic box and enough marbles for the box to overflow.

Strategy:

1 Explain that the box is the classroom and the children must put one marble in for each child in the class.

2 Explain that hypothetically in 50 years' time, the class could have twice as many children if the population grows too much. Put into the box the right number of marbles to double the class.

3 As the box overflows, talk about how there would not be enough room for everyone, not enough chairs, paint, pencils, etc.

4 [This could be done at the same time or at a later date.] Discuss how this relates to the developing world and people's lack of food and water if the population continues growing at a high rate.

On the subject of population growth (for Key Stage 2)

Activity 1

Let the children work in pairs. They will need paper, pens and perhaps scissors, glue and felt pens. Tell them that they have been asked to prepare a leaflet for a city council informing people of the problems associated with an increasing population of the city. The leaflet, which can be illustrated, should:

- suggest some ways to relieve the pressure on the city and some solutions to an overcrowded area
- not just concentrate on solutions for the city to adopt, but also think how people could be prevented from moving into the city in the first place.

Activity 2

Give the children the following information:

Towns of the future

Some towns are being built with the future in mind. One such town is Arcosanti which is being constructed over 100 km north of Phoenix in the USA. It is similar to something out of a science fiction book. The use of an alternative form of energy to the conventional fossil fuels or hazardous nuclear energy has been a major consideration in its development. It is planned to house 6000 people and to supply them with all their energy needs through solar power. Being in the Arizona desert, there will be plenty of sunlight. The sun's rays will be captured by massive solar panels and turned into a usable form of energy like electricity.

- The task is for the pupils to design a town of the future for themselves.
- Use certain questions as stimuli:
    What would you put in it?
    What would be the most important things?
    What sort of environment would you put it in – a forest, by the sea, on a lake, by mountains?
    What would you call it?
- Make a model of it.
- Discuss the advantages it may have over towns of today.

SUMMARY

In conclusion, we reinforce the key message of this chapter, which is that planning for environmental education must take account of the complete threefold framework, and of the essential place of first-hand experiences in the environment. These, together with issue-based content, should promote the development of knowledge, understanding and appropriate behaviour. In the primary school effective programmes of work will incorporate a balance between local and global issues, and will promote the links between these. Programmes are likely to be topic based. They will almost certainly be linked to the attainment targets and programmes of study in geography and science, and it is highly likely that they will also incorporate other curriculum areas. We recommend no particular teaching style or approach to classroom organization. These are matters for individual schools and teachers to decide. The all-important aim of planning is to promote *effective* environmental education, wherein pupils will be encouraged not only to learn about issues ranging from local to global, but will also be helped to appreciate the need for decision making and the importance of personal concern and action in relation to environmental matters.

Chapter 6

Primary to secondary: a time of transition

Some pupils transferring to the secondary phase have passed through the system of teaching adopted by Miss Fairfax and some through that of Mr Bailey and Mrs Castle. Many will not have had experience of either type of competent teacher. Unless they take the trouble to visit the feeder schools, the secondary teachers who teach the new entrants will be unaware of the past mode of learning to which the individuals in their charge have been subjected. They will soon discover that not all the incomers had the good fortune to attend an environmental study centre regularly; their knowledge and understanding of the natural world and the built environment will vary enormously. It is no wonder that some secondary cynics decide to start all over again. Applefield Comprehensive School receives an annual intake of up to 300 pupils from nearly 30 primary feeder schools with the majority coming from six in the locality. Teachers at Applefield have learned that they can assume nothing where the environmental experience of each individual is concerned. New teachers are told the story of the time that a group of 11-year-olds were set the task of replanting the lupins rescued from the bulldozer, about to level the local allotment land for playing field space. For three months the plants had been piled against the boundary wall so that any leaf evidence had long since disappeared. The after school activity ended with an inspection of the work – true all had been planted in neat rows as directed: all with their roots in the air and their stalks in the ground! 'Assume nothing, even the most basic of knowledge and understanding' was the message.

Applefield, like all secondary schools, has its ration of Miss Fairfax and Mrs Castle/Mr Bailey types; it also has its Mr Careless BA whose classroom discipline and lesson planning is not all that it might be. The world of the secondary school, through its complexity of size, timetable domination and constant movement from place to place, is hard enough on the new pupil, without having several teachers with varying styles and levels of competence. But much can be done to alleviate many of the difficulties of transfer both before and after the event. Surprisingly little investigation has been devoted to this, although past efforts still have relevance today, as with the project conducted by Birmingham's Education Development Centre some time ago (Neal 1975).

Environmental education is one special case in the transition process, able to contribute to liaison between primary and secondary teachers and, in so doing, aid both the pastoral and academic interchange. The primary school head, and the head of lower school of the secondary, should welcome positive intervention by environmentalists. It is essential that the coordinators for environmental education work through these two senior staff members when initiating any contact between schools. The primary/secondary liaison over environmental matters is well exemplified by the following comment from the coordinator for environmental education in a Glasgow secondary school:

> Secondary schools too, should liaise on environmental education with feeder primaries. A co-ordinated policy can bring higher order skills as a starting point to the environment in the first year of the secondary phase. It can also save duplication of effort and avoid fragmented knowledge at that stage. Secondary school environmental enthusiasts (staff and members of our environment club) can help the environment programme in the upper stages of feeder primaries. Secondary expertise and resources may thus be appreciated and the danger of underestimating primary pupils and methods overcome.
>
> (Letter to the author as secretary to the NAEE)

The transition process is not something which is to be left to the summer term before transfer. It needs to be one part of an ongoing process for cooperation. It is true, as in the case of Applefield School, that the concentration of effort falls on those primary schools from which the majority of the intake comes. The primary school will need to deal mainly with the school(s) to which most of their leavers go. Nevertheless some broad liaison needs to take place with the other schools involved in the transfer process. It is particularly useful if the local adviser for environmental education has set up interchange meetings as with the case described later on page 150. In each neighbourhood there are a number of facilities to be used for environmental enquiry. It is essential that cooperation between schools takes place to ensure

1 overuse of any single one does not occur
2 that some local resources are not neglected altogether
3 secondary schools are not plagued with the problem of some of the intake already having used one of the facilities.

In general terms it is of great advantage if, at transfer, pupils are already well versed with the use of, for example, the local public library. It is useful, too, that pupil transfer records show what local or other environmental centres have been used and the topics undertaken. Publishers are understandably keen to sell their products and invariably fail to stipulate target ages, except in very broad terms. Some series, and we have been involved as authors, are written in such a way as to be suitable for upper juniors and lower seniors. This is good for business but not good for the secondary school needing to have fresh material for the eager newcomer. Liaison and agreement on who buys what, or who goes where, is desirable in order to avoid the dreadful, but triumphant, put-down of 'we did that with Miss Green in our last school!' from one group in the class. This applies to books, local field work and other matters but in particular it applies to visits outside the area – to a National Trust historic house for instance.

It should be possible to enable teachers from one phase to experience life in the other phase. It is all a question of 'where there's a will there's a way' including making a positive use of surplus staff time arising from the departure of years 10 and 12 (the fifth and upper sixth forms) when external examinations are concluded. The secondary school often has large grounds available for natural science investigations which can be used by local primaries with the minimum of fuss. With more determination, laboratories and equipment can be shared on a limited basis. But it is not all one way, for there is much cooperation where the primary can contribute to the benefit of the secondary school. Local circumstances will dictate the possibilities. Even in the most unlikely situations we know from experience that it is possible.

Environmental education can help to overcome the trauma of transfer and we would like to suggest that too little attention has been given to the matter of a cooperative combined project. This can take one of several forms and will depend on individual locations, the proximity of schools to each other, rural, suburban, inner city sites, even the willingness of staff to spend time and effort on pupils from another school who may not eventually transfer between them. There are two broad types of cooperative venture. The first is where pupils from the first year secondary join with youngsters from the top juniors to carry out a combined project. The second is a consecutive venture where the final year juniors start a project which is finished when they themselves are first year pupils in the secondary school after transfer. With the latter it is important that the work in both schools is self-contained, so that those who go on to a different senior school, or who come from a different junior school, participate in what to them is a whole involvement, although to the others it is the first or second part of a continuing enterprise.

The choice of topic needs to be compatible with local conditions and the school curriculum. From the secondary viewpoint it must either be a timetabled ongoing commitment or else part of humanities, or some form of combined subject grouping – in other words 'school' time must be allocated if it is to succeed; it must not be taken from the limited subject period allocation which could lead to teacher opposition. Experience at Applefield has shown that investigations into local traffic, roads and public transport are suitable topics. If the road system is investigated by the juniors they will inevitably learn of the location of the local secondary school. If public transport is scrutinized by the same students, when they have transferred, they will become acquainted with local services. This will be an asset for future environmental study involving local bus travel. The NAEE have a useful publication *Traffic Study and Surveys* (NAEE 1987) which contains a whole range of ideas for transport activities. Other projects which fit easily into this cooperative classification are those making use of local parks. At Applefield the junior work included making maps of the grounds later used for studies carried out in the secondary school, thus providing a physical bridge between the end of time in one school and the start of time in another. This is one project where the contrast between a place in spring and summer and the same place in autumn or winter can be a continuous investigation, recorded through an art form or with a camera – the polaroid is an indispensable tool for quick field study results!

It can be argued that the common age of 11 years for transfer could not be worse, coming as it does at the time of momentous physical change with puberty. It is possible, however, to remove at least some of the stress of changing schools and at the same time advance the cause of environmental education.

Chapter 7

Planning and practice at the secondary level

That part of the lecture billed variously as 'questions', 'discussion', 'comment from the floor', had come. The talk on environmental education as a cross-curricular theme had gone well – the transparencies had been clearly visible – not too many nor too few – they had well illustrated the views being put. Overhead projector acetates had summarized the points made and were legible for all the audience, even those at the back of the room. Their content was brief and precise and as copies were available there had been little need to take notes. The first question – the second – the third – all were relevant and positively answered apparently to the satisfaction of the questioner. 'One last question, please' asked the chair – it came:

> 'How can I do what you suggest when I have to follow the set examination syllabus, the timetable prevents my going out on even limited field work and my head teacher will not introduce a new subject?' – the latter despite the fact that the talk had emphasized that environmental education is not a subject but a curriculum area and requires no extra lesson time, only a different approach.

Content – time – extra work – lack of priority in school: all brought to a head in this one question – had all the input been in vain? To the questioner his school organization prevented the straightforward implementation of environmental education. Some encouraging words in return but nothing more in the time available to convince him it could be done. The niggle is that this questioner probably represents the views of a majority of teachers interested and willing to further environmental education but lacking local guidance.

We do not pretend to have all the answers where the secondary phase is concerned but, perhaps, the experiences of some of our colleagues and ourselves will cast a little light. Cross-curricular environmental education can become an essential part of the school curriculum without turning the whole establishment upside down. This has been done successfully in schools throughout the UK and across the world. What follows is intended to illustrate some examples of how it can be achieved within the constrictions of a 'normal' school facing all the changes demanded by society and their elected representatives. Nevertheless some sympathy for the 'cause' has to be shown by the head and senior staff. It is their professional duty so to do.

THE SECONDARY SCHOOL

In UK secondary schools the organization of both the pastoral and academic sides of the curriculum varies. The former may be on a year-by-year basis or divided into lower, middle and upper schools – possibly some still retain the enlightened house system. These are not pertinent to our present discussions except to say that out of school field work and other activities in environmental education inevitably involve social interaction.

With regard to the formal curriculum, the organization ranges from the simple (cross-curriculum friendly) grouping into areas of learning at one end to the pomposity of the mini-university faculties at the other, with the straightforward breakdown into subject departments somewhere in between. Where does our cross-curricular theme come into these? How can it be properly reflected in the welter of stronger statutory demands? With secondary schools in England and Wales compared on the basis of examination results, set out for the world to see in league tables, just what demand is there for effective environmental education?

The organization and delivery of the curriculum is a matter for the individual school to decide. After the greater emphasis on the integrated approach of the primary school there is likely in the secondary school to be teaching through a combination of separate subjects, integrated subjects and a modular approach. Whatever the form of organization, schools must deal with environmental education coherently, recognizing that the usual forms of across-the-year setting are based on certain academic abilities and are not necessarily a true reflection of environmental competence. The child in the least academic part of the year group is entitled to as much environmental education as his or her peer who has been assessed as having a more fertile intelligence. In any setting or streaming system, there will be a 'corridor of uncertainty', to borrow a cricketing expression much in favour with commentators, between the ability bands (in cricket between the off stump and the slips!). It is totally unjustified to present environmental issues to those deemed to be less able in a simplistic or patronizing manner.

The principle of differentiation has been well expressed in many curriculum statements, and that from Wiltshire encompasses most of what has been said.

The school should recognise that each child is different in terms of ability, aptitude, interests, motivation and social and ethnic background. This demands a curriculum which is *differentiated* – a curriculum that provides learning experiences which meet the needs of the individual child.

However pupils are grouped together, teachers need to use appropriate approaches according to the individual needs of different pupils. These should both challenge and extend all pupils including those with special educational needs, whether they are the most or the least able. Special consideration will need to be given to cases where the national curriculum does not apply either in whole or in part for any pupil.

Differentiation may be achieved not only by pupil grouping but also by:
— the language used;
— the selection of materials;
— the problems posed;
— the pace set;
— the outcomes expected;
— the assessments demanded.

In all aspects of teaching and learning teachers need to have high expectations so that all are able to achieve the best of which they are capable.

(Wiltshire County Council 1989)

We repeat our commitment to the view that it is totally unjustified to treat any section of the school population in a manner whereby they receive a less than 100 per cent opportunity to become environmentally aware. The secondary curriculum should be balanced, not only in the allocation of time and resources to different subjects and cross-curricular themes, but also to the way in which the subjects are taught. Let us begin by accepting that a total cross-curricular, holistic and fully integrated approach is, at present, no more than a dream to be realized occasionally in special timetabled events. The pressures of the English National Curriculum inhibit such an idea and the Scottish (Appendix B), Welsh (Appendix C) and Northern Ireland equivalents, though much more encouraging, have, at the time of writing, yet to be translated into statutory approval. We have experienced the consultative process and know that (when politicians are involved in educational reform) night does not necessarily follow day.

The conclusion, therefore, is that at present we must work through the subject base, ensuring that those who dispense their curriculum material do so in a way sympathetic to environmental education. Fortunately the ground to be covered can be a fertile field for the environmental approach. How to influence these subject 'farmers' is something to be discussed later when dealing with the implementation of environmental education as a cross-curricular theme. Time now to look at particular cases.

SOME SUBJECT-BASED EXAMPLES

Whatever the organization of the secondary school and the approach to cross-curricular themes, the majority of environmental education will take place in the context of a timetable of separate teaching units. The lesson occupying a single or double period will be the norm. As we have seen with the primary school, the approach within the lesson may be different between one teacher and the next, but a set amount of time has to be filled day after day whatever the teaching style. At secondary level the teacher must plan the lesson meticulously in order to occupy the set time in as productive and interesting a way as possible. If, as we have said, it seems inevitable that the subject base will remain for some time to come, it also follows that the bulk of environmental matters will form part of history, geography and science lessons, hopefully taught by staff sympathetic to cross-curricular work. In this section our model for teaching and learning in environmental education, described on page 38, has been used to plan and assess the cross-curricular approach of the particular example under review. The result, each time, is shown in an accompanying figure. We would hope that lesson planning by subject teachers would take their environmental responsibility into consideration and that the plan which follows might be typical of a geography teacher's lesson notes.

A geography lesson (Figure 7.1)

In this example for a third year class (i.e. Key Stage 3) the following extracts from *Geography in the National Curriculum (England)* (DES 1991a) are behind the plan for a series of lessons.

An enquiry approach should be adopted for classroom activities
Pupils should develop skills in interpreting data
Enquiry should be supported by the use of secondary sources
During Key Stage 3 pupils should study the local area
Pupils should be taught
● why people move homes
● the concept of a settlement hierarchy
● patterns of urban land use

The lesson is a double period (80 minutes) geography lesson in a series, the aim of which is to increase awareness of the built environment.

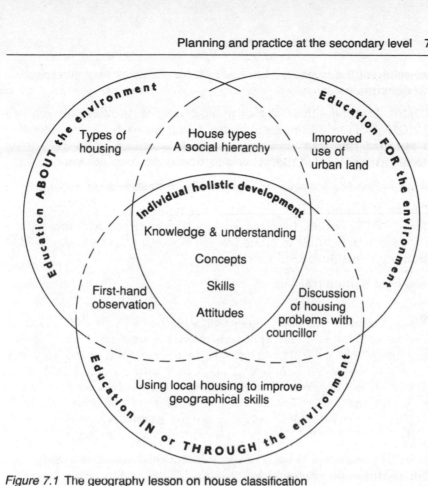

Figure 7.1 The geography lesson on house classification

LESSON PLAN

Objective

To determine a classification for types of domestic dwelling.

Resources needed

Local street map on 1:10000 scale. Collection of photographs of dwellings obtained from local property estate agents after a trawl of their back files.

Method

10 mins. Recall previous work on urban development, including the variation in housing in the local area (both older and new housing).

25 mins. Ask all class members to describe briefly the dwelling in which they live (option to 'pass' if desired). On chalkboard or overhead

projector list the basic features of dwelling places as they emerge from the descriptions.

20 mins. Distribute three or four photographs of dwellings to each pair of students. From pictures and house details for each classify according to age, exterior style, building materials, number of rooms, utility rooms, garage, garden. Locate each property on copy of local map.

15 mins. Receive suggestions for house type classification.

10 mins. Set homework – preparation for types of housing elsewhere in the world. Choose one from anywhere which contrasts with those in the UK – encourage pupils to locate places on world map from atlas and to photocopy any illustration found.

Total time 80 minutes.

This is typical of the work a geography teacher will do with a class of third years. However, the approach reflects a cross-curricular appreciation and involves direct investigation, secondary sources and both local and global issues. Without losing subject identity it can link with other subjects. It is a requirement of the National Curriculum for history and geography that attainment targets and programmes of study contribute to cross-curricular themes, including environmental education.

History for example requires pupils at Key Stage 3 to have:

. . . opportunities to use a range of historical sources including:
- pictures and photographs
- buildings and sites

Use words and phrases related to the passing of time, indicating . . . decade. They should have opportunities to ask questions, identify sources for an investigation, collect and record information. A study of homes could be a thematic unit designed to deepen pupils' understanding of chronology. . . . This unit should be drawn from British history.

(DES 1991b)

Science requires pupils at Key Stage 3 to participate in activities which

- encourage systematic recording
- involve the use of secondary sources

Pupils should be able to:
- link the use of common materials to their simple properties
- sort materials used in building into those that occur naturally . . . and those that are manufactured
- describe and recognise signs of weathering on the stonework of older building . . . in their locality

- be able to relate the properties of a variety of classes of materials to their everyday uses
- explain why certain materials . . . are used in buildings. The materials . . . should be studied in everyday use.

(DES/Welsh Office 1991)

Technology and mathematics are able to present individual subject lessons which can encompass the geographical work on the classification for types of domestic dwelling – materials, plans, measurements are basic elements. The scope for relevant English work is wide.

But it does require some cooperation and interdepartmental communication!

An art project

Art is an obvious subject for raising awareness of the built environment, so it may be convenient to describe at this point a project which involved 'buildings' through a series of lessons of art, craft and technology in a residential secondary school in East Anglia for pupils with moderate learning and/or emotional and behavioural difficulties. One set of buildings was a series of garages in various states of disrepair located within the school grounds. They were aptly named the Ramshackle, a local eyesore. Individuals had to use any medium to express the visual effect artistically. Each group of four or five pupils was asked to make observational drawings of the structures with the ultimate aim of creating scale models. Photographs were taken to aid the work, the processing of which was carried out by the pupils. With the aid of the maths department individual scale plans of the buildings were recorded on squared paper and from these miniature scale models were built in a variety of materials. The result was a series of realistic constructions which when placed together were a remarkably accurate representation of the real thing. All of this activity promoted discussion, cooperation, team work and a general spirit of job satisfaction as well as heightening each individual's awareness of the local environment. The important thing was that youngsters had been motivated by real observation of their environment and, during what some might suggest was a fairly routine set of tasks, examined in detail one aspect of the built environment. Follow-up work involved the planning of a redevelopment of the Ramshackle, a natural progression from the original starting point. Again this reinforces our claim that environmental education adds no extra load to the subject teacher; all it requires is an awareness of an approach which encompasses the environmental dimension.

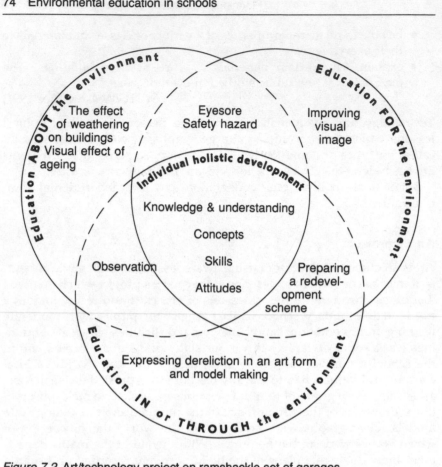

Figure 7.2 Art/technology project on ramshackle set of garages

INDIVIDUAL EFFORTS – LITTER AS AN EXAMPLE

It has long been said that in the English-speaking world all teachers are teachers of English. Now it is equally important they realize all are teachers of environmental matters. With a subject-based curriculum this must be emphasized with secondary school staff. Hopefully there are no cases where all subject departments refuse to cooperate with environmental learning. There may be many who are not prepared to alter their work scheme in order to participate in a cooperative environmental programme. That being the case it does not prevent an individual subject area responding to environmental pressure and directing some of their subject teaching towards an environmental issue. This can be part of the environmental audit which we hope will be a common feature of the whole curriculum before too long. One local issue will be litter prevention and litter control.

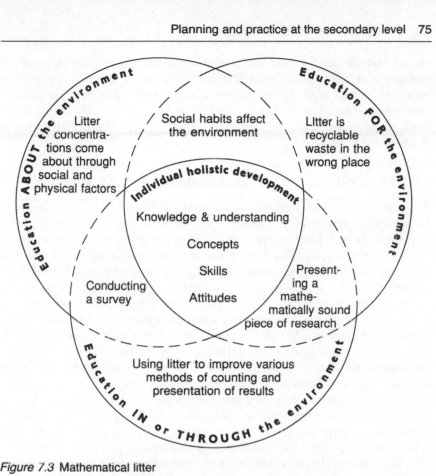

Figure 7.3 Mathematical litter

Of all topics with an environmental orientation none is more 'popular' in schools than 'litter', both on social and environmental grounds; see Figure 7.3. Usually it will appear through some form of social education in response to an anti-litter campaign or an award scheme organized by an outside body. Yet subject teachers are in a good position to bring realism to their own scheme of work through the medium of litter abatement. The mathematics department is well placed to take litter 'on board'. Mathematical litter can include counting, estimation, pro-portion, area, scale, density, weight, volume, costs and statistics and can lead to block graphs, histograms, pie charts, surveying and map-ping exercises. One school 'divided' the neighbourhood into litter 'habitats' (playground, corridors, classrooms, playing fields, foyer, entrance gates, bus stops, parkland, estate play area, front gardens, shop frontages, proximity to fast food outlet, and others) and directed their investigations to different times and different days. For the record, playing fields were lowest, and outside the fast food outlet (fish and chip shop) after school midday break was the highest. The participants found that a proper and valid mathematical investigation involved considerable time in the planning and that the reliability of statistical evidence varied with the effort put into the task. One thing is certain, resource material is available in abundance for litter investigations. How such an environmental topic can be integrated into other subjects is well documented elsewhere.

THE SCHOOL AS AN ENVIRONMENTAL ROLE MODEL

However much we emphasize the responsibility of individual teachers to approach their subject lessons with environmental awareness, a far greater responsibility rests with them to provide an environmental role model to the pupils. Together with the senior management and the ancillary staff they must ensure that the corporate image of the school passes on to the students, and any visitors, the fact that the school is environmentally sensitive. The hidden agenda goes far beyond the lack of litter, although that is important and in itself can provide an environmental learning vehicle. This is not a matter for the secondary school alone, but it is probably more difficult to exude the message 'we who work here care about the environment', simply because of the design of the buildings and because territorial areas are allocated to subjects rather than teachers. So much movement along corridors and common space, invariably far too narrow for comfortable passage, provides a constant hazard to display material. We in the UK have much to learn from school design in the USA, Canada and elsewhere.

A large comprehensive school in the West Midlands has given much thought to creating an environmentally friendly atmosphere. The approach to the school welcomes visitors, particularly parents; a notice points the way to reception and suggests simply how unexpected 'guests' can best avoid the inevitable wait. Internally someone is always on duty to receive visitors including those who have called without warning. The 'NO DOGS' sign has been replaced with a polite message inferring that uncontrolled animals are a danger to pupils' health and safety and if it is necessary to bring the family pet it must be kept on a lead. Delivery drivers, postal workers, refuse collectors and others are asked to observe a few guidelines so as not to clutter foyers, entrance doors and driveways with parcels, bins and vehicles. Positive provision has been made for parking spaces at the rear and not between the main gates and the school entrance. The local ground maintenance staff ensure that this entry area is something of which both they and the incumbents are proud. Thanking the maintenance staff and inviting them to school events works wonders.

There are several points around the school exterior where a small magnet fixed to a wall has a large recycling bin either side, one for steel and the other for aluminium cans – the magnet enables a correct choice to be made. Inside, each classroom has a box for clean waste paper, which recycling monitors empty at the end of each day into a main collection skip. The walls of classrooms and corridors have pupils' work on show, all of it properly mounted on coloured card, reusable on other occasions. At various strategic points there are noticeboards, not only for the normal notices for club and sporting activities, but also for conservation events and awards. Beside each light switch is an admonition to switch off unnecessary lights and a similar sort of notice encourages water saving in cloakrooms. At home time the last act in each room is to close all but one of the curtains so as to retain heat – the cleaner draws the remaining one. There are special campaigns to raise environmental awareness and much is made of the presentation of 'green awards' for outstanding effort every week by the respective heads of school. The school has a students' environmental council with representatives from every class whose job it is to plan future events and to evaluate the success of past and current efforts. It is their task to see that national and international environmental news is displayed in the school library and that suggestions for assembly topics are passed to the head of school.

The result is a workplace where it is difficult not to be environmentally aware, and where continual attempts are made to involve pupils in conservation activities.

A CHILD-CENTRED APPROACH TO A GLOBAL PROBLEM

It could be said that creating an environment-friendly school is a child-centred approach to environmental responsibility. Pupils can be inhibited by the adult frame of mind which closes around them, stifling imagination and creating a barrier to an understanding of environmental issues. Consider the problem of ozone layer depletion (OLD) as an example of a current global environmental issue likely to affect the living conditions of today's young people (see Figure 7.4). It is possible to take a standard adult approach with lessons planned along traditional lines beginning with the definition of the ozone layer, its make-up and properties, with pollution leading to a hole in the layer above the south polar region. From this would follow an analysis of the ensuing problem of danger to human health from an excess of UV-B rays. With the upper secondary age range this may well be an acceptable and successful format for a series of lessons in science or geography. With younger secondary pupils, building on their creative imagination is a far better starting point, especially if the initiative comes from an unexpected quarter of, say, English and art.

One secondary school, learning of the Anti-Cancer Campaign of Victoria, Australia, through the environmental education coordinator, was persuaded by her to settle for a child-centred approach to OLD by considering slogans and catch-phrases for various advertising promotions – from 'I'm a fruit and nut case' and 'XXX washes whiter' to 'smoking damages your health' and 'a xxx a day helps you work, sleep and play' – and by creating their own for various products. All such phrases seemed to be best conveyed to the public through succinct visual images. Thus the English and art departments started cross-curricular cooperation with the development of advertising characters and slogans for products and health campaigns. A consideration of sun protection lotions led to a consideration of the Slip-Slap-Slop slogan of the anti-skin cancer campaign fronted by Sid Seagull. [Sid Seagull is the cartoon character created to promote the anti-skin cancer campaign in Australia. His message is SLIP SLAP SLOP – slip on a shirt, slap on a hat and slop on some sun lotion. Details of this campaign can be obtained from the NAEE (see addresses on pp. 202–13).]

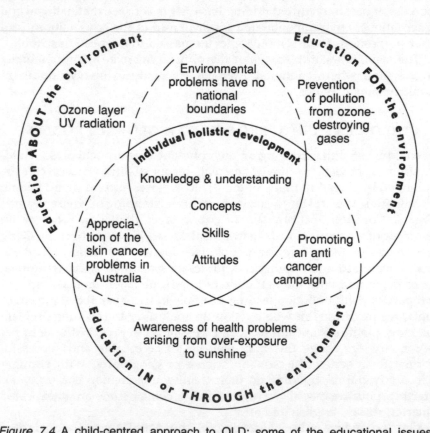

Figure 7.4 A child-centred approach to OLD: some of the educational issues raised

It was time to bring in other subjects and the cooperation of other colleagues. Geography and science agreed to cover various relevant subject matter such as the location of the polar regions and their wind systems, Australasia, emissions from the sun, the spectrum, ultra-violet rays, skin cancer, CFC gases, methane (at the time sadly highlighted by the tragic deaths of two children on a cross-Irish Sea ferry from leaking sewage gas), methyl bromide as a pesticide and the UV barrier properties of various substances. An exchange of letters with pen pals in a Melbourne school was initiated. Real campaign posters from Australia were displayed around the school.

From this child-centred approach to a global problem arose the suggestion that the whole year group should spend a length of time free of the formal timetable to investigate refuse disposal (methane gas creation in landfill sites) including the collection of unwanted fridges and freezers (CFC refrigerants) and the dilemma of built-in obsolescence as an economic factor. Strong stuff for 12-year-olds but, as with much of environmental awareness, free of the 'inhibitions of the adult frame of mind'. With some observation of the world of the growing child it does not take too much insight to realize that a study of beefburgers could lead into Rainforest Destruction, starvation in the Sahel into Global Warming, the crumbling monuments in the local cemetery into Acid Rain, debris on the tide line at the seaside into Ocean Pollution and peak hour traffic jams into Air Pollution. It is also quite apparent that these introductory routes could involve RE, technology, health education, citizenship, economic and industrial understanding and other areas of the curriculum not normally associated with environmental matters.

SUBJECT COOPERATION TO ENCOMPASS A GLOBAL PROBLEM: A CONCENTRIC APPROACH

The concentric approach to environmental learning is one borrowed from geography teachers, many of whom were using it before 'environment' as a term was any more than an alternative for 'neighbourhood' or 'hinterland'. With this method children relate the topic under discussion to something of relevance in their locality, moving out from this to a study of a national example and then beyond that to one from the wider world. A very simple example would be:

Study of a local stream – the Clyde and Clydeside – the Amazon and the forest

First of all it is necessary to consider the knowledge content needed to study a global problem; after that the concentric approach can be tackled. Of all the problems facing the world that of overpopulation, with its ensuing social difficulties, must be paramount. No student should pass through the secondary school stage without the opportunity to appreciate the many-faceted aspects of the 'population explosion'. The implication of this goes much further than a mere treatment of family planning and contraception. The study of overpopulation would be ideal for general studies at sixth form level, but this would mean some students leaving school without a coherent approach to the issue. Presumably much of the content would have been covered in a fragmented way during their five secondary years. A complete 'treatment' in the third year might be ideal. The following is a list of topics which could constitute the content basis for an across-the-year project or for the agreed content for cross-curricular cooperation.

Mathematics	exponential increase graphical representations statistical forecasting

History	past limitations on growth (emigration, disease,
	    famine, war, genocide, ethnic cleansing)
	Irish potato famine, Black Death
	Malthus
	contemporary events (Bangladesh floods, Sahel
	    starvation, Yugoslavian civil war, Irish
	    sectarianism, Belsen)

Geography	population distribution demographic factors natural controls (climate, soil fertility, water supply) greenhouse effect location of modern disaster areas
Economics	affluence and family size state social support education (literacy, statutory age) wealth distribution world wide
Religious education & social studies	world relief organizations (WHO, UNICEF, Oxfam, etc.) social customs (infanticide, marriage age) political (sterilization laws, family benefits) plagues of Egypt sectarian views on birth control
Science (biology, rural science,	population dynamics (yeast experiments, plant dispersal) mammalian reproduction (abortion, contraception)

environmental science)	ecological balance (predation, natural selection, habitat destruction)

environmental
science)

ecological balance (predation, natural selection,
    habitat destruction)
pest control
modern medicine (antisepsis, organ transplant,
    preventative medicine, chemotherapy,
    radiography, genetic engineering)
diet
water purification (sources, sanitation, sewage
    disposal)

English

appropriate fiction (e.g. *Brave New World*, *Animal
    Farm*, *On the Beach*)
appropriate non-fiction (e.g. *The Population Explosion*,
    Gaia Atlas of Planet Management, *Silent Spring*)

It is hard to envisage such a list being totally acceptable to all subject departments and much will depend where external curriculum forces suggest individual items are relevant. At what point in the overall time scale of the project or year schemes of work each particular topic should be placed is also a matter for close cooperation. It can only be a matter for the individual teacher to decide. One would hope that the students would be given an outline of the programme they will be following so that a coherent whole is apparent to them. Whatever the secondary curriculum in whatever subject, it is unusual for students to be given a plan of their work schedule for the term or year at the start, with the possible exception of work directed towards an external examination – even then the content timetable is rarely openly discussed. The coordinator for environmental education will need to be on top form to achieve success with the plan discussed above and others like it. The treatment of this global problem serves as a reminder, if one is necessary, of the way that environmental education straddles subject areas. To the students a rationalization of the work they are doing across the curriculum must give them some sense of purpose and may even cause them to realize the relevance of those subjects which they find less pleasing to those which they enjoy. We can take this particular list of content to illustrate the concept of the concentric approach to the environment. Linked with it is the overworked, but nonetheless appropriate, cliché 'Think globally, act locally'.

Take mathematics as a case in point. Exponential increase (as in Figure 7.5), graphical representations and statistical forecasting can all be linked to:

Local (school) – school population, class sizes, school dinner consumers, heights, weights, eye colour, etc. of peers, shopping surveys, traffic counts – the list is endless.

Billions of people

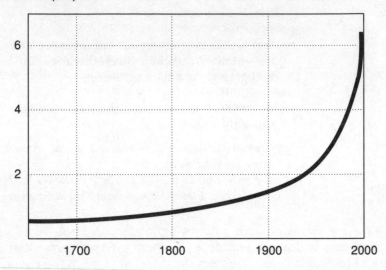

Figure 7.5 World population
Source: United Nations

Local (neighbourhood) – population, local taxpayers, voters on register, political constituency size, election results, household statistics. All the local examples could be exploited through 'field work'.

National/regional – census returns, tax matters, inflation, football/cricket results, environmental statistics.

Global – population growth, decline of elephant numbers in Africa, population growth of individual countries, travel times over the the past 100 years, refugee numbers.

We will not labour this concentricity with reference to every subject area. Outside the classroom there are opportunities through assemblies, drama productions, national competitions and awards, international events and charitable activities to provide school events which also reflect the theme of 'population explosion'. The only danger is overkill!

BLOCK TIMETABLING – ANOTHER APPROACH TO ENVIRONMENTAL EDUCATION

In order to provide for a whole range of cross-curricular matters in a positive and flexible way, a ten-form entry comprehensive school in the West Midlands block timetables one afternoon a week for the fourth year and a different afternoon for the fifth year. The whole year is involved in each case, organized into the mixed ability tutorial groups employed for the basic pastoral administration of the school and for subjects (music, PE, art, RE) where mixed ability teaching is the norm. The fourth year has ten topics lasting about three weeks each and the fifth year six topics of three weeks each as the summer term is unavailable due to external examinations. Tuesdays, Wednesdays and Thursdays are used in various academic years as seem appropriate at the time, for the other two weekdays are more likely to be affected by half-term holidays or national and local closures. Typical lists of activities are given below, the selection of which is dependent on staff interest and availability, the availability of outside sites on a regular basis throughout the year, and the availability of extra adult assistance on a regular basis for some activities.

Parental consent is gained for the principle of going out of school on the appropriate afternoon for the whole year, the scheme being explained at parents' meetings and through simple explanatory leaflets. At the beginning of each new activity individual arrangements are explained but the original consent is taken to hold unless a contrary negation is received. Apart from the occasional 'hiccup', consent proves to be no bother at all and over the many years that the scheme has run, parental problems have been very few.

The school is located in a municipal suburban area, markedly parochial; where youngsters' travel-independence is limited to visiting the local shops, the nearest supermarket, the local football stadium (top division league club) and similar venues. Surprisingly, travel elsewhere in the large urban area is very limited, with some pupils, including the older students, inexperienced in public transport travel out of their own environs.

Unless the distance to any one of the activities necessitates private transport, all participants are given the location of a meeting place, travel tokens if required, and are expected to be there on time. Similarly travel back to school (*always* the place for dismissal) is an independent exercise. Failures to arrive are surprisingly few. This independence of travel is deemed to be an important part of 'course study', as the overall activity is called, a phrase coined before its application to external examination work.

Some 13 or 14 teachers are timetabled for each of the year groups, which, for a school used to breaking subject teaching into four or five sets for each block of three 'normal sized' classes, is quite economical. Obviously ten of the teachers selected are directly chosen for their ability and interest to organize one of the topics in each of the two years. Some who are particularly keen on the system appear in each year. Other staff are chosen on the grounds of availability and, where possible, new staff are introduced to the system. Excluding 14 teachers for a whole afternoon from the rest of the timetable produces many difficulties for the compilers. It means that this blocking must be given priority at the start of timetable construction and remain sacrosanct throughout the rest of the compilation. Unless the head teacher is convinced of the value of cross-curricular activities being properly organized, administered and staffed, and of the importance of the pastoral spin-off effects, such a programme will be less effective and possibly carried out with no real staff conviction. As with all else affecting subject-flexible timetabling, resistance from 'traditionalists' will be constant.

Over the years the topics have been varied and wide in content according to the particular talent of individual teachers. The working of the magistrate's court was a popular activity for two years when a senior staff member was a Justice of the Peace. An international gymnast introduced aspects of training programmes before the days of in-depth TV coverage of athletics. The conversion from coal to natural gas provided a topic for two years, while planning procedures and a public inquiry for a new shopping complex was another. Throughout, certain topics retain their place and popularity, particularly one of the local authority field centres, the disposal of refuse, police control of the local motorway network (which includes the famous Spaghetti Junction) and community service. Perhaps it is not immediately obvious that one great advantage for this scheme, for the individual teacher, is that the meticulous preparation required for all individual topics can be used ten times

Topics: a sample of some activities

Fourth Year	Fifth Year
Careers	Careers
Local historic hall	The National Trust
Leisure facilities	Local leisure clubs
Power supply	Alternative technology
Mapping local estate	Role of council surveyors/ architects
Repertory theatre	Two-minute TV advert (video)
Motorway control	Urban parking
Estate agency	Stock exchange
British Rail safety	Canal safety
Wholesale markets	Supermarket stock acquisition
Community service	Community service
Acid rain (cemetery monument study)	Air pollution
Local public transport	Going abroad
Local field centre	Animal welfare organizations
Noise pollution in school	School recycling action

over during the year, with all the benefits of refinement and adjustment to the original presentations, a chance not always available to traditional topic work. Weather, changing seasons, staff absence all keep the over-all coordinator on her/his toes. In such a large school this task became the responsibility of one of the three deputy heads. It involves not only the supervision and approval of individual topics but the development of new ones – an eye to the future is essential. The coordinator visits the sites of the activities and, on occasions, provides emergency transport, staff cover and diplomatic representation when things go wrong. Detailed planning and periodic evaluation of topics prevent all but minor adverse incidents.

Space does not permit detailed analysis of individual programmes. Perhaps one example will give the flavour (Figure 7.6). The field centre run by the local authority was chosen because it is within half an hour's coach ride of the school, is situated beside an electricity power station, has a pool with a hide where kingfishers can be seen (and that is 'magic' in anyone's experience) and where the warden is sufficiently flexible to permit the same school to book an afternoon once every three weeks throughout the year. This was despite the original hostility to the idea of the 'powers-that-be' in the central office who operated a free transport system to the centre and felt that one school appeared on paper to be getting more than a fair share of the facilities (even though different pupils were involved each time). Over the three-week programme the first afternoon is a preparation for the visit, the second is the visit and the third, follow-up work. Such is the rapport built up over the years that the school provided cover at the centre when the warden was away ill on one occasion. Even the 'powers-that-be', aforementioned, were impressed. Particular attention is paid to each group producing a piece of work which can be displayed at the end-of-year open week, mainly in order to reassure parents (and other staff) that much basic learning results from the topic work undertaken. It also provides those outside the school, without whose cooperation the programme is not possible, with an opportunity to visit the school and to receive both formal and informal thanks.

Cross-curricular work always requires detailed planning. Field work always requires detailed planning. Course study is a combination of both with the planning more than just the sum of the individual aspects involved. On a purely practical note an ongoing insurance policy was negotiated with the company responsible for school journey insurance. If nothing else it seems to reassure the parents and staff!

This particular block timetabling proved to be popular with the local initial teacher training institution before it closed. A certain number of students attended the school on these afternoons to add to the super-visory team and to give their own individual contributions to the topics. At the same time they were gaining invaluable experience and could themselves make suggestions for improvements which could be tried in the next cycle of repeated events. Team teaching was not imposed but for many of the topics it evolved in a most positive way. It is not the time or place to discuss the merits of such staff cooperation except to say that where it arises naturally it can bestow high benefit on both teacher and taught.

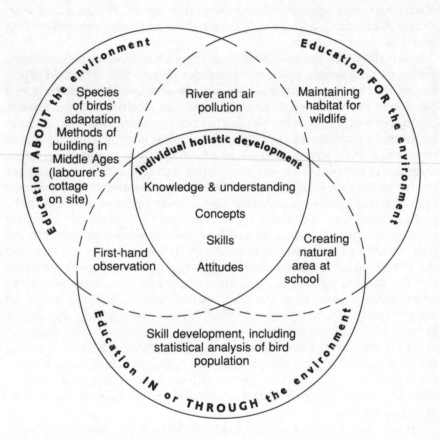

Figure 7.6 Visit to environmental study centre

THE SPECIAL EVENT

In our view, environmental education is not to be seen by teachers or students as something unusual such as the annual sports day or the Christmas theatrical production. Nevertheless we recognize that it is difficult to cover any environmental issue in depth unless there is time to do it justice and a flexibility impossible within a restrictive timetable.

The abandonment of the normal work schedule for a period of time can thus be justified, particularly if a full week is dedicated to the project. For practical reasons, after the completion of the external examination sessions is convenient, although it does have the disadvantage of being interpreted as an end-of-year 'treat' with less than full academic rigour applied by some staff. But it can work, as many have experienced. A school in the north west of England is now into its third year of week-long environmental projects. The most recent of these involved an investigation into energy and formed part of an environmental audit. This theme was chosen because work for this was already a part of the teaching of individual subjects which could be coordinated in a fairly straightforward way. Teachers in other subject areas were invited to cooperate – all agreed to help. The planning group of teachers, with representatives from each class in the third year, the year chosen to participate, met several times to plan the overall programme, although the detailed contribution was left to each subject department. A block of time was allocated, so that, for instance, the art department had two full days with one group and two full days with another. Other departments had blocks of time according to their particular needs. Thus any individual pupil would find her/himself following the theme of energy with, say, two days following an art approach, a day with modern languages and two half days with science. Providing the time allocated balanced with the student groups formed, the timetabling was relatively easy. Each student opted for a block of subject-based input, although in practice the teachers made her/his contribution as cross-curricular as possible.

Subject areas were retained as staff felt less intimidated than with a totally integrated approach, but as each project progresses more cooperation and a great deal more flexibility is apparent. Greater multi-disciplinary work is to be built into the next project, probably based on the theme of world population.

As well as increasing specific subject-based knowledge and skills, certain cross-curricular skills were identified and every teacher encouraged to promote them. For example the head teacher asked that verbal communication and clear speech were given specific emphasis. Each subject, or group of subjects, was committed to a definite outcome. Modern languages produced a brochure for foreign students concerning recycling in the UK; English, geography and history simulated an enquiry into proposed open-cast coal mining some miles away from the school, which involved a visit to the site with a National Coal Board representative; technology and science produced instruments to measure wind speed and air pollution; mathematics designed a questionnaire for energy conservation in various parts of the school and carried out a survey of fuel consumption, analysing and presenting the

Technology

During my time in technology I was able to:

Collect information from several sources in order to help me make an instrument for measuring air pollution or wind speed ☐

Choose tools and materials for making the instrument ☐

Complete a number of design ideas for the instrument I constructed ☐

Seek advice on the way to proceed ☐

Review and explain why I would change my design next time ☐

Talk about labour saving devices we have at home and how energy efficient they are ☐

Understand some of the things I should look for when buying a piece of equipment from an energy saving point of view ☐

Only tick a box if it fits what you did

I wish I had been able to do the following:

_____

_____

Figure 7.7 Third year energy project – an evaluation form

results for public display; art produced an exhibition of work in various media expressing the concept of energy flow as well as cooperating with mathematics with graphical displays of energy consumption. A half day at the start answered the general question of what is energy in a series of group activities designed by the environmental education coordinator. A further half day was devoted at the end to the presentation of results and the final act was for each student to complete a project evaluation profile for use in planning future projects, for assessing the success of the current project and for transmission to tutors for student profile files. The evaluation for technology is given in Figure 7.7.

This project, carried out in the way it was, staffed and planned in the way it was, suited this particular school at the point it had reached in its development of environmental education as a cross-curricular theme.

We emphasize the warning that individual conditions of school size, location, staff skills and cooperation and many others determine what and how environmental work can take place. This example is just one approach to a week-long joint project. For this school it worked quite well and students seemed to relish the complete change from the normal timetable.

THE SIXTH FORM

Students in years 12 and 13, traditionally known as the lower sixth and upper sixth in UK schools, are mostly those preparing for higher education leading on to professional careers. It could be said that they are the potential decision makers of two or three decades to come. Without doubt they need to be environmentally aware. Hopefully general studies will be taken seriously and those universities now paying only lip service to the value of such studies will change their attitude. A leading part of general studies must be environmentally based, backed by a course on environment which has field work at its heart. The idea of some sort of residential experience is to be commended for both pastoral and academic reasons. It would appear that this is easier to arrange in a school-based sixth form than in a sixth form college or tertiary institution. This is not the place to argue the case for and against the location of 17- and 18-year-olds in the educational process, but it has to be said that in our experience the greater flexibility of the school programme is supportive of environmental experience for all.

A secondary comprehensive school in Mid Wales encourages environmental awareness in many ways similar to examples quoted elsewhere in this section. One extra dimension directed at the lower sixth form (year 12) is a residential conference held in a large country mansion used in the county for a whole range of activities (Figure 7.8). The conference has been held annually in December for the past three years on environmentally related topics. The latest was organized under the general title 'Challenge of the Environment'. The set task was to 'Decide how your group will envisage the town in the year 2000 with regard to environmental, social, and industrial issues'. The town in question was a fictitious place based on a real town about 20 miles from the school. The planning for the weekend extended over a full year with regular committee meetings of over a dozen people including teachers, students and guest 'experts', e.g. local planner, computer programmer, representatives of the RSPB, local wildlife trust, etc. (Readers are asked to note the essential element of long-term planning – the success of any environmental work can be measured in a direct ratio to the amount of forward planning. Every week the NAEE office receives requests for help and information with variations on the theme 'this information is needed urgently as the work begins in two weeks' time'!)

For the actual weekend an invited person in a position of some importance relevant to the topic – for this topic the secretary of the NAEE – acted as the evaluator. The work of each group was judged by experts – the district council planning officer, the county council economic development officer and the evaluator.

At the beginning of the autumn term, during the school induction week, a meeting of participants was held to allocate individuals to one of ten groups. Each group was to name the town and choose a logo for it. Each group of nine individuals received a description of the town and were instructed to obtain brochures from various organizations. They were, in effect, role-playing as members of a town council. A month before the conference a talk was given to the participants by a representative of the (real) local council purporting to come from the fictitious town.

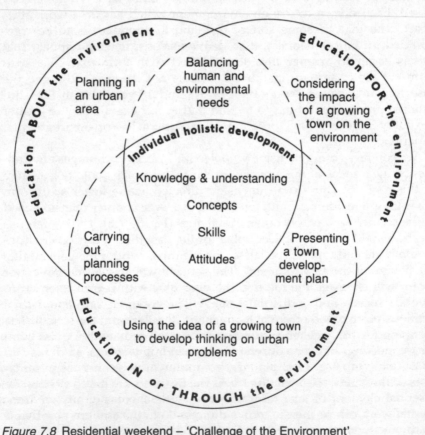

Figure 7.8 Residential weekend – 'Challenge of the Environment'

At the end of November all participants received a folder containing:

- Map (A4 size) and several area maps
- Description of the town as it was at that time
- Planning guidelines under the following headings:

Industrial	Tourism
Housing	Recreation
Retail	Motorway
Agriculture	Environment

- Several sheets of suggestions as to what groups might do, prepared by an officer of the local district council
- A short article on 'How to develop a neighbourhood'
- Extracts from the county council's (real) Development Plan
- Population review and projection up to 2001
- Visitor figures for the recent past for Mid Wales for use if the group wished to develop tourism in their town.

The description of the town at present contained smaller area profiles. One such profile is reproduced in order to show both the extensive nature of the information the students were handling and the depths to which the planning of the weekend had to go in preparation.

Area C
1 Conservation area produces many restrictions on development
2 Listed buildings occur throughout the town centre
3 Motte and Bailey must be protected
4 Public open space
5 Disused canal with derelict turning wharf
6 Geological SSSI in disused quarry which has limited extraction rights
7 Culverted water stream must be considered
8 Agricultural market place
9 Half hour hold-ups occur in the centre as the main road bisects the town and the main shopping street crosses this trunk road.

The actual weekend followed the plan shown in Figure 7.9, a poor reflection of the all-absorbing, exciting and fulfilling experience for participants, staff and visiting 'experts'. That so many individuals should have given of their time and effort (teachers and learners) reflects great credit on a school where lip service to environmental education is not enough – total commitment is only just sufficient.

A follow-up task was set which was intended to capitalize on the enthusiasm generated. In this case it was to prepare a plan, and possibly execute part of it, to enable pupils of a local school catering for special needs to have an aromatic garden and pond. It was also possible that an environmental audit of the school would be carried out.

PROGRAMME   DAY 1

10.00 am	Introduction to the Conference
10.15 am	Introductory Activity
10.45 am	Group Activity I—Leadership Exercise
11.15 am	Report Back
11.40 am	Main Group Activity begins with Brainstorming I (how do we start?)
12.00 noon	Group Activity II

Specialist Groups meet with Representative of:

Housing	—Mid-Wales Housing
Agriculture	—Agriculture Training Board
Retail	—Chain Store Grocery
Forestry	—Forest District Manager
Industrial Development	—Rural Wales Business Park
Recreation and Leisure	—Montgomeryshire District Council
Highways	—Powys Highway
Tourism	—Wales Tourist Board
Environment	—Countryside Commission for Wales

1.30 pm	Penpictures	—Landscape Architect—Landscaping
		—Local Supermarket Manager—What the Company has done to help the Environment
2.15 pm	Group Activity IIIa	—In 'Town' groups
5.00 pm	Guest Speaker	—A Town Planner

CONFERENCE DINNER

7.00 pm	Guest Speaker	—An Environmentally Aware Industrialist
9.00 pm	Group Activity IIIb	—Continue Meeting of Group Committees to Prepare Plans

PROGRAMME   DAY 2

9.00 am	Introduction to the Day
9.10 am	Talk—Manager of Public Utility
10.15 am	Groups prepare for Final Exhibition
10.40 am	Final Groups, Presentation and Exhibition of the Towns
12.45 pm	'Clean-Up'
1.30 pm	Report by Judges and Presentation of Awards
	Close of Conference

Figure 7.9 Sixth form 'Challenge of the Environment' conference

SUMMARY

The subject-based approach, with its rigidly timetabled day, inhibits cross-curricular work including that of environmental education. We have tried to show how it is possible to overcome these restrictions within the confines of typical secondary schools, with examples that represent some of the ways and means whereby environmental aware-ness can be promoted. As it is not possible to undertake a comprehen-sive review in limited space, it is fortunate that much case study material is to hand as listed in the resources later. Yet nothing is possible unless some effort is made by the school management to enable cross-curricular work to be undertaken. Part III will provide some guidelines for the implementation of environmental education in schools at all levels.

Chapter 8

The out-of-school (field work) approach

Environmental education is based on as much first-hand experience as possible so that the idea of moving out of the confines of the traditional classroom is one well rooted in the environmental approach. Although we prefer to talk about 'out of classroom studies' we recognize that the term 'field work' is firmly entrenched and in common use. What must be emphasized is that long journeys are not necessarily an essential part of field work – it can be a study entirely within the walls of the school, for instance an investigation into noise pollution. The school estate is part of the field work scene and the immediate neighbourhood will provide ample opportunity for activities of short duration and repetition. It goes almost without saying that study of the built environment is as much a part of field work as study of the countryside and other aspects of the natural world. The National Association for Field Studies Officers and the Field Study Council see field work as 'relevant at all levels of education and requires the application of skills not easily demonstrated or used in the classroom. Field studies provide a most effective way to study environmental issues' (NAFSO 1992). Field work to them

- is essential in a cross-curricular environmental approach to both core and foundation National Curriculum subjects.
- gives relevance to topics which could otherwise remain as second-hand learning.
- is concerned with *real* people, *real* situations and *real* issues.
- enables pupils to observe, record, analyse, present and interpret their own investigations.
- provides pupils with opportunities to talk about their own world, to listen to others and to share their knowledge.
- provides pupils with opportunities to look closely at aspects of a local environment and introduces the idea of environmental responsibility.
- provides opportunities for pupils to work cooperatively using academic, practical and social skills.

(NAFSO 1992)

They go on to argue the value of field centres, something we would not dispute, although much sound study out of doors can be based in the school itself. The Geographical Association emphasizes the importance of field study as

. . . all developments in education demand that pupils have first-hand experience of real people, real situations, real action and real places. Field work provides this opportunity. Living in today's challenging world demands skills such as observation, keeping records, analysing data, experimenting, problem solving, decision making, communicating and cooperating. Field work develops all these skills.

(Geographical Association 1992)

At this point we could give innumerable examples of good traditional field work but we imagine that most of our readers are well versed with examples of both nature and built environmental study so we shall proceed without them. Most primary school courses and geography, history and science in the secondary school contain regular out of classroom studies, the most fortunate students participating in residential field centre work. The borders between subjects are blurred when study in the field is undertaken – field work is essentially cross-curricular.

OUT OF THE CLASSROOM

There is a discussion going on among environmental educators that too much of the environmental curriculum is natural-world based and much more should be centred on people. Nowhere is this felt to be more true, by the protagonists of this view, than with activities outside the classroom. The very term 'field work' is felt to imply a nature-led series of investigations. As with so many educational arguments there is good and bad on both sides. Those who emphasize the need to understand the natural world in order to appreciate the problems brought about by human activity are opposed by those who see every environmental issue as humankind led. We see it as a question of balance and believe that any field work activity can be so structured that both nature and people are included – or at least neither one is ignored. The basic approach to field work is essentially similar no matter where in the world such a programme is to be followed. To provide a particular statement of aims and objectives for one area will underline the universality of this environmental education approach. We could have taken examples from the UK, continental Europe, New Zealand, Canada or the USA. We have chosen to take Australia as an exemplar not only to bring variety to our text but because their emphasis on community action is an approach we wish to underline. We doubt if any teacher anywhere will find much at variance with good practice in their own local area, or, indeed, anything very different from what is being done in any good environmental school.

AUSTRALIAN FIELD WORK: LOCAL ACTION FOR A BETTER ENVIRONMENT

Field work, particularly local action in their own community, is seen as a fundamental introduction to, and support for, environmental education in Australian schools. 'It is vital to recognise that actively involved people generally undergo far greater development of abilities, understanding and environmental commitment for the future than do passive receivers of information or those who theorise but do not act' (Malcolm 1990). Nevertheless emphasis is placed on the premise that positive action in the environment must provide the framework for education rather than vice versa.

It is considered that the ideal local action programme:

- is seen by the students to be their idea and under their control
- takes all viewpoints into consideration including attitudes and values
- aims to involve those beyond the school itself
- considers the overall effect on the environment, working with, rather than against the natural state of affairs
- encourages individuals to become environmentally responsible
- is cross-curricular in approach
- involves creative problem solving
- emphasises the value of individual action
- where possible involves follow-up activity.

Successful programmes tend to follow a basic pattern although they are not necessarily sequential. The pattern is:

1 creating a desire to take action
2 investigation
3 selection of the action plan
4 implementation including on-going evaluation of success.

1 Creating a desire to take action

The idea for a local activity may come from the students who have by personal observation, from hearsay or from local publicity realized that something is amiss or needs extra support. Raising the issue in the normal course of classroom learning may be sufficient to develop an interest in the particular matter but a site visit, possibly accompanied by an outside 'expert', is beneficial. The site does not even have to be off the school campus; wherever it is, it should be within easy access of the school.

2 Investigation

Any time spent on investigation will repay itself in the end if a successful project is to ensue. In particular attention needs to be paid to:

- the resource need, which includes that of finance, as well as time and the extent of physical endeavour required
- the actual details of action involved and which of the subject areas of the curriculum may most beneficially contribute their expertise
- the selection of the possible courses of action
- the reaction of others to the action plan – will they approve or not?
- the broader context in which the local activity can be placed; a case for 'thinking globally and acting locally'.

It is part of the skill of the teacher to see that all the participants appreciate the wisdom of giving due consideration to all points of view based on the fullest understanding of the local problem. The students should be encouraged to assess their own individual impact on the well-being of the environment and to realize that together with others, they make up a community whose combined lifestyles can create a serious pressure for good or evil, in conservation terms. The best local activity depends for success on everyone involved feeling a personal responsibility for its fulfilment. Within the bounds of the school's collective responsibility, a democratic approach to organization is to be encouraged.

3 Selection of the action plan

Since any plan will need to be flexible to deal with the programme as it develops the initial choice will reflect its outline rather than its detailed organization. Nevertheless it is as well to select something which will show rapid initial progress: it is essential not to 'bite off more than you can chew'. A small start, which enables confidence in the project to be established quickly, coupled with skill development, will form the basis for a more ambitious expansion later. It is essential to involve all project participants from the outset.

4 Implementation

This will depend so much on the activity itself that only general guidance is possible here. Early realization that each small step taken is worthy of immediate evaluation with a view to improving the approach right from the start, i.e. getting it right at the beginning, will pay dividends and lead to that prime objective of maintaining motivation of all the group and not just of some individuals. Bringing in outside help and advice can be done in such a way that participants see it as constructive and not as an unwelcome intrusion. Some local action projects do go wrong – calling a halt with 'dignity' can be necessary. The follow-up enquiry process can be a valuable contribution to environmental awareness.

The following case studies illustrate some of the ways in which some Australian schools have approached local action projects. The first was classroom based following an investigatory visit to the 'problem' site.

Our Lady of the Sacred Heart School, Alice Springs

Human problem – understandable antithesis to sewage disposal ponds in urban area. Sewerage disposal ponds at Alice Springs provide a habitat for a wide diversity of bird life. In drought years they provide one of the few sources of large, permanent surface water in the centre of Australia. During a bird observation visit to the ponds one class from the school not only discovered the extent to which these ponds were used by birds but that, contrary to popular perception, the area was not over-smelly and that plans even existed for landscaping the area into a tourist attraction. However there were other plans for the relocation of the ponds away from the town with the site to be used for urban development. The students decided to carry out a public education programme to change the attitudes of local people to the ponds, to that of a bird habitat worth preserving. Basically the members of the class contacted the local authority to discover the status of the rumoured proposals, and, having confirmed it as a possible future course of development, they organized and analysed the information and proceeded to raise public awareness by writing letters to the local press and other activities such as a display in the town library. The programme of drawing public attention to the importance of the sewerage ponds as a bird refuge was successful and has caused the local planners to reconsider their proposed actions. As a footnote to the project it is worth mentioning that controversial matters can be dealt with in the classroom if activities are properly controlled.

Apollo Bay School, Victoria

Human problem – disciplined use of a natural area for recreation. It was a ranger in charge of the Otway National Park who suggested the school became involved in the Tall Trees Nature Trail, a proposed 3 km trail near to the school. After much initial hesitation, due mainly to a change of staff, the matter was taken up by senior students following an environmental studies course. After investigating the need for such a trail and deciding that it was desirable, the students developed a detailed proposal for the trail and gained financial backing from a successful entry in an environmental award scheme. The intervention of a major road construction restricted activity to surveying the fauna and flora. When, at last, initial clearing of the trail began the project activity really started. Timetable restrictions brought frustration (see p. 82) as it was impossible to spend any worthwhile length of time on the trail during school time. A full afternoon of activities did provide about two hours at the nature trail if the preceding lunch time was sacrificed by teacher and taught. ('What's new?' will be voiced by field study teachers around the world!) Students have been involved in tree planting, signposting and, when the trail is in operation, with trail management. That the field activity has given rise to much classroom work and enquiry goes without saying. This particular activity is to be seen as one which involved succeeding groups of students rather than as a one-off local action.

Glen Dhu School, Launceston, Tasmania

Human problem – derelict site left after urban development. The reconstruction of a major road system in the suburban outskirts of Launceston resulted in a piece of land about the size of a football pitch being left for development. It had been zoned as an industrial site but over the few years since the completion of the road scheme it had been left neglected to become a play area for children, a 'walking the dog' place for adults and a general decrepit area for litter, graffiti, land erosion – quite simply an eyesore. Glen Dhu school was close by. As part of a classroom exercise each child was asked to walk over the site and name five good and five bad things to be seen. When the problem had been identified each student was asked to choose one and to come up with a solution. To enhance the process of evaluation, visits to the school were made by local politicians, landscape experts and others. Role play exercises were carried out where the various interest groups argued their case; not surprisingly when put to the vote the majority were in favour of a park although some did see benefit from a combined park/factory development. The 'Campbell Gardens' project was set up following research into the history of the site which revealed a previous occupier to have been Campbell's Pottery. Letters, questionnaires, and visits to local council departments became part of the extensive enquiry. A six-page proposal was set up using a word processor and launched at a public meeting attended by local and national dignitaries. Perhaps the best summary of Glen Dhu's efforts in out of school local activity is to reproduce the conclusion of the staff involved.

> . . . we saw the development of an awareness and sensitivity to the environment and a basic understanding of how humans interacted with it. We saw kids actively involved at all levels in working toward understanding or resolving complex environmental problems. We saw them make informed decisions.

> The program has a message for others contemplating environmental work of a similar nature. Firstly, the outdoors is a tremendously fertile stimulus for meaningful environmental work with kids. . . . It provides a focus for valuable learning modes and behaviours that are difficult to achieve in classrooms. Secondly, we were continually amazed by the support we received from the public. The wider community, it appears, thoroughly approves of children getting out of their schools and into the community.

> The real classroom is indeed 'out there'. Our challenge is to find ways of empowering teachers to realise this.

Rivendell High School, Victoria

This is a residential school for secondary age children with behavioural problems.

Human problems – improving the look of a neglected watercourse; improving relationship between special school and local residents; integrating special needs pupils into the local community. The River Parramatta flows near to the school and, over the years, became a repository for rubbish along its banks. A student raised the issue in conversation which led to enthusiastic support for a clean-up operation. Together with a thorough investigation into the ecology and natural history of the local river area, a project on clean-up was started. Use was made of a video camera to make a documentary record of the project which involved students' learning to write scripts and prepare story boards as well as camera techniques. The idea of selling recyclable rubbish collected brought mathematics into the venture. The 'Clean-a-thon' event itself raised $150 and was repeated once a term during the year in which the project was held. The whole conservation idea gained public recognition including several environmental awards. Remembering the background history of the individual student it is not surprising that staff found that this out of doors cooperative effort had many social behavioural benefits and that the hidden social agenda was of equal importance to that of the overt environmental aspect of the project. Interestingly the school action stimulated a local horticultural college to start a bush regeneration scheme and during the course of this a rare example of salt marsh was found among the mangroves.

None of the four community-based case studies described would be claimed as extraordinary by the teachers involved; but each is unique to the school itself. Similar projects may be undertaken elsewhere but any attempt to copy another school's activity in precise detail is a recipe for failure. Imitate, gain ideas but do not copy slavishly. It is not necessary to detail here the obvious cross-curricular nature of the work resulting from all four examples – English, mathematics, art, technology and physical education featured in most of them along with the more obvious geography, history and science. Social education has been emphasized already as one of the aspects of the hidden curriculum. The encouragement of a positive attitude to the environment must be another.

The success of these activities depended on sound organization and the cooperation of the rest of the school. The Tall Trees Trail was held up by a change of teacher – it is always worthwhile ensuring that several staff members are involved from the start to avoid delay or collapse of a venture by an unexpected teacher move.

Reading the Australian case studies will have highlighted the fact that the field work approach is comparable worldwide. To underscore this point: the following guidelines for local study were adopted by the town of Wolverhampton in the industrial Midlands of England. They could have been written for the Australian examples.

The following ten-point Guidelines give some idea of the approach schools are asked to consider:

1 The Study (Topic or Theme) should be based on the immediate school surroundings, the local neighbourhood or town.
2 The Study should focus on particular features and areas and on local issues and problems that affect the quality of life of the community.
3 The Study should be directly related to the basic aims of Environmental Education.
4 When possible, the Study should be a local educational experience

that may be related to a national or international environmental problem or issue.

5 Pupils should be involved in direct personal exploration of their locality and town and be required to make first hand observations.

6 The work should improve the pupils' understanding of the processes and people that plan, manage and change our surroundings.

7 The Study should involve local agencies such as Environmental and Technical Services, Parks and Gardens, Architects, Planners and Safety Officers.

8 The Study should encourage pupils' appreciation of the importance of involvement in maintaining and improving the quality of the built environment.

9 The Study should teach specific skills, techniques and concepts and encourage the operational use of basic skills, especially in language.

10 The work should reflect the overall Environmental policy of the school.

It also suggests that school projects have some value to the local community by achieving at least ONE of the following:

a) A specific contribution to a particular debate within the local community e.g. use of land, conservation proposals, play area design.

b) The creation of resources for the future use of the local community e.g. trails, photographs, historical records.

c) The physical improvement of an aspect of the local environment, including school grounds and gardens.

(Wolverhampton Environmental Awareness Unit 1984)

FIELD STUDY CENTRES AND FIELD WORK

We have emphasized the fact that neither long distance travel nor residential experience is essential to field work, yet it would be remiss of us not to place on record our support for the use of field study centres by schools. The UK is fortunate to have many thousands of centres for both day and extended visits. Some are named in our resource section. Local education authorities have been a main provider and supporter of study centres but the financially led approach to education is placing such provision under severe threat. Even as we write we learn of cases of closure threats and forced 'privatization'. We can only express our anxiety that we may lose what others have called the 'jewels in the crown' of British environmental education.

Part III

Practicalities

This Part provides some guidelines for the implementation of environmental education in schools at all levels, considering particularly the issues of coordination, management and school policy.

Chapter 9

Developing and coordinating a school policy for environmental education

Curriculum planning, at least in my own school, seems to be in a state of constant change. My present concerns as the co-ordinator for Environmental Education are:

- teacher priorities centre on core and foundation subjects (of the National Curriculum)
- cross-curricular themes are of secondary importance
- attainment targets are too prescriptive and are being translated too literally
- trends towards subject teaching are being reinforced and, therefore in future, themes may not be properly integrated
- the increasing number of attainment targets 'to get through' put staff under pressure
- pressures of time limit opportunities for first hand investigation and increase reliance on secondary sources
- not enough emphasis . . . on developing attitudes and values of responsibility (to the environment)
- implementation of environmental policy too dependent on the enthusiasm of one or two members of staff
- 'chasing up' already overworked subject specialists.

Such was part of the content of a letter from a member of the NAEE seeking help with implementing a policy of environmental education in her school, in this case a large primary school in an area of the country with good local support for environmental education. The fact that she starts from a position of being in charge of environmental education in the school is an indication of the responsible way this curriculum area is being tackled by the school management. As a result her colleagues will recognize they have an obligation to cooperate with her attempts to implement environmental education within the whole curriculum of her school.

She is in a strong position compared with another correspondent realistically assessing the mood of teachers on his staff.

The present situation finds teachers bewildered by statements of intent/support stemming from the great 'above' in terms of priority/ content/method, and presents staff with an enormous workload in very real terms when dealing with core (especially) and foundation subjects of the National Curriculum, so much so that muttered asides in support of 'cross curricular themes' are given little heed.

What of the dozens of enquirers who need to ask for guidance on creating an environmental education policy: how can they persuade colleagues and governing bodies to pay more than lip service to environmental education? What of the hundreds of teachers who are not yet motivated even to ask for help? How many times have we heard the phrase 'the battle for environmental education has been won with its recognition within the National Curriculum', as if such recognition implies that everything will now fall into place with teachers wholly committed to the environmental approach? If only they had no other educational responsibilities, no other curriculum matters to consider – then the battle might be won. And this for teachers in England and Wales who have the National Curriculum to back them. What of the rest of the UK – and for that matter the world – where attempts to establish environmental education in the curriculum is still an aim to be fulfilled by its protagonists? To these suppositions one of us would add, 'what of the subject barons of the secondary school, defending their territory against all attempts at cross-curricular activities?' Do you remember those valiant attempts in times past of team teaching enterprises, attempts which effectively failed through the lack of real conviction by the historian (or geographer or mathematician or modern linguist or whoever)? Often it was not an actual lack of conviction but a lack of perceived time for 'covering the set syllabus' inevitably geared to external examinations: cooperative deviation from this was just not on the cards however attractively they were dealt.

Our first correspondent began by highlighting the fact that 'curriculum planning seems to be in a state of constant change'. We wonder if this has not been the case in most schools over the years for a variety of reasons, not least of which is the fact that school-based learning inevitably reflects a changing society with its ongoing social, political and technological advances. Perhaps the difference now is that the imposition of curriculum planning is from outside, supported by a document mountain and complicated by the vacillations of political expediency and dogma. It is difficult during the crowded, busy and time demanding school day not to feel overwhelmed by the whole paraphernalia of an imposed National Curriculum with its targets and tests, foreign to the traditional ways of school-based learning and in many cases at variance with previous practices. Yet when the overburden is stripped away educational aims and objectives remain much as before and the curriculum content similar to that of the past, altered only by the need to match a changing world. Certainly this applies to environmental education, where for at least the past 25 years the need for a school curriculum policy, planned into the overall school programme, has been recognized by a relatively small number of enthusiasts. They perceived the need for an increase in environmental awareness, the teaching of which inevitably crossed subject boundaries and necessitated an integrated approach. The recent recognition by the general public of 'environment and environmental issues' has reinforced the call for environmental education, echoed by politicians and educationists alike.

Earth Summits of the world's leading statesmen, meetings of environmental experts and global forums of non-government conservation organizations proliferate with report after report, often at odds one with the other! Media coverage is strong, though not as strong as for football, baseball, cricket or the Olympics. Yet the feeling remains that environmental education is an essential part of the preparation of young people for the world they will 'inherit'.

In Europe, the USA, Canada and Australasia, the major change is the acceptance of the importance of having someone on the teaching staff responsible for producing a policy for environmental education, and of promoting its implementation. The NAEE (UK) emphasizes the importance of coordination:

> It is difficult to see how environmental education can be delivered effectively unless schools have a member of staff responsible for its co-ordination. Those involved should study the contents of all subjects and identify the environmentally relevant information in each. This done it is important that environmental education is presented to pupils in a cohesive rather than a disjointed way. It is important that within subjects reference is made to environmental causes and effects beyond the particular discipline.

> (NAEE 1992)

It follows that this requires coordination in a way suitable to the individual school. One deputy head teacher put it this way: 'Coordination of such an environmental programme in secondary schools is essential if it is to be effectively focused, avoid overlap and reap the benefits of interdepartmental cooperation.' Positive steps need to be taken to ensure cooperation and communication among the whole staff – but this ought to apply throughout the curriculum with environmental education slotting into the processes in a natural and unexceptional way.

COORDINATION

Every school is unique; location, size, age range, student ability are essential elements which will condition the way in which coordination for environmental education is set up. This has been expressed succinctly by saying that the various approaches to coordination should always suit the changing 'micro climate' within the school. As geographers we approve of the analogy. A small primary school, for example, usually has insufficient staff to designate environmental education as the sole responsibility of an individual teacher, yet, in contrast, in a large secondary school it may well be that a single teacher cannot carry the whole workload for a full environmental education programme.

Experience has shown there to be many variations on the following basic patterns:

1 an individual coordinator
2 an individual responsible for all cross-curricular themes
3 a committee for coordinating environmental education
4 a committee for coordinating all cross-curricular themes
5 no 'official' structure but an understanding that an individual has the task of coordinating environmental education.

We shall not comment further on the last variation except to say that many schools with a thriving programme for environmental education rely on this loose pattern of organization, particularly where the school is small and the staff cooperative.

Our aim would be to have an individual in a position to coordinate environmental education throughout the school, backed up by an organized, formal system of communication between the teachers involved, resulting in an informal and happy working atmosphere which leads to genuine and willing cooperation of people pursuing a common goal. We recognize that this is not always possible. Typical of the solution adopted in many smaller secondary schools is that of one situated in Kent which has about 450 students on roll with a staff of 25, a staffing ratio to be envied elsewhere. The whole curriculum is managed by the senior management team of head teacher, deputy head concerned with pastoral matters supported by a pastoral coordinator, a senior teacher for curriculum, and a curriculum coordinator who has responsibility for cross-curricular themes including environmental education. A larger school had the difficulty of integrating cross-curricular issues into the five full years with some 1000 plus students on roll and over 50 teaching staff. Its solution was a curriculum overload committee which corresponded to our pattern (4) above, although later, as environmental education gained a firmer foothold, a coordinator, with a coordinating committee solely for this theme, evolved. In the rest of the discussion where we refer to an individual coordinator we accept that most of what is discussed can apply equally to a committee or other coordinating organization, except where it is obvious that only a single person can be involved. Individual status is one example. Ideally the coordinator needs to be someone of seniority by virtue of experience and salary. Yet commitment and enthusiasm are almost certainly as import- ant as rank. This person must be able to command the attention of colleagues and in the secondary school of those heads of departments who defend their territory by insular attitudes to learning, often enhanced by the subject-based curriculum. The need to stimulate, coerce, persuade, facilitate, innovate, synthesize and analyse will mean that above all the coordinator must be tactful, understanding and appreciative of the fact that environmental education is not the only cross-curricular theme in the school. The coordinator for environ- mental education must have a precise knowledge of the head teacher's expectations in the task of overall planning and fostering cooperation between staff.

Yet every school situation will be different and, indeed, the same school will be different at various times reflecting the changes in staff and staffing levels, the number and abilities of the pupils, the views of parents and governors, the nature of its organizational status, and the attitudes of the officers who control it, the local political structure and government ideology – as we have said both its 'micro climate' and its national setting. The evidence from inspections is that where objectives have been defined clearly and where cooperation and coordination across subject boundaries have been conscientiously implemented, the standards achieved in environmental education can be very high indeed.

The task of the coordinator

The task of the coordinator must be to facilitate the implementation of the school's policy for environmental education. If there is no policy one will need to be established, together with general guidelines towards its implementation. This can be a daunting task if the head teacher is not convinced of its necessity and if the rest of the staff are anticipating extra work on top of the full load carried already. If a senior teacher or well respected committee is fulfilling the role of environmental education coordination then the task of establishing such a policy is considerably eased.

Curriculum Guidance 7 (NCC 1990b), the NAEE's *Statement of Aims and Objectives* (1992), the Department of Education and Science's *Curriculum Matters 13* (DES 1989) and the publications and research documents of the Council for Environmental Education (such as CEE 1987) will aid this task, as will local guidance. However, three points need to be made:

1 Each school is different and presents a unique circumstance for an environmental education policy.
2 Staff consultation and discussion in establishing a policy, if not essential, has considerable merit. Personal involvement in the planning is important and aids future cooperation and communication.
3 In most circumstances it is advisable to set up a working group to draft the policy and to set the guidelines for its implementation.

It may well be that the head teacher both wishes, and is the best person, to guide the policy making group and that the future coordinator will be the planning group rapporteur or will emerge naturally as a result of the working party activity.

The ways and means of coordination

The coordinator must recognize that there are several stages in establishing thriving environmental education in a school. Experience has shown that it is expedient to begin with some environmental activity which precedes the second step, that of the creation of a written policy for environmental education. The third is the implementation of that policy and the fourth is the continuation of that policy after the initial enthusiasm has waned, various alterations and adaptations to the whole school curriculum have inevitably taken place and staff changes have occurred. Finally there is the continual assessment of success and the need to stimulate fresh ideas and reinforce resource availability. To emphasize the role of the environmental education coordinator in creating environmental awareness leading to a written policy, we quote from the experience of one such person from a junior school to the north east of London:

The Headmaster is very enthusiastic about developing the school grounds as an educational resource. Apart from creating a conservation area and planting over 500 native hedging plants alongside a perimeter fence, under construction is a geological rock garden, maps, amphitheatre, orienteering trail and a maths/science area. He is equally interested in providing a well maintained, attractive internal environment and there is emphasis on children and teachers to take a pride in the appearance of the school building. My contribution as Environmental Education Co-ordinator is in involving children in the creation and maintenance of wild-life habitats, the conservation area, scented butterfly gardens and borders. This includes identifying areas in need of improvement, raising money, planning, writing letters, shopping, telephone calls and carrying out the task. As part of their theme on Environments this term, Year 4 pupils will be making a survey of the plants and animals present in the conservation area – pond, banks, woodland, butterfly garden, hedging, meadow. As a result teachers with their classes have enhanced facilities to study and appreciate the natural environment outside the classroom. I run Watch [see p.166] type activities such as the Ozone Project and Riverwatch and have a conservation notice board. We have an aluminium can recycling scheme and litter patrols. So that every teacher would have some commitment towards Environmental Education, I am preparing an Environmental Education policy.

(Letter received by NAEE in 1992)

THE CREATION OF A SCHOOL ENVIRONMENTAL EDUCATION POLICY

That all schools should have a written policy for environmental education has been recognized by all those who, over the years, have cared about ensuring the place of environment in the curriculum. It was pleasing to see that recommendation 1 of the UK's response to the education section of the World Conservation Strategy read as follows:

Aim
For all schools to have a written environmental education policy with specific reference to living resource issues.

Proposals for action
a) All schools should have a written policy for environmental education within the total curriculum policy of the school and the LEA. This should include environmental education objectives, and guidelines on how the school can achieve these objectives. All teachers should be involved in the formulation and implementation of the policy.

(*Conservation and Development Programme for the UK* 1983)

Our opinion that the whole curriculum policy for a school should contain an environmental education policy section is reinforced by this explicit recommendation. Few seem to be aware of this World Conservation Strategy response as it rests on the library shelves. What is certain is that any environmental education policy will need to take heed of the curriculum policies produced by national and local governments for those schools within the maintained sector. Hopefully non-maintained schools will still feel inclined to follow the guidelines laid down by the local and national 'experts'.

It is not possible, even if desirable, to quote extensively from the curriculum policies of local authorities. For England the NCC's *Curriculum Guidance 7* is available for all to read (NCC 1990b). For most other countries similar documents exist in one form or another, or are in the consultation stage (see Appendix F). However we think it appropriate to quote from the Curriculum Statement for Kent which, under the title 'Education for Life', encapsulates much that others have to say. Emphasizing the multidisciplinary nature of environmental education, it says environmental education 'provides a particular style of teaching, allowing teachers to extend their work beyond the confines of the classroom into the immediate environment of the pupil, extending gradually from the home and school to the natural and built environments'. It goes on to suggest that successful environmental education teaching requires

i)   Using relevant first-hand resources and experiences from the immediate environment where this is possible and appropriate.
ii) Working outside the classroom as a natural extension of the learning environment.
iii) Developing the skills of enquiry and exploration in both local and contrasting environments.
iv) Developing communication skills, particularly through discussion and debate, leading towards practice of decision making and value judgement.
v)   Developing the pupils' self-reliance and ability to organise work programmes in the school and in the field, with an increasing degree of responsibility for their own learning.
vi) Building an understanding of place, time, change and relationship using concrete phenomena that pupils can perceive and relate to.

(Kent County Council 1988)

The Scottish Environmental Education Council (SEEC 1987) have grasped the nettle firmly and produced curriculum guidelines for environmental education. In brief the council suggests some guiding principles:

It is possible to characterise further the approach to environmental education by means of a set of guiding principles. These combine philosophical, pedagogical and organisational considerations, and together they amount to a checklist of essential elements. Environmental education should:

• be a coherent, continuous and progressive lifelong process which should start at the pre-school level and continue through all stages of formal education and beyond. If this idea is to be realised it will require a co-ordinated approach, particularly at school level, based on carefully devised whole-school policies for environmental education sustained by appropriate management and organisational structures.

(SEEC 1987)

It continues by recognizing six further considerations. Environmental education should:

- be firmly rooted in direct experience
- adopt a concentric approach (i.e. local to regional to global)
- be essentially interdisciplinary in character
- use an issue-based approach when appropriate
- use as wide a variety of teaching and learning approaches as possible
- be conspicuously pupil centred.

The SEEC produced a framework for the production of a school environmental education policy which is reproduced in Figure 9.1. It contains a useful list of 13 headings under each of which staff should receive guidance. For our part we would suggest that a policy document may be broken down into eight sections.

1 Aims
2 Objectives
3 Methods and timing
4 Content (knowledge, understanding, skills and concepts)
5 Resources and the organization of resources
6 Assessment, record keeping and evaluation
7 The school as an environmental stimulus
8 Other matters.

Aims and objectives have been discussed earlier and elsewhere examples of these pertaining to a particular school are given. We would plead that statements go beyond generalities which although they are supportive of an environmental approach, are not specific enough for a local situation. Such statements as 'have a degree of insight into other people's environment, lifestyles and predicaments' are just not good enough – their scope is often almost limitless. We believe it is for each school to make positive recommendations in order to limit the scope of environmental education.

Some may argue that having stated aims and objectives it is up to individuals to work out the rest. To us this is the recipe for a lack of coherence for environmental education work and, though we do not advocate rigidity, we feel a better defined structure is essential.

Where methods and timing are concerned our plea is for a flexible approach. Yet this flexibility should not lead to some pupils having an adequate diet of cross-curricular environmental education while others

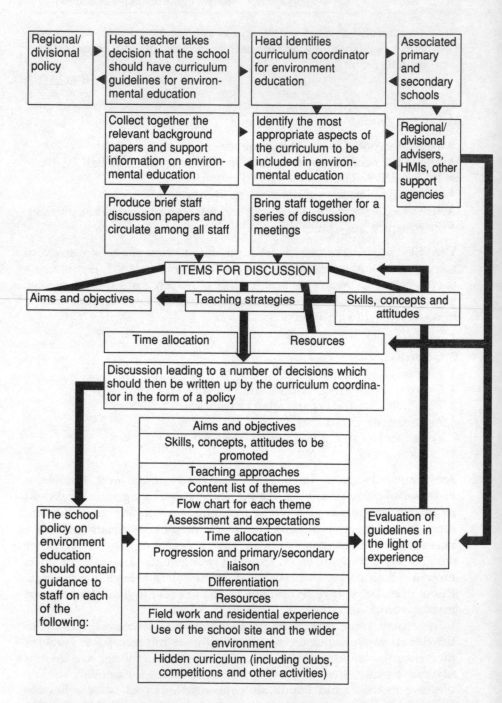

Figure 9.1 Framework for the production of a school environmental education policy

Source: SEEC (1987)

never seem to become involved. It is the policy document which should bring order to this state of affairs, so as to avoid repetition for some and omission for others, with some gaining a high quality of experience, but others a limited diet both in terms of content and the chance to extend their thinking. Attention needs to be given to sequential learning and progression, where the latter is conceived as the acquisition of increasingly difficult concepts and skills.

How comprehensive the listed contents for environmental education should be is a matter for the individual school. Much will depend on the way in which cross-curricular themes are tackled, guided by the curriculum statements of the governing authority, and those of the National Curriculum subjects. It is not necessarily even desirable to specify in detail the environmental content for every subject; often it is more the way in which subject matter is treated rather than the content itself which is environmentally important. In their environmental education guidelines the New South Wales Department of Education summed it up neatly:

> In general, this can be achieved by using the content of a particular curriculum area to develop students' understanding of key environmental concepts and by providing students with learning experiences from the processes and strands of environmental education.
> (New South Wales Department of Education 1989)

Whereas we believe the policy document is the place where the local relevance of wider environmental issues and problems should be recognized we do not believe it to be the place for listing school-based resources often seen to occupy most of the content. It may be sensible to mention the sort and variety of environmental aids appropriate to environmental education and where the material garnered in previous environmental projects, the archive material, is to be located. Others may argue that a separate guide to environmental resources is required and a policy document is not the home for such information. Does it matter as long as the basic reference is easily to hand?

It may well be that the difficulty of assessment and evaluation of environmental education is such as to cause any reference to be omitted. Perhaps it may be left until sufficient experience of organizing environmental education has been gathered in, but eventually guidance on these must be included in the policy documentation. It is to be hoped that what we have to say elsewhere will help coordinators to consider their own particular situation.

We think the school itself as a physical and thoughtful establishment plays an important part in environmental education. To us it is the main strut of the hidden curriculum for environmental education in the formal education service. For children and teachers the school is their environment for most weekdays and for much of the year; it is up to the school management to ensure that the fabric of the place is functional and attractive – for instance a noisy environment is often the fault of architectural structure and interior design rather than poor conduct from the taught. One of us ran a school officially designated as 'structurally acoustically deprived'! Yet it is possible to do something about deadening echoes if the problem is recognized and seen to be important to the quality of the environment. It is up to the head and the staff to ensure that the school is a positive place from a 'living together' viewpoint. Wall spaces and display areas should stimulate the visitor and incumbent alike, so that at any one time every child can say quite simply 'It's a nice place'! Establishing this as part of a written policy is probably harder than making it happen on the ground.

We have mentioned the 'micro climate' of each school, in other words the uniqueness of each place. The environmental policy must reflect the special nature of each school. Despite the differences it is interesting to note that schools following an environmental approach have considerable similarities of spirit and purpose, as reflected in the attitudes of teachers and students.

One interesting approach to cross-curricular environmental education through subject departments in one school, prior to creating an environmental education policy, was to examine the environmental content for some subjects in the National Curriculum and to select areas where more than one subject was involved in the same or similar task. In other words they audited the particular contribution subject departments made to environmental education and where else it appeared in the day-to-day running of the school. Here is the result (as listed in the school records):

Geography   All the geology of the National Curriculum is sub-contracted to the work in geography associated with environmental geography in the National Curriculum.

Science   All meteorology of the National Curriculum is sub-contracted to science. A Countryside Council for Wales externally funded project 'Water in our community' is being followed and includes sections on (a) acid waters (b) water flow analysis and (c) leisure and tourism associated with water.

Technology   All designs include environmental assessment. Energy-saving devices are being investigated.

Humanities/IT IT capability for environmental work is developed. Local and national databases are assessed.

Personal and social education	Simulation exercise of a planning inquiry concerned with industrial development in a national park is part of PSE work.
RE	Third World issues are addressed through the Bugosa, NE India and Tear Fund projects.
Sixth form general studies	A weekend residential conference on 'Challenge of the Environment' is being organized.
School based	Recycling of waste throughout the school community. Improving the working environment of the school buildings and estate, especially tackling the litter problem.

This initial exercise was by way of fostering the idea of the need for a full environmental audit. As it stood it certainly increased departmental awareness but lacked the rigour of a properly planned procedure. It also raised the problem of involving other subject departments not seen at first to be of environmental importance.

Much of the suggested guidance is applicable at one or more of the five stages detailed earlier; some of them are ongoing throughout. For example, one continuing task is to stand back from the day-to-day scene of activity and to observe and reflect on the 'culture' of the school during the time when everything seems to be established and proceeding well. A living school has a habit of altering its tone because of staff changes, change of status, political pressure particularly at senior level, external interruptions (break-in, fire, rebuilding, extension, alteration) and variations in pupil numbers. Three other dictums should be borne in mind:

1 Perceived success will show other staff the advantage of environmental work better than hundreds of pages of documentation.
2 There is nothing more suffocating to enthusiasm than excess paperwork.
3 A deliberately slow process concentrating on one innovation at a time is more likely to achieve the required goal than a broad rush along several fronts.

This latter point is well exemplified by a large secondary school in Essex of some 1600 students aged 11–18 which had been active in the Training and Vocational Enterprise Initiative (TVEI) and its subsequent extension, so that cross-curricular initiatives within the school had been developed in line with National Curriculum guidelines. From this grew a central part of the school programme to develop cross-curricular themes and dimensions across the whole age range. Originally there was a management team of four people each with a particular role, for example the coordination of initiatives for the 11- to 13-year-olds. The planning demands and whole-school involvement proved to be too great so, instead, a working party was created with a member from each of the subject departments.

The cross-curricular themes were already running through the fourth and fifth year special courses. They were economic and industrial understanding; citizenship; health education; careers guidance; information technology; and environmental education. It was felt to be important to introduce cross-curricular based work into the first three secondary years as pupils would be made aware of the concepts involved and so develop their skills and learning strategies. They were already accustomed to working on projects which encompassed various subjects, and in their first year all had had residential experience. A move to a project based completely on environmental education in a cross-curricular setting was thus fairly straightforward.

Initially the working party concentrated on the second year students. The first planning point was to identify the environmental work already being taught in the subject areas. This was then reviewed to see where established and new work could be introduced into the second year schemes of study. Careful planning was needed to ensure that cross-curricular links were made. It was deemed appropriate to tackle the problem through a well defined and easily recognizable project. That chosen was to develop a natural resource region within the school estate. The aim was to nurture positive attitudes and values towards the environment by giving pupils an opportunity to develop opinions and strategies so they might realize the environmental implications of their own and other people's decisions and actions.

The establishment of a natural area is not unique and similar schemes are well documented, so that detailing the tasks is unnecessary here (see Part IV, p. 167). Highlighted, however, was the emphasis placed on opportunities for work across the curriculum, with pupils encouraged to develop their knowledge and skills while working in a practical environment. Liaising with and joining local and national organizations was given a priority so a school reference and database of information could be set up. Outside involvement was seen to be particularly important, for the project was never envisaged as being entirely school based.

The working party soon realized that whole-curriculum planning required effective staff training and that in order to do this the management team needed to attend courses specifically designed for environmental education. Through school-based INSET (In-Service Education and Training), information gathered was to be transferred to all teaching staff. The awareness of 'green' issues and the environmental attitudes of all staff were seen to be particularly important in order to create a caring attitude in pupils, impossible if the school does not lead by example.

The working party was flexible in any approach and planning it adopted, and actively sought the experiences of other schools whose advice and information were valued, made possible by an environmental education forum and sound networking locally.

As the project progressed other offshoots, for instance, dealing with a serious litter problem, enabled the basis for a school policy and implementation programme for environmental education to be established, one which grew naturally rather than one which was imposed from 'above'.

This example can be used to highlight some very important aspects of initiating an environmental education policy. Early on the identification of environmental work already in hand was given priority so that new work could be introduced with as little fuss as possible. Careful planning was the foundation stone for success. Again the concept of building on a 'well defined and recognizable project' is reinforced. Perhaps less common is the recognition of the aid which can be obtained from liaison with environmental education organizations. In some areas a far-sighted local adviser for environmental education will ensure that all schools are affiliated to local and national organizations – inevitably this leads to effective local networking and the establishment of some sort of environmental forum (see p. 144). The importance of in-service training was also recognized, as was the value of reporting back to other staff.

Throughout, the coordinator should aim to produce a minimum of paperwork. There will need to be a brief initial discussion document, as a clear statement of intent. It will contain the philosophy of the proposed innovation but not the content, skills or methods to be employed in the classroom. It should be a clearly stated stimulator and not something where various interpretations may lead to destructive forces gathering against it. It must encourage the idea that the project is a team effort and that it is not a case of throwing overboard existing practice but of building on current work by extending it, with little extra work, to develop a greater environmental emphasis. It will point out that small changes in current practice will give the desired result in a painless way. It is a case of transferring teaching skills rather than the implementation of new ones. It must be clearly relevant to the implementation of the whole curriculum. There are several routes into achieving this, one of which is the environmental audit to be discussed later. Most existing policies have begun by requesting the cooperation of all primary school staff or the secondary school heads of departments, in completing a matrix which shows just what each individual department is contributing environmentally. Such a survey not only shows what is happening but it also shows the gaps that need to be filled.

The size and complexity of the school will determine how full such a survey should be. It needs to be right so that time is not wasted in

Knowledge	English	Mathematics	Science	Humanities	Art & Design	Music	Technology	Drama	Modern languages
I The natural processes which take place in the environment	None of the knowledge areas forms a compulsory Key Stage 3 topic. We all agree to 'explore an issue' in each of years 7, 8 and 9 and an aspect of the environment is a popular choice with staff and students. However, there is no guarantee that any class in a year group will actually cover an environmental topic.	Effectively the mathematics faculty would support the college's environmental education 'policy', but it would be difficult for us to be specific about where we may fit into the 'knowledge' matrix. Of course in our Handling Data ATs we could look at an environmentally based topic but we feel as a faculty that we enable students to become mathematically competent	Weather (water cycle and air currents) It's our Water (cycle utilizing and conserving)	Geography – The work of the sea/rivers D Weather B C F	A C D E F Observational drawing	Pop music A Enhancing quality of school life, e.g. concerts, care of materials E 3 4 5		Through movement ...involve A E 2 3 5	
II The impact of human activities on the environment			Living and changing (changing environment and pollution) It's our Water	History – enclosures, Industrial Revolution Geography – present-day industry, tourism	Murals/art-work enhancing colour		AT1 and AT2 identifying a need and research A C D F	Project on homelessness or disgraced peoples. Begins with appreciation of a 'wasteful' society, e.g. throwaway mentality over indulgent use of resources A D E 1 2 3 4 5	Market and produce environmentally friendly product, e.g. washing powder, petrol adverts, TV, radio, commercials, packaging
III Different environments, both past and present				A B C D 7–9 RE A E F		Music of past C D E 1 2 3 4 5		Industrial Victorian environment, e.g. mining disaster and mills A D 1 2 3 4 5	
IV Environmental issues such as the greenhouse effect, acid rain, pollution			It's our Water (pollution and effect of acid rain)	The effect energy consumption has on the environment Geography D		Pop songs, folk songs, protest songs A C E		Noah, modern version A D E 1 2 3 4 5	
V Local, national and international legislative controls to protect and manage the environment; how policies and decisions are made about the environment				Local planning issues–local councils Rainforests – reserves, treaties, etc. Antarctica – treaties A B D E			AT2 possible solutions A B C D E F	Legislation about canal boats/effect on traditional longboat owners/travellers A D E 1 2 3 4 5	
VI The environmental interdependence of individuals, groups, communities and nations—how, for example, power station emissions in Britain can affect Scandinavia			Living and changing						

Topic				Awareness of resources made and used	Folk music A C D E	AT4 evaluation A D E	'The Island'—ritual, famine, threat of western takeover, etc. A E 1 2 3 4 5	Packaging, TV, radio commercials
VII How human lives and livelihoods are dependent on the environment	It could be built into our curriculum that a project on the environment is undertaken by all students at some point in Key Stage 3. We would involve skills A, C, D, E and attitudes 1, 2, 3, 4, 5		RE – Repercussions of IV A D E Indigenous Indian tribes in the rainforest A B C Religion and environment A C E					
VIII The conflicts which can arise about environmental issues	enough to apply themselves and their mathematics across the curriculum and specifically in subject areas where the environment and environmental issues more naturally arise	Role-play exercise – a public inquiry into a proposed new building development	Geography – local planning issues, e.g. Tesco's supermarket. Development of rainforests, Amazon, Antarctica A D E	Graphs to highlight plights. Visual persuasion		AT4 evaluation A D E	Role-play exercises D 1 2 3 4 5	
IX How the environment has been affected by past decisions and actions		The Foxley Mound Plant	History – enclosures Industrial Revolution Agricultural Revolution	Discussion when working from imaginary – attitudes		AT2 and AT3 Taking action		
X The importance of planning, design and aesthetic considerations			Geography C Planning for settlements Redeveloping a derelict area	As I and II	Conditions imposed on music / composers and within school over the year	A B C D E F		
XI The importance of effective action to protect and manage the environment			Geography Acid rain Rainforests A D				This 'special place' improvisation based on a fictitious beauty spot under threat of development	Packaging, TV, radio commercials

Figure 9.2 Environmental education Key Stage 3 matrix

Key:

AT Attainment Target, as detailed in National Curriculum (England)

A B C D E F refer to skills: (A) Communication; (B) Numeracy; (C) Study; (D) Problem solving; (E) Personal and social; (F) Information technology

1 2 3 4 5 refer to attitudes: (1) Appreciation, care, concern for environment; (2) Independent thought on environmental issues; (3) Respect for beliefs and opinions of others; (4) Respect for evidence and rational argument; (5) Tolerance and open-mindedness

	Year 2	Year 3	Year 4
Language work	Description of direct observation of reservoir 'Lost' village of Llanwyddyn—reaction to news of loss Character studies—imaginative poetry Creative writing—'The day of the flood', 'Vyrnwy as a nature reserve' Mystery story: *The Straining Tower*	Descriptive writing 'Under the surface' 1st person singular *Tarka the Otter*—story to be heard *Wind in the Willows*—fantasy Punctuation—speech marks, paragraphing, dictionary work	River and town guides Letter writing *Legend of Sabrina* Creative writing
Mathematics	Capacity—conversion graphs from old to new measure Volume—symmetry Scale drawing	Capacity Volume Weight wet/dry Rate of flow	Capacity Histograms Graphs Measuring river length Areas of flood plain Speed
Geography	Plans and maps of Vyrnwy Distance from Liverpool Model of area Valley formation Atlas—Wales and England	Bridge settlements Mapping and scale Stream source and flow Valley development Meanders Atlas—major world rivers	Location of Severn River basin Contours and profiles Crossing points Ice Age and effects Mapping Atlas—main British and other European rivers
Science	Properties of water Geology of lake bed Problem solving Plants and the need for water Local flora and fauna Materials in water Dissolving solids	Floating and sinking Dissolving Bedload and trap Boreholes Water cycle Adaptation of plants and animals to life in water Breathing in air and water Food chain Identification and classification	Water cycle Properties of water Filtration of water Bacteria Chlorination Fluoridation

	Year 2	Year 3	Year 4
History	Census returns Social conflicts Need versus settled lives Change and results Comparison then and now	Crossing the stream Fords and bridges Place names	Place names River transport Study of bridges Spectacular events
Art and craft	Marbling Collage work Model making Drawing and painting	Marbling Tie and dye Water colours Spatter prints Claywork Shapes/symmetry Fabric paints	Range of art work
Music and drama	Rhythm of flowing water Small-group compositions of water moving Appropriate composers—Handel's *Water Music* Role-play of Llanwyddn villagers and flood Drama of need for water in Liverpool	Water rhythms Own short composition Development of watery sounds Vibration Movement in water	Role-play—Severn boatmen Musical composition Music and movement
Religious education	Moses and rock Red Sea Jesus and the storm at sea	Red Sea Jonah and the whale Water into wine Baptism in water Call of disciples	Holy waters Sacred rivers Water in different religious faiths

Figure 9.3 Primary school matrix: environmental education project (Theme: Water)

unnecessary detail nor is it necessary to go back afterwards for further information. In fact one of the first cooperative tasks is to compile the matrix and/or questionnaire (Appendix D). Perhaps the simplest is a grid construction with topics listed. Such a matrix used in a large secondary school for the 11–14 stage (Key Stage 3) is shown in Figure 9.2 and another for a particular environmental project in a primary school is shown in Figure 9.3. It is at the point when staff are drawn together to talk about the discussion document and the matrix procedure that the very important matter of clarifying the aims and objectives of environmental education in the specific school will emerge. Nothing will hinder the work of the coordinator more than the fact that even one teacher, or one department, is not fully aware of such targets. It should be possible to ensure coherent environmental education without detracting from the specific objectives of the core and foundation subjects and without creating too much pressure on individuals.

It is obvious that curriculum guidelines will need to be produced eventually, but this is not an immediate task, at least not for public consumption. The real task is to create the right atmosphere for change. It is, for instance, necessary to see potential areas of resistance and either to break it in a pleasant way or to work with it as a recognized constraint. Enthusiasm is the keynote to success, but this must not lead to lack of tact towards colleagues or a lack of consideration for their other activities.

Another school pursued cross-curricular themes for several years which led, eventually, to a written environmental education policy. A community college in the south of England, catering for students of secondary age (11–16), it had set up a cross-curricular activities week in 1989 entitled 'The Summer of '39' which was a celebration of the 50th anniversary of the outbreak of the Second World War in Britain. Evaluation of this work convinced the staff that this approach was well worthwhile and led on to two similar weeks in 1990 (Air, Space and Flight) and 1991 (Frontiers). To programme these weeks a committee called the Curriculum Overlap Working (COW!) Group was set up under the chairmanship of one of the deputy head teachers, and consisted of ten other members, another deputy and a representative from each of the departments (humanities, English, mathematics, science, personal and social education, modern languages, special needs, technology and expressive arts), the titles of which say something of the philosophy and organization of the college. In the words of their own in-school publication:

> With the introduction of the cross-curricular themes in the National Curriculum the College was also looking at the wider implications of delivering cross-curricular work throughout Key Stage 3 and eventu-

ally Key Stage 4. The COW group set itself the task of mapping the curriculum in 1989/90 in Key Stage 3 to see where the overlap was already occurring. The rationale for developing cross-curricular links and themes was to extend the basic curriculum, as required by the Education Reform Act, to meet the personal and social developmental needs of the students across the curriculum.

The staff had gained valuable experience through the activities weeks and a more holistic view of the curriculum was developing. This involved a range of teaching and learning styles, both core and foundation subjects, extra-curricular activities, hands on experience, field trips and producing a presentation or final outcome of the theme being studied. All these features gave clear opportunities for students to enhance their personality and social development. The publication of the five cross-curricular themes and how they should be integrated into the curriculum is a daunting task for all schools. An audit of all the themes was the obvious answer but COW decided to concentrate initially on environmental education and, at the time that an Energy Project was being conceived, the Curriculum Overlap Group started to map environmental education across Key Stage 3. As a result of this mapping exercise and the audit, and *considerable consultation*, the College Environmental Policy was drawn up and adopted by the College Curriculum Committee.

(From school internal brochure 1992)

This is the environmental education policy which they created·

Environmental education policy

Aims
To raise students' environmental awareness.
To give opportunities for students to develop their skills of research and enquiry across the curriculum.
To encourage students to believe that both individual and collective action on environmental issues can make a difference and effect change to solve environmental problems.
To give students the opportunity to study the environment from more than one perspective and sometimes through a common theme.
To provide students with opportunities to meet a range of National Curriculum Attainment Targets in a cross-curricular framework.

Delivery
Environmental education is already being delivered in a variety of different ways. The following check list is not finite. Environmental education can/should be delivered through:
• individual subjects
• field work

- assemblies and tutor time,
- work experience,
- community service,
- water sports,
- College Activities Week,
- Cross-curricular Activities Week,
- use of College grounds,
- practical awareness through recycling cans, paper and by keeping the College environment litter free,
- staff leading by example to encourage all students to be environmentally aware.

The COW group was concerned about progression and assessment in environmental education. Again, in their own words they commented:

Tracking and evaluation
Initially this seems a daunting task. When faculties are preparing schemes of work it would be useful to highlight where environmental education is being delivered using the KS3 matrix and eventually the KS4 matrix. The evaluation within faculties will obviously be covered by the National Curriculum where statutory orders are in place and in GCSEs. A major task will be to develop an environmental education profile to cover cross-curricular modules e.g. Energy project Year 8, Spring Term 1992.

Outside agencies and the LEA advisers would be useful in giving us support and advice as to the effectiveness of our delivery of environmental education in the curriculum.

Celebrating students' work is also very important in the evaluation process. Students should be encouraged to evaluate each other's work. Exhibitions both within the College and in local schools, libraries and banks might provide public areas for displaying students' work. Students would be encouraged to write for a local newspaper many of which now have an environmental section. The use of questionnaires and interviewing students regarding their work could provide a valuable source of feedback in appropriate circumstances.

Inevitably the success of raising environmental awareness in the college, and indeed, in the community in general, meant that the idea of an environmental resource area gained support. It proved to be an excellent example of cooperation both within the college and with outside individuals and organizations. The project was 'up and running' in April 1992 and is open not only to college students but also to local primary schools and interested local community groups. The enthusiastic environmental education coordinator gained financial assistance from several sources and the help of local businesses with equipment loans, reduced prices and other services. Parents, governors and friends of the college raised money in all the usual ways. The coordinator in question has now left the college to guide environmental education in a wider context within the same county area – his in-depth planning over the years appears to have left a firm base for the continuation of cross-curricular work in the future. This last comment emphasizes the need for the coordinator for any cross-curricular theme, environmental education included, not to work in isolation but to ensure 'succession'. No sadder sight is the overgrown, neglected, litter-strewn environmental area, testimony to a previous enthusiast whose 'passion' had not permeated the rest of the staff! The coordinator will need to compromise, adapt and cooperate to avoid difficulties which may arise. With a well motivated staff the path towards successfully achieving the ultimate aims and objectives for environmental education should proceed smoothly. Inevitably setbacks will occur to the fulfilment of such aims. If individual targets are set they can be viewed as tactics within the main strategy of the complete integration of an environmental approach across the curriculum. Good generals know that it is success overall which matters even if minor setbacks occur along the way.

Chapter 10

Implementing a school policy for environmental education

A WHOLE-SCHOOL APPROACH

Elsewhere we have said that changing to an environmentally focused curriculum does not mean that the whole school will be turned upside down. Yet it is also true that, for local reasons, a total alteration of attitude may be needed by students and teachers with environmental awareness used as the vehicle for such change.

A secondary school in Etobicoke, one of the districts of Toronto, Canada, with its own Board of Education, illustrates this thesis in a remarkable way. The school is 25 years old, serving a mainly municipal housing zone with a highly mixed ethnic population. Morale generally at the school was low, reflected in all the usual signs to be found in such circumstances and which need not be listed here. Through the enthusiasm of several individuals and with positive backing from the school board and the involvement of pupils and staff, it was decided to make a positive difference to life on Planet Earth by becoming a focus school that would pilot and share an environmentally sound curriculum. We quote from a paper written for the school environmental education brochure by the environmental coordinator for the school whose vital role in this new approach is recognized by the fact that her job is now a full-time funded appointment.

> This decision [to become an environmentally focused school] is the result of a process which began in the 1989–90 academic year. In March 1990 the Program Leader for Outdoor Education for the North York Board of Education [another Toronto school board] conducted school assemblies on environmental issues. In April the students organised a Humber Valley clean-up, and a school recycling program was implemented by the students' council. A tree planting event was held and environmental concepts and issues became a part of all staff letters, staff meetings, newsletters and student magazines.

A Strategic Planning Committee was formed to forward the project by intense and extensive investigation into present attitudes and interests. The committee 'developed the school's mission, values and beliefs in cooperation with students and parents' groups. In October 1990 all staff members were interviewed individually to assess their interest and concern about moving towards an environmental focus.' The school produced a mission statement and belief as follows.

Our Mission:
In a safe and caring atmosphere the school will graduate individuals who advocate concern for the environment and act with an environmental conscience; who are able to anticipate and adapt to accelerating change and who can cause positive change; who strive for personal excellence; who explore a broad knowledge base with a global perspective; who are enriched by cultural diversity and not limited by economic circumstances.
WE BELIEVE THAT:
— each person must recognize and respect the individual worth and needs of others;
— we must practise and promote a respect and active concern for the environment;
— we benefit from different cultures, races, religions, ages, and genders working and learning together;
— the learning environment must be safe, caring and personal;
— individuals must take responsibility for their actions;
— staff, students, parents, and many other groups in the community are partners in the educational process.
These beliefs are leading the school to a vision of what the school can be at its best.

(Etobicoke Board of Education 1992)

Various committees were set up all containing members from teaching and ancillary staff, students, parents, a trustee, program advisers, *feeder school teachers*, as well as other appropriate individuals. The driving force for the project is the Environmental Steering Committee which includes all committee chairpersons.

The basic premise is that curriculum forms the foundation of the focus school concept. All too often we expect students to accumulate theory without putting knowledge to practice. An environmental curriculum, we believe must be interwoven with an environmentally sound school life-style. This is essential to bringing substance to learning.

The project, completely supported and funded by the local school board, has now received an enormous boost from a charitable foundation which, through the Ontario Society for Environmental

Education, has granted $90,000 (about £45,000) to develop curriculum materials at the school which will lead to piloting them at schools across Ontario. The change brought about in the ethos of the school has, according to the school itself and outside observers, been enormous and for the better. Not only has environment topped the school agenda but social attitudes have altered to bring a harmony to the institution evidently lacking in the past. There was even a move to change the name of the school to emphasize the emergence of a fresh culture. That all of this has been done through a dedication to environmental education is not only exciting but it must be thought provoking to those schools who find themselves in a similar position. In effect the school carried out an environmental education audit, a method we will now examine in more detail.

USING THE ENVIRONMENTAL AUDIT

The 'environmental audit' is a concept well established in the world of commerce and industry. Environmental auditing is becoming as important a practice as financial auditing. In itself it is spawning a new service industry, and texts concerning its use and application are being published. For instance the International Chamber of Commerce (ICC), the world business organizations, set up a working party to examine the concept of environmental auditing and published their findings in a short document (ICC Publishing 1989) which sets out to answer the questions:

- What does environmental auditing mean?
- Why should industrial companies arrange for environmental audits?
- Who should be responsible for them and to whom should they report?
- What sort of methodology should be applied?

Among its other objectives the paper is aimed at 'helping to establish audits as credible and trustworthy instruments in the minds of the workforce, local community, environmentalist associations and the general public'. No direct mention of educational institutions here, but it takes little lateral thinking to apply some of their considerations to schools (student teachers, parents and governors). That the document immediately received endorsement from 20 leading international organizations is testimony to the universal acceptance of environmental auditing as a way into greater environmental awareness and action. From UNEP to Greenpeace, from the World Health Organization to the WWF the concept is found to be 'environmentally acceptable'. The UN Economic Commission for Europe commented that 'Environmental auditing is an appropriate management tool *to promote policies* for environmental protection and rational use of natural resources.' Had the present authors been asked to comment it is likely that, to paraphrase, we would have included in our reply 'Environmental auditing is an appropriate management tool to promote policies for environmental education in schools and elsewhere.' The ICC adopted a definition of environmental auditing for commerce as follows:

A management tool comprising a systematic, documented, periodic and objective evaluation of how well environmental organisation, management and equipment are performing with the aim of helping to safeguard the environment by

1 facilitating management control of environmental practices;
2 assessing compliance with company policies, which would meet regulatory requirements.

One great appeal of environmental audit is that it not only appeases the environmental conscience of the organization involved but it can lead to both financial and environmental advantages. This must be an attractive proposition for boards of management and shareholders – in a school setting for governors and parents. With the popular, if partially misguided, view that schools should respond to market forces, be economically viable, be run along commercial lines and be seen to be following 'sound' business principles, what could be better than using an emerging business technique and applying it to the school situation? We will not labour the analogy between business and education much longer for it is not our intention to suggest that management of schools and the management of business companies is similar, or even a comparison which we endorse. Every teacher and head teacher knows the chasm of difference between them – but also recognizes that some commercial ideas are well worth further investigation. In business parlance the 'practice of Environmental Audit involves examining critically the operations on a site and identifying areas of improvement to assist the management to meet requirements [of the National Curriculum for instance]. The essential steps are the collection of information, the evaluation of that information and the formulation of conclusions including identification of aspects needing improvement' – we quote from the ICC report, except they made no mention of the National Curriculum with environmental education as a cross-curricular theme!

For such an audit to be successful it is necessary for there to be full management commitment by, in the case of schools, the head teacher, her/his senior assistants *and* the governing body. They should endorse, better still, lead, in an overt manner a purposeful and systematic environmental audit programme. The leader(s) of the environmental audit, hopefully the staff with responsibility for coordinating environmental education in the school, should be sufficiently detached to ensure objectivity with well defined and systematic procedures published for all to follow. Eventually the results should be well documented and from this a precise policy should emerge – a policy for environmental education in the school.

The environmental audit programme for each school will be designed to suit the specific needs of the individual institution. What, then, should be the content of an environmental audit? The emphasis will depend on whether the school already has a policy for environmental education or whether the audit is being used as a way into establishing such a policy (there will be areas of common investigation – in the latter it will be a case of intention; in the former of auditing what has been introduced earlier). For the pupils' involvement, the emphasis will be on first-hand investigation into the management of the school in an environmentally friendly way. Much should be made of energy conservation – it is here where better practice will result in financial saving as well as environmental improvement. Heating (and cooling) and lighting will be first and foremost in this investigation. Not only will pupils need to examine ventilation procedures, heating efficiency, draughtproofing, double glazing, floor, wall and roof insulation, the type of heating installation, the electrical efficiency of workshop, laboratory, kitchen and other equipment, but they will require access to past records of payment and maintenance of utility services. The use of water will be an important area for investigation with an examination of the relative merits of metering as opposed to standard charging. Economy measures, with all services, are but part of the conservation investigation; many interesting direct observations can be made concerning the use of lighting unnecessarily and the possible installation of energy-efficient light bulbs including costs relative to normal lights. One such audit carried out by a secondary school in Powys, Mid Wales, revealed a recurring payment to the electricity board of £400 per quarter for the last decade. Each account was shown as an estimate, and apparently paid without question by the local council's treasury department. Further investigation showed it to be a supply to a temporary classroom unit on a site adjacent to the school itself, once used for teaching purposes – but that was before a reorganization programme many years previously when the unit had been removed without telling the treasury. The account had been transferred with other accounts when procedures were altered and nobody had bothered to check on such a 'trivial sum' (as the treasurer's department put it later!). The repayment to the school, now responsible for its own budget, is awaited in eager anticipation.

Another area of investigation will be into the use of materials and the disposal of waste. Recycling, the use of tropical hardwoods in furniture and workshops, glossy paper, environmentally 'unfriendly' products in teaching and in servicing the school . . . the list is not endless but it could go on for a considerable time. Time. . . ? Is the school day planned in an environmentally sensible way – so as to make the best use of daylight for example?

What of the school estate? Is that planned, used and maintained in an environmentally positive way? The school transport – hired coaches, the school minibus, staff cars, local authority vehicles visiting the school – are they using unleaded fuel – what levels of pollution arise from their exhaust systems? Are there areas of the school surround which attract a diversity of wildlife – if not what could be done to improve the situation? Does the school know about its own environment – weather for example – is there a regularly used and properly recorded weather station?

Staff investigations need to include the way the school is responding to curriculum guidelines – in England and Wales to the National Curriculum, and in particular to environmental education as a cross-curricular theme. Is field work a part of the school scheme of things – how is it planned – is it part of a planned progression of environmental awareness? Are staff aware of *Curriculum Guidance 7* and *Curriculum Matters 13*, both referring to environmental education? Do they have their own copies? What of the hidden curriculum for environmental education – the school itself as an expression of a pleasant learning environment? The approach to school, the entrance area, corridor walls, classroom displays – are they interesting and reflective of the rich diversity hopefully to be found in every school? Does the school fabric indicate an interest in environmental care? Are global issues made relevant to the school community through assembly material, charity involvement, extra-curricular activities? All in all is the school a 'nice' place to attend? And the teachers themselves, together with the ancillary staff – do they all present a good environmental example? Is this too much to expect – or at least too much to discuss?

Outside organizations, as we shall see later, provide resource material and encouragement for their particular interest in the environment. The environmental audit should address itself to the extent to which the school is taking advantage of these opportunities. Are members of the teaching staff active in the local environmental education association and is the school itself an institutional member of such a group? Is there a proper display of environmental education material, for instance the monthly newsletter of the Council for Environmental Education and the termly journal of the National Association for Environmental Education? Are there assessment and evaluation procedures for environmental education in the normal record keeping of the rest of the school curriculum? Are records kept of projects/field work so that future endeavours can take advantage of previous experience? Does the school library/

resource centre have a separate area for environmental issues and a system for referencing the daily/weekly/monthly articles and press reports concerned with environmental affairs?

It is obvious from the above that a full environmental audit can be all-embracing and requires detailed planning and the cooperation of all 'ranks' of the school hierarchy, including the governors and the local advisers for the environmental subject areas. If one can bring such a project to fruition it is hard for any individual to deny the importance of a planned environmental education policy for the school. The great advantage of the environmental audit is that it needs to be repeated at regular intervals in order to assess the benefits gained from the initial enquiry and the investment made in time, trouble and cash. If, as a result, the working environment of the school is improved and economies have been achieved, thus leaving more for direct educational resources, the environmental audit and its resulting environmental education policy will become as essential a part of the school as any of the curriculum policies for the foundation subjects. The NAEE has produced a pioneering document *Towards a School Policy for Environmental Education: An Environmental Audit* (NAEE 1992). Krysia Baczala, its author, suggests there are ten main questions to be asked:

1 How is the school as an institution encouraging environmental education?
2 How is environmental education managed?
3 Is the school developing appropriate and useful documentation relating to environmental education?
4 What evidence is there that environmental education is being integrated into the curriculum?
5 How do pupils perceive the relevance of environmental education in their learning?
6 What arrangements does the school have for field work?
7 What are the arrangements for assessment in environmental education? Is achievement acknowledged?
8 Is there evidence that the school estate is used as a learning resource?
9 What are the arrangements for coordinating the management of the school estate?
10 To what extent does the school manage itself with respect for the environment (practise what it preaches)?

A subset of questions applies to each of the main questions. For instance 'What evidence is there that environmental education is being integrated into the curriculum?' has seven sub-questions:

(a) Is there cross-departmental discussion?
(b) Does topic work have an environmental focus?

(c) Are there lessons that emphasize links between subjects?
(d) Do schemes of work show evidence that environmental education has been incorporated?
(e) Are staff members linked into local environmental teachers' support groups?
(f) Is the school linked to national environmental associations such as the NAEE?
(g) Is there a student environment council, linked to others locally, nationally, internationally?

The book quotes from a secondary school's audit report:

> The findings of the audit revealed that environmental education was not only taught by those subjects with obvious environmental interests, but was keenly supported by other, less biased disciplines. At a meeting which followed the completion of the audit, plans were drawn up to heighten the school's level of environmental awareness to embrace pupils, staff and governors.
>
> To this end, a meeting of staff and governors was held to examine ways of encouraging pupils to become more involved with environmental projects and to agree a list of measures to improve the pupils' working environment.
>
> The views of pupils were given substance by the founding of the Students' Environmental Council, whose officers and members would have direct access to the staff running the project. The availability of some funds meant that certain suggestions could be carried out immediately.

A typical school policy for environmental education in a primary school resulting from the imposition of an environmental audit is highlighted:

A School Policy for Environmental Education
Within the context of environmental education, the school will hope to bring about an understanding of the environment, an appreciation for the environment and a sense of caring for the environment.
    From first-hand and real experiences, the pupils will learn:

- in, through and from the environment (as a resource)
- about the environment (knowledge)
- for the environmental (values and attitudes)
- skills to assist in the study of the environment

Successful teaching will involve our pupils in learning *through* the environment:

- using relevant first-hand resources and real life experiences as a basis for learning

- working outside the classroom as a natural extension of the working environment
- developing skills of enquiry and exploration within the local area and contrasting environments elsewhere
- developing communication skills such as reporting the results of research
- developing self-reliance, responsibility and independence especially while exploring the school grounds
- building an understanding of place, time, change and relationships using actual phenomena

Successful teaching will involve our pupils in learning *about* their environment. Pupils should develop knowledge and understanding of:

- the natural processes which take place in the environment
- how life is dependent on the environment
- the impact of human activities on the environment
- differing environments past and present
- how the present environment has been affected by past actions and decisions
- how decisions are made about the environment at local, national and international level and how we might affect them
- how what we do affects others, for example factory emissions in Britain can cause acid rain in Scandinavia
- environmental issues such as pollution, the destruction of rainforests, the designation of Antarctica as a world park
- arguments which can arise from environmental issues
- the importance of planning and design considerations
- the importance of effective action to protect the environment

Successful teaching will involve our pupils in being educated *for* the environment. Our children should:

- develop an interest in and learn to appreciate their environment through the care of living things and their habitats in and around the school
- develop a respect and liking for their environment through relevant and interesting studies of it
- seek solutions to environmental problems within the school and the local area, taking account of conflicting interests

Successful teaching will develop the *skills* of our children by using environmental education as a channel to develop:

numeracy
communication (including reading, writing, speaking and
    listening)

study skills
problem solving skills
personal and social skills
information technology skills

Environmental education will be closely linked, not only to subjects of the National Curriculum, but to the other cross-curricular themes of economic and industrial understanding, health education, careers education and citizenship.

First-hand experience of different environments will be offered wherever possible to allow pupils to develop a personal response to their environment and to enable them to gain awareness of environmental issues. Field-work will have an important role to play in this as it provides opportunities for drawing on the environment as a stimulus to learning. Every attempt will be made to ensure progression in environmental education to keep a record of progress, to reward achievements and to encourage participation in practical conservation activities.

To supplement the policy and to highlight the day-to-day actions needed to encourage environmental care, schools may wish to adopt an environmental charter. One such charter is displayed prominently around one primary school and reads:

At all times the pupils, staff and friends of Snodland CEP School will try:

- to keep the school and grounds clear of litter
- to save energy by switching off unwanted lights and heaters and keeping doors and windows closed
- to recycle as much as possible, ranging from cans to stamps
- to use environmentally friendly cleaning materials
- to use recycled paper products
- to develop and improve the school grounds and plant more trees
- to keep the school a non-smoking zone
- not to waste natural resources like food and water
- to teach everyone about the importance of caring for our environment.

The environmental audit, as with all other school projects, needs extensive planning and preparation. The subject-based approach of most secondary schools demands an overall curriculum plan whereby each subject prepares the way for the audit by introducing pupils to the various knowledge and skills required. One such subject-based work scheme is given in Appendix E as a guide to what may be attempted. No claim is made to it being fully comprehensive and it is up to the individual school to consider at what stage in the school such an integrated approach should be attempted. It may well be expecting too much to plan a whole-school project along these lines. Experience has shown that some of the best results have been achieved with 11/12-year-old entrants and with first year sixth form students. Adaptation to local circumstances will be essential.

The environmental audit approach is being used in New Zealand in its Eco-School project where an integrated whole-school approach to environmental education is developing. The audit examines practices used in the maintenance, care and improved use of school grounds; school caretaking practices, use of energy, paper, plastics, aluminium, including recycling strategies which can earn money or provide materials for art and other programmes. Curriculum guidelines for environmental education have been developed from this and published by the New Zealand Natural Heritage Foundation (1991) based at Massey University, Palmerston North (see Appendix F). As in the UK, organization of the curriculum will take place either through the various subjects of the New Zealand National Curriculum or through the various forms of integrated studies, recognized as being easier to introduce in primary and intermediate schools, although some forms of block integrated timetabling have been introduced in a few secondary schools. The Eco-School programme recognizes that a whole-school policy for environmental education comprises four components:

1 The school curriculum: how environmental education is introduced and organized in the subjects and courses offered
2 The school environment: how the school environment is enhanced and waste is avoided
3 Decision making: who is involved in making decisions (students, teachers, community, etc.) and the processes and structures put in place
4 School management and leadership: how the school is run to motivate and encourage involvement and reduce stress and to manage resources (including human resources) effectively.

It may be of interest to readers to know that it is the intention to develop an international Eco-School network with the New Zealand Natural Heritage Foundation in a coordinating role. The relationship of environmental education to the National Curriculum for New Zealand, through the concept of Essential Learning Areas, is shown in Appendix F.

Summary

The environmental audit:

• should not be seen in isolation, but as just one important element in a comprehensive approach to environmental education

- where properly applied shows that self-determination is more effective than outside guidance or official regulation
- is an important component of voluntary policies
- will strengthen environmental awareness within the school and credibility with parents and governors
- helps safeguard the environment
- substantiates compliance with the National Curriculum
- facilitates the interchange of information and cooperation between teachers and between subjects
- increases teacher and governor awareness of environmental policy and responsibilities
- identifies potential cost saving and minimizes waste
- evaluates INSET programmes
- provides an up-to-date environmental database
- enables credit to be given at all levels for good environmental performance
- is a concept whose time has come.

Assuming through whatever method employed, that the environmental education policy has been established, the coordinator will need to give attention to many tasks.

TEACHER APPRECIATION

Appreciation is a two-way process - from the coordinator to the teacher and from the teacher to the coordinator. Within this dictum is encapsulated the hazards and the easy paths to the successful implementation of an environmental education policy. Unless the ideology and philosophy of the environmental approach has been completely explored, clearly stated and thoroughly disseminated, teachers may be confused. An incomplete appreciation of the aims and objectives may lead to frustration with only a partial or inappropriate response. In order to appreciate a 'new' non-traditional curriculum demand, motivation must be kept high.

Genuine innovation does not happen unless a personal commitment to ensuring success is built into each individual. Experience has shown, almost invariably, that staff members will take on extra tasks if they are seen to be realistic and valuable. Rejection will come only if the demand for change is too fast and too unrealistic. The best examples we have noted of assimilating environmental education into the curriculum have taken place over several years. Some cynics may claim that the aims and advantages of a fresh approach have less influence on the individual than the ultimate effect on their work load and work routine. It is up to the coordinator to ensure that teacher cooperation does not break down into adversarial components and that no established role in the school situation is a bar to progress. It is vital for the coordinator to recognize the overt and the covert structure of the school, and the attitude of the personnel.

Change is only possible with cooperation and it is necessary to work alongside each teacher, to recognize the particular relevance their subject has to environmental education, and to exploit the particular teacher talent or subject skill to the best advantage. It is equally difficult not to overburden the willing horse. It is essential that the coordinator is aware of the total school commitment of teachers and not to make extra demands such that other important areas of the school organization suffer.

In view of these comments the tasks to be highlighted are to:

- Ensure that all teachers appreciate the basic environmental entitlement of every child of whatever age or ability.
- Be quite clear that the aims and objectives for environmental education in the school are understood by all of the staff.
- Evaluate the special talents and interests of teachers and departments and build on them.
- Create a programme of active participation and involvement in the policy.
- Advise staff on differing methods of environmental approaches and assessment and establish which is best for their particular current needs.
- Sound the staff water to discover the 'shallows and the rapids' which may restrict a full and willing participation and to work to remove or reduce these restrictions.
- Cooperate with subjects and other cross-curricular themes, even if they are of little personal interest. 'Give and take' must be the motto for success.

PUPIL INVOLVEMENT

The natural interest of pupils in the environment is a vital plus for environmental education. They may be apathetic, bored and even hostile to the basic elements of learning, yet using the environment may provide an acceptable stimulus. What is very important is not to underestimate the potential of pupils to tackle complex environmental issues, provided they are presented to them as an understandable package. Pupil investigation in major projects from Watch, the junior section of the RSNC (p. 166), namely, stream pollution, acid rain, ozone and riverwatch, points the way to the fact that every school has many potential researchers on its roll. Numerous national or local award schemes and environmental competitions are designed to stimulate pupil involvement. The astute coordinator will exploit these to advantage, particularly in building up an environmental resource library. The coordinator should:

- Examine the schemes of environmental work to ensure that there is no direct relationship between the age and ability of the pupil and the triviality of the pursuit. On too many occasions the academically least able are thought to be environmentally backward as well. Experience proves this not to be correct.
- Create a programme of active involvement and participation of children in environmental activities, particularly conservation activities.
- Cooperate with the school librarian and establish a newspaper/magazine reading panel to set up a database of environmental information available for project and other work.

PRESSURES ON THE SCHOOL CURRICULUM

It is the coordinator's prime task to ensure that environmental education does not lead to excessive extra pressure on the whole-school curriculum. It certainly has to dovetail into the fabric of other activities within the school. The skill of the coordinator will be severely tested as this involves content, resources and time. The following are but some of the key issues to be borne in mind:

- Whatever schemes are developed ensure that they do not increase pressure on the curriculum excessively.
- Determine the restrictions placed upon environmental activity by the timetable and the allocation of space and resources, e.g. part-time staff, swimming and games commitments, assemblies, school bus collection times, school meals, INSET programmes, holidays and special events. Determine, too, the national and local regulations conditioning special activities (see 'communication' later).
- Examine the established school curricula and recognize programmes of environmental study in the core and foundation subjects and other cross-curricular themes.
- Be aware of common skills across learning areas and coordinate strategies for dealing with them. This has been well exemplified by the matrix in Figure 9.2.
- Relate, where possible, each piece of individual subject work to the environmental education curriculum as a whole.
  Ensure that individual projects of the curriculum which draw on periodic issues/statistics are placed in the context of ongoing research, e.g. school weather station, and that full records are kept for future use. Far too much splendid research is carried out in isolation, the

results to be used once and then abandoned. One hopes that information technology provides a unique way of keeping useful data in a
compact and accessible way (see p. 198).
- Recognize that there are other cross-curricular themes which need to
be planned into the school menu and which demand support.
Exclusivity for environmental education must be rejected.

METHODS/APPROACHES/ASSESSMENT

One of the main tasks of the coordinator after the environmental policy
for the school has been agreed will be to indicate the ways in which
environmental education can be approached, the methods for teaching
and learning to be employed, and the way in which assessment of
progress can be made. Details appear in Chapter 11. It may be useful to
list the essential jobs to which attention must be paid:

- Time will need to be given to formation guidance on out-of-classroom
work both in the school estate and away from it.
- Close attention will need to be given to the reports of statutory
bodies.
- Define the patterns of content to be studied, and environments to be
investigated, at different stages and different times in the pupil's
progress through the school.
- Formulate a policy for drawing on the experience of all out-of-school
activity and not only that pursued for direct environmental purposes,
e.g. trip to a museum, outing to France, visit to a local factory.
- Ensure that everyone realizes that work outside school must be part
of a planned experience and needs as much consideration of aims and
objectives as any schoolroom work.
- Set up a system whereby teachers not involved in any out-of-school
activity are aware of what is planned by others. Thus they may
request some special attention to be given to the opportunity to
further their own specialist area.
- Be aware of award schemes, competitions, exhibitions, and other
opportunities in which pupils or classes may participate where there
is an environmental content.
- Plan contributions to the themes and content of school assemblies.
- Help staff to formulate and carry out assessment procedures.
- Devise evaluation methods using the experiences and ideas of other
departments. Evaluation should be of environmental awareness as
well as of factual knowledge and skill development.
- Above all else the coordinator must give the lead by organizing and
being the key figure in the first 'Across the school environmental
project'. This may well be the most crucial of all the steps taken by the

coordinator, for much of what has been preached will be revealed to the public gaze.

ENVIRONMENTAL ISSUES

Much of the work of environmental education will be associated with the many environmental issues which beset the world at present. It is essential that a coherent approach to such issues is made across subject areas. A balance must be kept and up-to-date information made available for teaching purposes. It is important to relate the worldwide issues to the problems of the neighbourhood, so as to satisfy the dictum 'Think globally, act locally'. The way to deal with environmental issues on a school basis, and the methods to be used for acquiring learning, are a separate topic in themselves to which attention has already been paid. (Part II). An example concerning ozone and ozone layer depletion given elsewhere as an INSET exercise (Appendix G) indicates but one approach to one global issue. In order to achieve a result the coordinator will need to recognize certain tasks:

- Identify current environmental issues and, with staff consultation, prioritize their relative importance within the school's programme of environmental work.
- Establish the relevance of such issues to the school neighbourhood.
- Recognize that certain aspects of environmental awareness have particular relevance to the individual school, e.g. traffic noise and exhaust pollution, litter from the local supermarket, lack of sports facilities.
- Deliberately integrate the cognitive and the affective domains within studies of issues and problems.

RESOURCES BEYOND THE SCHOOL

Government departments, the local education authority and other local council departments (environmental health, planning), people and agencies in the neighbourhood and national organizations are all available for professional exploitation in the cause of furthering an environmental policy. First and foremost is the local advisory service, hopefully led by an adviser or inspector for environmental education supported by an advisory team, probably including the heads of the local authorities' environmental study centres. Again hopefully, such study centres are provided as one of the major resources for environmental teachers locally. The current trends in UK education have led to the disappearance of full-time local environmental education advisers – we believe all without exception now have other duties to perform and many have been replaced by advisory teachers, often on short-term contracts. Nevertheless the local advisory service provides an essential back-up to schools. One adviser for a large English city has listed ten important tasks in implementing environmental education as a cross-curricular theme, tasks which he is attempting to fulfil in his area:

- presenting a clear and unequivocal message that the core and foundation subjects are only a part of the curriculum
- making information on environmental education instantly available to all who need it by providing them with a personal copy of all curriculum guidance documents
- ensuring that environmental education is to be found in every school's curriculum development plan
- transforming the blandishments of environmental education curriculum documents into practical ways of working, by planning for this curriculum area in as detailed a way as for any of the more prominent aspects of learning
- gathering together human, physical and financial resources to match programmes of activity and learning
- seeing that initial and in-service training of teachers takes account of environmental education
- encouraging all organizations with an interest in the environment to avoid unintentionally giving the message that environmental education is extra-curricular, special or only a game or competition!
- identifying the personnel in every tier of the local service who have a responsibility and accountability for the provision of environmental education
- encouraging the professional associations to establish formal links in order to explore ways of working together on all cross-curricular themes
- pursuing the objectives of environmental education as part of the school curriculum so that it achieves permanency – monitoring, evaluation and review to be included in this process.

Another adviser for a large county in England has set up a number of regional environmental education groups which carry out their own programme of events. Many are of an in-service training nature which are repeated for other groups. These efforts are overviewed by an environmental education forum of cooperating council departments and voluntary/commercial organizations. Some local council authorities have established wide-ranging environmental plans which include an element of environmental education. The initiative for this probably comes from outside the education service itself which is of help where, for one reason or another, the educational advisory service is not set up to provide all that could be desired. Happy is the area where a combination of overall environmental improvement initiatives combines with an excellent environmental education advisory service backed by several study centres.

Assessing the success of environmental education is difficult. One adviser for environmental education has made it a major personal task to evolve an assessment basis which can be applied in schools (Appendix H); others have organized exhibitions, displays and environmental fairs in order to stimulate and reward outstanding environmental education. At least one adviser has promoted a database for environmental education available to all those schools in the area provided with inter-communicating IT equipment (p. 198). For example the production records of a local farm are made available, to be used directly by the teachers of science, mathematics, geography and others in an outstanding example of cross-curricular environmental education. We are not suggesting that these activities are unique – indeed the encouraging thing is that so many exist – but they are not universal, more's the pity.

It seems appropriate here to interject that the legislation for environmental education in the USA (Appendix J) together with the trilateral agreement between Canada, Mexico and the US will set up a formal system of cooperation to increase the environmental literacy of young citizens. This will provide at a national and state level the guidance which will lead to many cooperative forums similar to those being promoted actively by most environmental education advisers in the UK.

Apart from working closely with the local advisory service the role of the coordinator can be summarized by the following points:

- Investigate the provision for environmental work in local teacher environmental study or professional development centres.
- Involve parents, councillors, governors, industrialists, local experts and all of those who contribute to the 'environmental' side of community life. Establish local contacts.
- Establish links with local environmental groups and, preferably, become involved.
- Establish links with national organizations. If possible become a school member, e.g. of the RSPB, CEE, NAEE.
- Encourage out-of-school individual study and research, for example by establishing a Watch group.
- Liaise closely with other local schools both primary and secondary.
- Cooperate with initial teacher training establishments.
- Remember to warn local people if the school embarks on a project which may include surveys or disturbance.

RESOURCE MATERIAL

Resource material for environmental education abounds – the environment itself is the greatest resource of all. For the coordinator it will be necessary to assess the potential of the locality with environmental learning in mind. The other task is to bring together the mass of material available, much of it free, from outside organizations. Again this is a vast undertaking requiring separate consideration. The Big Green Envelope (BGE) scheme of one local authority is their adviser's answer to the task (see Appendix K).

Things to be done are:

- Keep up to date with and publicize television and radio programmes. Arrange to make video recordings within the restrictions of copyright.
- Arrange to display the regular incoming items produced by such bodies as the RSPB, CEE, NAEE, CT, WWF, etc. Some items, for instance the newsletters of the CEE, the journal of the NAEE and the Countryside Commission news-sheets, need to be properly displayed in staff common rooms.
- Cooperate with the school library and/or resource centre to build up an environmental picture and wallchart library.
- Build up a special 'open-ended' resource section of videos, pictures, etc. which enable pupils to establish their own individual attitudes and evaluations.
- Establish good relationships with the local library, museums and teachers' centre for resource loans.
- Investigate the usefulness of simulation exercises and games in environmental matters, especially those which stimulate value judgements and the heightening of attitude awareness. Tape recording in sound or video of news events, such as a major oil spillage, can be useful source material to stimulate classroom discussion.

IN-SERVICE TRAINING

Numerous surveys have shown that few teachers involved with environmental education have had any formal training for this curriculum area. In particular they lack confidence to make the best use of out-of-classroom studies. It is essential that the coordinator attempts to rectify these omissions. In-service training can be used not only to point the way to different teaching methods in environmentally based learning but also to enhance the role of the coordinator and even to attain the objective of establishing a written policy for environmental education in a school. One such day-long programme presented the problem of dealing with a global environmental problem 'ground level ozone and the depletion of the ozone layer' in a subject-based secondary school. The aims and objectives were clearly stated:

Aims
- To initiate a debate on environmental education as a cross-curricular theme to stimulate the environmental awareness of each subject department.
- To encourage cooperation between subject departments.
- To establish the role of the coordinator for environmental education.

Objectives
- To contribute to the preparation of a school environmental education curricular policy.
- To explore the ways in which each subject department could contribute to the student's understanding of a global environmental issue.
- To introduce staff to a major global issue and its relevance to the school curriculum.
- To establish the concept of an environmental audit.

The exercise has been referred to earlier and is detailed in Appendix G. Other in-service resources are described in Part IV. Suffice it to say here that all of these training sessions require long-term planning on the part of the coordinator and almost certainly need the cooperation of the local advisory service, if, indeed, they do not emanate from that source. We are aware that with one local adviser the initial planning for a series of INSET days in secondary schools across the region took place two years before their implementation. In some ways the planning involved was also a method by which school head teachers were encouraged to nominate a coordinator and for this person to prepare the way in an individual school. It may be necessary for the reverse to happen with the school coordinator needing to convince the local adviser and the local teachers' centre to organize INSET courses for environmental education.

One of the aggravations of teaching is to learn of a useful training event after it has occurred. Often this is the fault of the organizers who sadly fail to realize the long lead-in time needed to ensure all teachers are aware of an event. More likely, however, is the fact that the information arrived in a school in good time but for the many reasons associated with a busy school life, it was not disseminated as it should have been. No doubt one of the tasks for a coordinator is to ensure that all courses, seminars and other events involving an environmental education approach are brought to the attention of every subject department or interested teacher. Another task is to make certain that those who attend such occasions are given the opportunity to report back for the benefit of others. Most schools are within reasonable distance of a higher education establishment which could consider running an appropriate diploma or degree course involving environmental education. The coordinator should investigate the possibilities for the organization of these courses. Again it is something which may be best approached through the local adviser.

RECORD KEEPING

Despite the trends to computerize school records it is not necessary to have a sophisticated retrieval system for record keeping. Quite simple box files can do the job – it is the conscientious updating of information and an adequate index method which justifies the time and trouble put into it by members of staff. Why duplicate effort when it can be easily avoided? But having said this it does follow that a computerized database operated by staff competent and confident to use it is, for now, the ultimate in record keeping. We do not doubt that at the secondary level much of the record system could be student operated – we need to be convinced that this is *not* possible with older juniors! Pupil records of environmental understanding, and school records of work accomplished, need to be kept. As with any other area of learning, progress in environmental education should be made and needs to be recorded in a standardized way. It is essential, too, that project and other work in environmental education is detailed so that similar events in the future can benefit from past experience. The coordinator needs to establish a reference system which records work in the environment including the useful contacts made. It is valuable to good relationships not to over-exploit any person or corporate body. Thus times when contacts were used need to be set down together with any fruitless avenue explored. The successes and the failures need to be recorded with ideas for the improvement of the project or possible extensions next time. A system of recording pupil progress in environmental matters, possibly through a pupil profile system, needs to be set up (see Chapter 11).

COMMUNICATION

The coordinator must consider communication within the school, bearing in mind it is always a two-way process. In addition communication with outside individuals and institutions is essential.

Communication within the school

A good system of communication within a school does not apply solely to environmental education. In any well organized school, an efficient system should be already established; environmental work merely needs to be added. Nevertheless the successful coordinator must give her/his own personal attention to it for any environmental policy might just as well remain on the shelf if it is not understood because of a breakdown in communication. Good contact may take place through the chance (or apparent 'chance') meeting in the staffroom between individuals or small groups. Reliance on this is not good enough and a structured system is needed in addition to formal staff meetings for other purposes. Ideally a structure needs to be established so that exchanges of information and ideas are easy and part of the ongoing school day. It should not be necessary to detail here the many ways in which schools ensure that groups of teachers may be enabled to meet together. The often complex timetables of the secondary school should be the servant and not the master. Much myth surrounds timetable construction. Essentially the coordinator must ensure that requests for special structures are made well in advance. Late in the autumn term is not too early for the following academic year. Discussing the matter with the person in charge of the timetable and offering to help can reap a reward. Although the content of what is to be taught is of importance it is probable that greater emphasis will need to be put on the teaching styles and methods for environmental education. There is no doubt that regular meetings to discuss these are essential, possibly in the context of dealing with all cross-curricular work. Local, national and world events of an environmental nature arise unexpectedly, an oil spill for example, so that the coordinator needs to be able to communicate quickly with colleagues ways in which environmental 'exploitation' of matters of the moment can take place. A balance must be kept – over-enthusiasm for environmental awareness may lead to an unwanted and undesirable backlash. Remember, too, that positive environmental observations abound and all doom and gloom can lead to acute environmental pessimism followed by a general feeling of 'well, what can we do anyway?' – to coin a phrase, a strong case of 'environmental turn-off'.

Communication beyond the school itself

Enough has been said already to underline the important role which environmental education advisers and their advisory staff have to play. It is an unfortunate school which is situated in an area where support services directed for environmental education are not provided. If this is the case it is part of the role of local groups of teachers and other environmentalists to put pressure on the local council administration to rectify the omission. Education committees (the equivalent of the school boards of the USA) have teacher representatives who could raise the matter; this is one avenue of approach – a local corporate association of the NAEE is the most effective pressure group to make the necessary contact. And it goes almost without saying that the school coordinator for environmental education should be active in that local association – if there is none she/he should gather together like-minded individuals and form one. There is much to be said for inviting the local chief officer for education to be the president of the group. Whereas the coordinator can make personal contact with helpful organizations, it is more effective, has greater input and is economic of time if the environmental education group is the channel for communication.

An active adviser can stimulate inter-school communication so much more easily than an individual teacher from one school. For example one splendid effort takes place in one local area. Every primary school has designated a teacher as the coordinator for environmental education, although it is not the only extra responsibility that person may have. Once a term at least, the adviser convenes a meeting of the group to promote ideas, exchange experiences, publicize matters of interest and to plan seminars, courses and the like. Secondary schools are being drawn into the planning. Other meetings of the group take place for special events, e.g. the contribution of schools to a local 'anti-litter' initiative or programming inputs into World Environment Day. Experience has shown that local field work planning can avoid over-exploitation of one resource. With several supermarkets in the area it has been found useful to 'share' them around so that no particular store suffers the multiple attention of shopping surveys by several schools. The problem of three separate schools surveying passenger travel on the same day at a busy main line station could have been avoided had inter-school communication been better, much to the gratitude of those hurrying people accosted about their travelling habits, one after the other, three times! The very act of discussing matters of interest and exchanging information may lead to exciting and useful project work.

Cooperation with the staff of the nearest institution involved with teacher training can provide mutual benefit. With work out of the classroom the school can always do with extra professional help and the college can capitalize on the invaluable extra student/pupil contact. Experience has shown that the students have access to more, and superior, technical aids compared with those available in the school itself. This also applies to cooperating with the nearest field study centre run by the Field Studies Council. It is always a surprise to discover just how many schools are within easy distance of one of these splendid establishments. We have found the wardens of these centres to be most helpful provided long-term communication is set up and the school is prepared to avail itself of the least busy time of the centre's programme, usually in the late autumn or early spring. The expertise and the technical facilities available at these centres is considerable. Whereas teachers are used to involving themselves with the excellent centres run by their local authority they do appear, especially at the primary stage, to be reluctant to approach the field study centre, and, for that matter, other privately run centres around the country.

Fortunately environmental concern has given rise to many organizations pursuing one particular topic of interest. Take the Royal Society for the Protection of Birds (RSPB) for example. This organization not only provides considerable resource material appropriate to its title, and centres where bird studies can be carried out, but it also provides a useful well illustrated series of wall charts directed at different age ranges. Most of this material is free. It also organizes a Young Ornithologists Club (YOC). Communication with the RSPB is, thus, an essential task for any environmental education coordinator. This is but one example. The RSPB and other organizations will be highlighted in the resources chapter later.

Not only must the coordinator know of these opportunities for assistance but she/he must ensure that other staff are aware too. In fact the broader concept of increasing teacher environmental awareness is an essential element of the coordinator's job. One way is to heighten awareness through the whole school by campaigning to improve the environment of the school itself, both inside and out. It has been said that a neglected school, hostile to learning, is hostile to environmental education as well. The quality of the school environment must exemplify all that the coordinator is trying to achieve. Signs of environmental initiative obvious to any visitor set the tone for caring. One school has mounted small magnets on the school walls set between two can-collecting bins. All pupils are encouraged to test their used drink cans for ferrous or aluminium content and to dispose of them into the appropriate bin. This leads to a constant reminder to conserve the world's resources (and removes dropped cans from the school estate as well)!

Busy teachers have their own interests and cannot be expected to be more than aware of global environmental problems. It is part of the task of the coordinator to see that the school library is well stocked with information books concerned with, for instance, rainforest destruction, acid rain, ozone layer depletion, nuclear issues and other matters. A good selection of these are now in print appropriate to the age of the pupils (see p. 171). For the staff shelves many of the books written for the secondary school library contain sufficient information and resource lists as to be useful reference sources for lesson planning. If the coordinator has insufficient time to prepare summary sheets it is possible to find such material from commercial and voluntary organizations. It is to be hoped that a section of the display boards in any staff room is the responsibility of the environmental education coordinator.

Chapter 11

Assessment and evaluation

If a school policy and individual schemes of work for environmental education are to be implemented successfully, then appropriate arrangements for assessment and evaluation must be in place. Progression in the theme can only be achieved through planned programmes of study which are devised and monitored to take account of the cross-curricular nature of learning; that is, that environmental education will be included in the progressive schemes of work of other subject areas. In the case of the National Curriculum for Schools in England, this will be interpreted to mean cross-referencing with the attainment targets and statements of attainment of the core and foundation subjects. Assessment should relate to the three central teaching objectives for environmental education, i.e. knowledge and understanding, skills, and concepts. The national framework for assessment will be an essential baseline since a great deal of environmental teaching and learning will occur through teaching of the core and foundation subjects. That aside, innovatory or original school-devised methods of environmental assessment are necessary in relation to other elements, notably the development of attitudes and concern.

We return to the model for teaching and learning in environmental education outlined in Part II (Figure 5.1, p. 39). This serves as a useful checklist when recalling components of environmental work which need to be assessed and evaluated. The following set of teacher-based questions arising from this model will form a basis for discussion and consideration when going about both planning and assessment tasks:

A

- Have I planned tasks which help pupils to learn *about* the environment?
- Have I planned tasks which involve learning in or *through* the environment?
- Have I planned tasks which involve learning *for* the environment?

B

- What specific elements and levels of knowledge and understanding are covered by learning tasks?
- What attainment targets/programmes of study do these relate to in core and foundation subjects?
- What skills are covered by learning tasks (both specific and cross-curricular)?
- What attitudes do I aim to promote through planned learning tasks?

C

- What personal experiences will each learner actually engage in while performing planned tasks?
- How will my planned experiences and tasks help to develop a sense of concern for particular environmental aspects and issues?
- What action (personal or class-based) may result from experiences and tasks which have been planned?

D

- How do I ensure that tasks and experiences build upon each other in a progressive way in each of these components of the overall model?

Documentation and methods of recording of the answers to these fundamental questions will inevitably vary from school to school, reflecting an institution's individual needs and circumstances. Pupil records should be be maintained by class teacher or subject coordinator and should provide a profile of environmental experiences and attainments across the curriculum. Complete documentation may comprise a wide range of written material, including pupil profile sheets, class and individual records, samples of children's work, overall schemes and specific learning plans.

In the absence of formal guidelines and standardized assessment tasks in environmental education, it is clear that a teacher's skills of observation, interpretation and questioning are crucial to the assessment task. The accumulation of evidence about progression and achievement in learning depends upon skills of observation, testing (in the formal or informal sense) and interaction with pupils – conversation, questioning and feedback. In short, assessment is about communication between teacher and learner, communication which helps the learner appreciate what has been learned, and the teacher to plan tasks and first-hand experiences that will promote future learning or development of attitudes/concern. In school classrooms this will necessarily involve time for discussion and questioning individual pupils and groups as well as written communication.

It is not the purpose of this book to provide a justification for assessment or an overview of the process; but we do focus further attention on the two teacher skills of observation and questioning, which are crucial to the curriculum theme of environmental education because of its emphasis on pupil interaction and experiential learning. Observation should be approached as a skilled and strategic task. Observations may be either planned or spontaneous in nature. The former will have a clear objective, for example, can Joyce organize the names of roads travelled on her way to school in the correct sequence? Does George understand why the shadows are made on a sunny day? Such observations and their results will be informative and help with future planning, confirming progress made in teaching and learning. When planning observations, it is necessary to decide exactly what will be looked for, ways in which it will be tested or checked, and whether the task will involve interaction with the learner or simply seeing what is taking place. Decisions must also be made about whether the interchange will be used to extend the learner's thinking at that time, and how the outcomes of the observations will be recorded. Spontaneous observations are an important aspect of all classroom situations, perhaps particularly so when pupils go about their environmental enquiries in an independent way, knowing what their tasks involve and the availability of the resources necessary to perform them. Obviously a teacher cannot possibly record what is happening in a classroom all the time. It is far better to focus on specific features or interactions, and to record significant events in a variety of contexts than to watch a class without a focus. Suitable contexts may include:

• Individual tasks, e.g. using appropriate equipment, asking relevant questions, constructing a sundial.
• Group work, e.g. classification of invertebrates extracted from the pond, involving discussion, sharing of equipment, allocating tasks, listening to the findings of others and collaborating to produce results.

Together with planned observations, spontaneous observations should be recorded carefully to assist the overall assessment procedure and the design of further appropriate learning situations.

The skills of questioning play a crucial role in the learning process alongside observation and testing. The range and quality of questions posed by a teacher will reveal not only ways in which the learner is thinking, but also the kind of thinking that is being encouraged and expected. Thus questioning results is important two-way communication in the learning process. In environmental education, as in other curriculum areas, questions could be posed at each of six levels (after Bloom 1956):

1 Knowledge
2 Comprehension
3 Application
4 Analysis
5 Synthesis
6 Evaluation

Each level produces a response that requires a different kind of thought process. By employing questions at all of the levels, learners will engage a variety of cognitive processes. This discussion will be pursued in the context of an example of a particular classroom situation, where pupils are engaged in environmental education.

MISS BAPTISTE'S CLASS

Miss Baptiste's pupils, aged 9 and 10 years, are seated in mixed ability groups, in a classroom characterized by colour and interactive display. Children's work is not confined to the classroom frieze boards, but trails around the walls and windows as a vibrant tribute to imagination in the context of meaning. Illustrated poems and stories appear alongside graphs and accounts of scientific experiments, plans, paintings, models and collages. Creative art work, needlecraft and the subtle textures of weaving mingle with information technology and published materials.

The children had visited the same Field Centre as that described in the accounts of Stonebridge and St Aidan's School in Chapter 5.

The topic being developed in the autumn term was one of field work related plans and mapwork. During their early visits to the Field Centre the children visited a variety of natural habitats, finding their way around by using a simple plan of the grounds devised by the teacher at the centre; they then measured the different areas (the field, the garden, the orchard, the nature reserve and the wood), collected various specimens of leaves, flowers and fruit, and devised their own imaginative symbols to indicate the plants growing there.

Back at school, the children completed written accounts of what they had seen on their visits, encouraged by purposeful discussion and questioning by their teacher. Being free of the stultifying effort involved in remembering and writing about every event in chronological order, the children were thus able to focus their attention on what really interested them, and had captured their imaginations.

Miss Baptiste: 'What was the most interesting thing you saw?'
Jo: 'I saw a wasps' nest! I wonder how they build one.'
Miss Baptiste: 'Where was it Jo?'
Jo: 'Outside the greenhouse, by the pipe.'
Miss Baptiste: 'What did it look like?'

Jo: 'Grey.'

Miss Baptiste: 'Go on Jo, what else can you remember about it?'

Jo: 'It was about this big [indicates with hands] and was kind of flakey with holes in it. Crumbly and soft.'

Miss Baptiste: 'Did you see any wasps near it?'

Jo: 'No, I think it must have been an old nest.'

Miss Baptiste: 'I wonder why we use the same word for wasps' homes and birds' homes. Are their nests the same?'

Julie: 'Birds build their nests out of twigs and bits. They fly around to find things to make them out of.'

Jo: 'Wasps fly around too.'

Miss Baptiste: 'But they are very different creatures and their nests are different in many ways. Can you think of all of the ways in which birds and wasps are different . . . and things that they have in common?'

Julie: 'Wasps are insects. Birds are . . . birds! . . . and they have feathers. . . .'

[discussion of the differences continues]

* * *

Jane: 'I saw some frogs in the nature reserve. They were hiding from us I think. I expect they can see us coming with their big, bulgy eyes. I wish I could jump like they do.'

Miss Baptiste: 'How far did you see the frog jump?'

Sam: 'Right across the pond.'

Trevor: 'What's the largest distance frogs can jump?'

Miss Baptiste: 'See if you can find that out Trevor. Can you explain why they are such good jumpers?'

Trevor: [provides a reasonable explanation]

Miss Baptiste: 'Very good Trevor. We could try frog jumping couldn't we. Do you think people would make good frogs?'

[discussion continues with comparison of human and frog physiology]

* * *

Miss Baptiste: 'Can you look at the plans we drew when we were looking around the habitats? Find the key to your symbols . . . to remind yourselves what we saw. How was the garden different from the nature reserve?'

Carole: 'The garden was maintained. Gardeners work there all through the year and they always have jobs to do to keep it tidy.'

Miss Baptiste: 'Go on.'

Carole: 'They choose what to plant and decide what is going to grow there.'

Miss Baptiste: 'What do we call anything that is growing in the wrong place in the garden?'

Jo: 'Weeds.'

Miss Baptiste: 'So can you explain reasons why the nature reserve is not maintained in the same way as the garden . . . why does it look different?'

Carole: 'Plants are left to grow most of the time . . . but the grass is cut twice a year. Wild seeds grow . . . so really nature is deciding what will grow there.'

[discussion of the differences in the two habitats, causes and effects, continues]

*   *   *

Miss Baptiste: 'What do you think would happen if the gardeners stopped maintaining that habitat?'

Jo: 'The grass would get longer and longer.'

Miss Baptiste: 'And?'

Sam: 'Wild seeds would blow there and grow. After a few years it would get like the nature reserve. Wild. More insects and birds may come.'

Jo: 'If it wasn't maintained at all the grass would just get taller and taller like a jungle.'

[other ideas follow in discussion]

*   *   *

Miss Baptiste: 'Which do you think is better for attracting wildlife, the garden or the nature reserve?'

Julie: 'The nature reserve.'

Miss Baptiste: 'Can you explain why, Julie?'

Julie: 'Wild animals and insects don't like to be disturbed so they live in the long grass.'

Miss Baptiste: 'Go on.'

Julie: 'Birds like it.'

Sam: 'We saw more birds in the garden.'

Trevor: 'That's because the gardeners put food out.'

Miss Baptiste: 'OK. Well when we write about these habitats we can decide all the advantages that each has for attracting wildlife.'

From maps and plans, the children moved on to consider aspects of the Field Centre recorded on them, including the various trees of the habitats. They identified specimens and collected leaves, fruits and flowers to take back to school. They painted tree pictures, measured their heights and girths, made leaf print patterns, measured their areas using squared paper, and carried out various other activities. When someone asked Miss Baptiste, 'Miss, what's the biggest plant in the world?' the search for an answer became the subject of extensive research. Yet these activities were never separated from reflection, imaginative portrayal of trees, discussion of field experiences, and further questioning.

The children also studied many of autumn's features, being particularly fascinated by the mysteries of hibernation.

Jo: 'I wonder how they know when it's time to go to sleep?'
Sam: 'They know because the weather starts to feel cold.'
Jo: 'How do they know when it's time to wake up?'
Sam: 'If they're asleep all that time, how come they don't starve to death? I would!'

Such was the interest roused that the children often spent their break times reading library books in attempts to find out answers to their own and Miss Baptiste's questions.

Questions that no one could immediately answer became the subjects for further investigation, and if not every answer could be found, there was enough knowledge to remember, and to apply to further reading.

Miss Baptiste: 'What do we call the green colouring in leaves?'
Julie: 'Chlorophyll, miss.'
Miss Baptiste: 'Right, can you think how we could do an investigation to find out about why chlorophyll is so important? Do you think all of the plants in our classroom have chlorophyll? Let's think more about this . . . how could we find out?'

* * *

Miss Baptiste: 'Can anyone remember where the stick insects come from? Which country? Vijay?'
Vijay: 'Vietnam, I think.'
Miss Baptiste: 'That's right. What colour are they? Watch how they move . . . what wonderful camouflage . . . they certainly have an appropriate name . . . think of other things that shape and size . . . are many living creatures shaped like this?'
'What sort of toad did Mrs Russell show us yesterday?'
Jo: 'Miss, I know . . . miss! It was a Xenopus toad.'
Miss Baptiste: 'Let's think of exciting words to describe the toad. Was it damp and shiny? What about the colour of its skin? How do you think it defends itself from its enemies? Did it move swiftly?'
'. . . and what sort of creature is a salamander? Can you tell me, Valdheer?'

Valdheer: 'It's an amphibian, miss. It can live on land and in the water.'

Miss Baptiste: 'Quite right. We've seen other amphibians this year . . . imagine what it would be like to be able to live in water as well as on dry land. . . . What shape is the salamander? What was it doing when we watched it? It seemed to be trying to hide. . . . What does the word camouflage mean?'

Questions were relevant as they guided the learners towards knowledge and understanding, yet always encouraged thoughtful reflection and recall of images and qualitative aspects of the topic under consideration.

Miss Baptiste is skilled in the use of questioning. Table 11.1 provides a summary of examples of questions posed by Miss Baptiste, their category, and levels of thinking required from the learner.

The classification of teachers' questions is based on the expected answer from the learner. A classification of answers would be based upon the level of thinking demonstrated. The effective teacher will aim to ensure a coverage of both lower order and higher order questions; that is, ones which require the learner simply to recall information and ones which require the learner to go beyond memory and use a wider range of cognitive processes. Lower order thinking involves retrieval of facts or information from memory. Questions involving thinking of this kind often begin with the words: What? Where? When? Who? The knowledge recalled will probably be in the same form as it was learnt and will not go beyond that basic information with which the learner is familiar. Higher order thinking requires a change in the form of existing knowledge, perhaps to compare or contrast, to apply it or extend it, explain or analyse, reorganize or evaluate, synthesize or solve problems. In other words, learned material must be recalled and then used or applied to provide an outcome or answer that is at a higher cognitive level. Both levels of questioning are essential for effective progression in environmental education. Lower order questioning will encourage memorizing of facts and rote learning; higher order questioning is essential for promoting more complex thinking processes associated with environmental issues and the promotion of concern. Neither should be left to chance – the effective teacher will plan for questioning with the same rigour as for any other aspect of the teaching role.

In summary, the use of questioning alongside observation and testing helps a teacher to ascertain:

- whether the pupil has learned the intended outcomes of specific tasks and activities
- the success (or failure) of specific teaching strategies
- how the pupil is performing relative to others of similar age

Table 11.1 Summary of teacher's questions and cognitive processes

Category	Required thinking	Examples
Knowledge	Recall of facts and basic understandings or observations	1 What was the most interesting thing you saw? 2 Where was the wasps' nest? 3 What do we call the green colouring in leaves?
Comprehension	Comparing, contrasting, describing, explaining	1 Can you explain why frogs are such good jumpers? 2 Do you think people would make good frogs?
Application	Applying knowledge to solve problems, classifying, selecting, using	1 Can you think of all the ways in which birds and wasps are different and things they have in common? (leading to further questions on classification) 2 Are many living creatures shaped like this?
Analysis	Drawing conclusions, making inferences, finding causes, determining and using evidence	1 Can you explain reasons why the nature reserve is not maintained in the same way as the garden . . . why does it look different?
Synthesis	Solving problems, making predictions, proposing	1 What do you think would happen if the gardeners stopped maintaining that habitat?
Evaluation	Judging, evaluating, deciding, appraising	1 Which do you think is better for attracting wildlife . . . the garden or the nature reserve?

- whether the pupil is ready for the next stage in a particular progression of learning
- the nature of particular difficulties (if any) that the pupil is experiencing.

Together, these skills form the basis for successful recording and assessment procedures, and make a substantial contribution to planning and evaluation of tasks, schemes, and programmes of work in environmental education.

Part IV

Resources

**Resource material and information concerning
environmental education (EE)**   163

Information technology   198

Other useful publications   200

Useful addresses   202

RESOURCE MATERIAL AND INFORMATION CONCERNING ENVIRONMENTAL EDUCATION (EE)

While it is apparent that the neighbourhood is the richest source of resources for environmental education, it is supported by a vast range of printed, visual, and electronic material. It would not be possible to describe all that was available both in the UK and elsewhere. In this section we pass on as much information as can be handled in a book of this size, and we have had to be selective. In our judgement the organizations and the resources listed are the major sources of help to the teacher of environmental education in schools. Also listed are the most useful addresses for obtaining information in the USA, Canada, New Zealand and Australia. Apologies are due to all who think their particular organization or resource should have been listed – we know how it feels to find a guide which fails to mention our own organization or products. We are fortunate in the UK to have the Council for Environmental Education with its excellent information service; always check with CEE if your search for appropriate help is difficult to uncover. Since we make this a general recommendation for those seeking help let us begin with the CEE.

Council for Environmental Education

The CEE is the main source of information about environmental education in the UK; although Scotland and Wales have their own organizations, they are smaller and therefore less comprehensive in what they have to offer. The CEE is the coordinating body for its 75 members (December 1993). It has an extensive library and information service set up to deal with all aspects of environmental education including schools and other sectors of the formal education service. It has a youth section which has promoted environmental education in the voluntary sector for young people and beyond. The Council has an important schools and tertiary section which seeks to reflect the views of the classroom and lecture theatre. Indeed readers are urged to pass on to CEE any of the difficulties and concerns which inhibit the full realization of the objectives for environmental education in each place of activity. The CEE has established close links with the UK government and is in a position to raise matters of concern. Increasingly the CEE is called upon to advise both government and business organizations on environmental education. Working parties research various matters and produce useful material. For example a series of packs is in production for guidance on in-service teacher training (see p. 200). A monthly newsletter goes to all schools where the local authority subscribes to CEE on a per capita basis. This brings to teachers news about events and details of the latest publications. It is worth checking that an authority is a subscriber, for the newsletter is a 'must' for the busy teacher needing to be kept up to date with environmental happenings. Regrettably some councils have a policy of not subscribing to outside organizations. If nothing can be done to change their minds then it is possible for individual schools to subscribe – well worth it in our opinion.

Council For Environmental Education,
University of Reading, London Road, Reading RG1 5AQ

The National Association for Environmental Education (UK)

The NAEE is a founder member of the CEE and has provided the main teacher input. It has been in existence for over 30 years and can justly claim to be the pioneering organization for promoting environmental education in schools and colleges. It has had a very small permanent staff since 1983 following the decision of the Department of the Environment to provide management funding for small environmental groups. The NAEE still relies considerably on a network of volunteers throughout the British Isles. The association is made up of individual and institutional (schools, colleges, libraries) members and groups of environmentalists in local areas. Over 20 local corporate associations are active and their location may be obtained by enquiry at the national office. Each local group has its own full programme of activity directed towards improving environmental education in their locality. It is usual for one of these groups to host the annual course/conference of the NAEE and provide the expertise with regard to their neighbourhood. A recent development, still in its embryonic stage, is the affiliation of all schools in a local area to the NAEE, tied in to a termly distribution of environmental education resource material.

The aims and objectives of the NAEE are set out in its publication *A Statement of Aims* (NAEE 1975, revised 1992) recently updated from the original 1975 version which pioneered the concept of environmental education in UK schools. The NAEE's prime concern is to help and encourage teachers to establish an environmental approach in every school. It provides an information service with the emphasis on initial and in-service teacher training, teaching methods and learning materials. Its main job is not to inform on environmental matters directly but to point enquirers in the right direction to obtain an answer. A termly journal *Environmental Education* is published which contains a News and Views section in order to update readers as to developments in the world of educating in an environmental way. It also publishes a series of practical guides and other books such as *Towards a School Policy for Environmental Education* (NAEE 1992). It tries to help researchers by providing a history of environmental education in the UK.

It is not a campaigning organization for particular environmental issues but it does take matters affecting environmental education to the highest levels. For example it has successfully applied its resources and influence to retaining threatened field study centres.

Although a UK organization it has many overseas members and contributes to international affairs.

> National Association for Environmental Education,
> University of Wolverhampton, Walsall Campus,
> Gorway, Walsall WS1 3BD

The Environment Council

The Environment Council (formerly CoEnCo) is a forum for individuals and organizations working towards solutions to environment problems. Through the Council's activities and those of its two supporting programmes – the Business and Environment Programme and the Information Programme – it identifies current concerns and defines processes which offer constructive ways forward on difficult issues.

A wide variety of interests are reflected in the Council's work and its members and supporters include representatives from voluntary organizations, educational institutions, government departments, professional associations and business. Full members participate in committee and steering group work.

The Council publishes various guides to sources of environmental information. *Habitat*, a digest of environmental news, and *NEWS from The Environment Council* are sent to Associates and Council members ten times a year.

As far as teachers are concerned the *Who's Who in the Environment* directories published by the Council are very useful sources of names and addresses of environmental organizations and their role. There is a separate directory for England, Wales and Scotland.

> The Environment Council, 80 York Way, London N1 9AG

Environmental Education Advisers' Association

National grouping of advisers, inspectors, advisory teachers and those with a responsibility for giving advice in schools. The Executive consists of advisers/inspectors employed by education authorities or in an independent capacity. All have a wide and long experience of environmental education, are actively involved in the modern curriculum and some are being trained in OFSTED (Office for Standards in Education) Inspection Training Aims.

Aims: To consider and promote environmental education and to provide links of communication between all advisers and inspectors. To offer an advisory and support service to all, in every aspect of environmental education, e.g. all aspects of the National Curriculum, cross-curricular themes and the development of an environmental education policy; INSET for advisers and teachers, educational development of school grounds and the wider environment; all aspects of the life, organization and ethos of the school and the development of environmental charters; all aspects of a school audit and a monitoring service for environmental education; review of books, publications and projects, etc., etc.

Secretary: Richard S. Moseley, Magic Hills Lodge, Rice Lane, Gorran Haven, St Austell, Cornwall PL26 6JF

The World Wide Fund for Nature

Previously the World Wildlife Fund, the retitled WWF is probably the leading national and international organization devoted to addressing the environmental issues and problems of the natural world. Their panda logo reminds the public of their long involvement with conservation campaigns, regrettably not always successful.

Within the formal education system, WWF produces resources for teaching and learning, conducts workshops and courses and provides other items for in-service training of teachers. Over the years those involved directly in schools have worked closely with WWF to develop a range of educational resources. These are described in the WWF catalogue.

WWF has launched a Teacher Representative Scheme designed to provide more support for teachers in schools. The aim is to have one person in each school to be the WWF point of contact so that full advantage may be taken of the resource material available. Schools receive the annual educational catalogue, a termly new resources leaflet, a termly *Lifelines* newsletter and are able to use a 24-hour answerphone 'hotline', both in and out of working hours, to obtain a response to queries or requests for information and support.

WWF, Panda House, Weyside Park, Catteshall Lane, Godalming, Surrey GU7 1XR

Royal Society for Nature Conservation

The RSNC has a young people's section known as Watch. It has a staff of helpful education officers who organize research projects which make a serious contribution to environmental issues. A stimulating newspaper, *Watchword*, is full of information on the natural world and the several projects currently under way. Schools can form Watch groups but their formation is not confined to the formal sector. Watch supplies research kits for their projects and these are useful even after the actual project has finished, particularly the descriptive material supplied. Some of the projects undertaken or in an active state at present are Acid rain, Ozone, Stream pollution, Batwatch, Frogwatch and Ladybird spotting.

Watch Trust for Environmental Education Ltd (Watch),
RSNC, The Green, Witham Park, Waterside South,
Lincoln LN5 7JR

Tidy Britain Group

The TBG is the organization mandated by the government to reduce litter and to stimulate pride in the environment. It has an education section which provides a whole range of resource material on anti-litter learning together with other teaching and learning programmes resulting from research projects. Teachers are advised to contact their regional office of the TBG when embarking on topic work associated with litter.

Tidy Britain Group, The Pier, Wigan WN3 4EX

Learning Through Landscapes

The LTL is a relatively recent newcomer to the environmental education scene as an independent institution. It was based on a research project which looked at school estates, particularly in Hampshire. Now, as a charitable trust, it promotes use and improvement of school grounds both with its members and others. It has published several books and pamphlets and takes a broad view of its remit with regard to environmental education generally. Schools considering developing their grounds should contact LTL for advice.

Learning Through Landscapes,
Southside Offices, The Law Courts, Winchester SO23 9DL

International Centre for Conservation Education

The ICCE aims to promote a better understanding of conservation. As far as schools are concerned, it provides excellent audio-visual packs dealing with environmental issues. For example, it provides a pack on tropical rainforests. The transparencies used are excellent and, for the busy teacher, the packs provide a rich source of illustrations to be used with the programmes or as support for individual topic work. A colour catalogue is available.

International Centre for Conservation Education,
Greenfield House, Guiting Power, Cheltenham GL54 5TZ

Royal Town Planning Institute

Town planning is becoming more and more a matter for any comprehensive course of environmental education. The RTPI has set up environmental education groups around the country. It is well worth discovering if one operates in your area – look in the telephone directory for details of the local branch. Many have published useful lists of planner contacts. Although many professional institutions take an interest in school education our experience is that the RTPI is way out in front where the introduction of urban studies is concerned.

Royal Town Planning Institute,
26 Portland Place, London W1N 4BE

Friends of the Earth

FoE is a campaigning organization which has a high profile and is well known for its many activities locally, nationally and internationally. It is essential that any teacher using FoE material seeks to balance it with other views. Nevertheless over the past few years FoE has developed an education section with education staff. This has meant that much of what is produced is sound resource material for teacher use.

Friends of the Earth,
26–28 Underwood Street, London N1 7JQ

Greenpeace

This environmental campaigning organization is very active internationally and has done much to highlight problems associated with whaling, the oil industry, nuclear power and the disposal of all kinds of waste. It produces some very useful material to provide background information on environmental topics. Again a balanced argument must be presented to pupils so that they may make up their own minds. Without doubt many of the advances in international conduct towards the environment have been stimulated by the brave (often foolhardy) activities of Greenpeace members.

Greenpeace, Canonbury Villas, London N1 2PN

Other campaigners

The nuclear industry is a resource provider for schools putting the supportive viewpoint. Its material and information service is readily available and whatever the views of an individual, teacher balance must be maintained. The Game Conservancy and the British Association for Shooting and Conservation support their view of hunting, shooting and fishing and also provide resource items for school use. British Coal, the Electricity Council, British Gas and many others have large and effective education sections which may be considered as campaigning although much of their literature is of an informative nature only.

Commerce and industry

Oil companies, chemical manufacturers, agricultural specialists, public service industries, insurance providers, banks, car makers – the list is almost endless – all provide resource material for schools. Many have full-time education departments which produce books, magazines, videos, films, wall-charts and other teaching aids. Much of what they provide is straightforward information on their particular product and a defence of their environmental awareness and caring production methods. However they do produce general environmental education resources, often after teacher input. The larger enterprises can provide speakers and environmentally focused visits to their sites. Many of the smaller enterprises cannot afford education officers and glossy publications but they are still willing to help teachers if properly approached. We have already commented on seeking help from outside agencies. The commercial world does give much financial and other support to education generally and environmental education in particular. The Council for Environmental Education has gained from the fact that our most famous High Street clothing chain has seconded senior executives to it to assist with organizational procedures. Without sponsorship it is doubtful if environmental education could have made the strides forward that it has. Unfortunately this aid is not organized and in our opinion much help has been misplaced, much duplication of effort has taken place and too often poor advice has been given by those remote from the classroom. So much material now gathers dust on school shelves and commercial warehouses. One national bank recently circulated environmental organizations to off-load, as constructively as possible, glossy and expensive material left over from an educational effort that went disastrously wrong. Since no one is happy to acknowledge a failure there is little learning from past mistakes. In particular, competitions and awards, which on the surface seem to have been most successful, are often unhappy experiences for the sponsoring organization. Most schools are reluctant to participate in more than a few of these ventures – they do take a lot of staff time and effort if the school is to do itself justice. Should any company executive read this text our plea must be to seek advice from those organizations directly involved with schools if the formal education sector is their target. In all fairness many do so already; for the record another bank abandoned its original competition plans after consultation with the NAEE and placed its help elsewhere.

Zoos and safari parks

Places which keep wild creatures in captivity may not be considered as ideal sites for educational visits. Zoos, safari parks, nature centres, aquaria, bird gardens and other similar institutions do, however, provide educational facilities and the best of them such as the Jersey Island Zoo and the Marwell Zoo, near Southampton, do splendid work with preserving some endangered species. It is worth a teacher investigating a site closely before deciding not to use the place at all. Some schools are misled into believing that the bringing of birds, beasts and insects onto the premises by individuals is acceptable as the individual creatures appear to be well kept. It is worth seeking the opinion of the local RSPCA who are better placed to assess the total care given to their charges by the exhibitors. Animals can be under severe stress even if their physical condition seems to be perfect. Health and safety are also involved and care must be taken to be aware of the local and national guidelines on these matters. We do not intend to list any addresses, in case these are taken as recommendations of acceptability. Your local environmental education adviser should be in a position to commend or otherwise possible venues for visits to captive wildlife. Unfortunately dire economic times are seriously affecting the running of zoos as the publicity over London Zoo and Windsor Safari Park has shown. It is essential that prior visits of inspection are made by teachers planning visits.

Groundwork Trusts (supported by the Groundwork Foundation)

Look in the local telephone directory for evidence of a Groundwork Trust operating in the school neighbourhood. They can be most useful contacts for all sorts of environmentally based activities. However no firm guidelines can be given by us because the way individual trusts work can be very different.

Groundwork Foundation,
Bennetts Court, 6 Bennett Hill, Birmingham B2 5ST

Urban wildlife groups

Again it is possible to discover from a local directory whether any particular urban area has a wildlife group. There are some very good publications available with regard to the wildlife living in built-up areas.

The Met. Office Education Service

As the UK National Meteorological Service, the Met. Office has always received requests for information about the weather from teachers, schoolchildren and parents. Since the introduction of the National Curriculum in England and Wales, and the inclusion of weather topics at all levels, the numbers of enquiries have increased substantially. Enquiries from England and Wales are dealt with by staff at Met. Office HQ in Bracknell. Edinburgh and Belfast Climate Offices have staff who spend some of their time answering educational enquiries from Scotland and Northern Ireland respectively. There are a whole range of resources available including the 'MetFAX' service described in the information technology section. Two teaching resource packs for primary schools contain workcards, games, wallcharts, project ideas and teaching notes. A set of weather phenomena wallcharts are also aimed at the primary age group. For secondary schools the Met. Office has cooperated with the BBC Schools Television service to provide a TV programme with accompanying video and teacher's pack. Information can be obtained from

> Education Services, The Met. Office,
> Sutton House, London Road, Bracknell, Berkshire RG12 2SY

Atmospheric Research Information Centre

As its name implies the ARIC provides information and lists of resource material concerning the global problem of acid rain. Acid rain as a term covers a much wider range of acidic-induced phenomena and is a learning way into air pollution generally. Although a specialist agency it does provide teachers with a balanced view of the overall problem.

> Atmospheric Research Information Centre,
> Department of Environment and Geography,
> John Dalton Extension, Room E 310, Chester Street, Manchester

Publishers

Inevitably much of the resource material for environmental education will come from the commercial publishers. It would be impossible to list all that is available but for schools certain companies seem to highlight environmental issues. There is a considerable amount of material, packs, books, charts, etc., directed at the younger years up to about the age of 12. Of these Wayland, Franklin Watts, Heinemann, Macdonald, Hamish Hamilton/Evans have published many titles covering the whole range of subject matter. The secondary phase is less well served but the *Considering Conservation* and *Conservation 2000* series from Batsford provide extensive coverage. Most other books written for the older age are texts suitable for the sixth forms as their authors, specialists in their own field, are not experienced teachers so present the information in a form which is not 'user friendly'. Teachers need to have resource material which provides them with the information they need for teaching in an easily accessible form. We have found that the books written by experienced teachers of environmental issues for older pupils fill the need better than the more academic texts. One problem is knowing what is on the market and their target reader ages. There is one reference book which is very helpful because it not only lists what is available but gives a short review of each publication. The book is slightly dated now but hopefully update supplements will become available soon: Richard Hill (ed.) (1991) *Green Guide to Children's Books*, ISBN 1-871-56601-0 (Books for Keeps, 6 Brightfield Road, Lee, London SE12 8QF).

Heritage education

The term 'heritage' is one which causes some discussion as to its precise meaning when applied to education. We take it to be that part of environmental education which deals with people living their lives in the past – their homes, their work, their artefacts – and in particular how these matters have influenced the environment in which we now live. It is not our purpose to provide an extended essay on the ways and whys of heritage education but rather to point out where further information, guidance and resource material may be obtained.

The Heritage Education Trust took over the organization of the Sandford Award given to heritage properties and, more recently, museums, from the Council for Environmental Education. Awards are given for those which provide a full education service according to the criteria set by the Trust. The first awards were made in 1980 and the list of winners shows the extensive coverage over the United Kingdom. The HET also organizes the Education Through Heritage and the Arts (ETHA) scheme which encourages role-play in properties and music performed by children in a historic setting. Details of the awards and ETHA appear in the annual issues of *Historic Houses, Castles and Gardens* and *Museums and Galleries* published by British Leisure Publications. These are the most comprehensive guides to places for school visits if history is the guiding force. We believe they are essential for the staff library. Not only are they useful guides but they can be used for many classroom exercises in geography, history, English and mathematics. Since they are classified in county sections it is possible to further local studies through the information they contain.

The National Trusts are most important to environmental education and they are dealt with separately. Other historic properties and natural areas are under the control of English Heritage, Historic Buildings and Monuments for Scotland, Department of the Environment for Northern Ireland and CADW, Welsh Historic Monuments, for Wales. The Royal Palaces are dealt with by the Education Services based at Hampton

Court Palace. English Heritage provides a full range of information and teaching and learning resources for their 350 plus sites. As with the other countries of the UK the aim is to provide teachers with as much help as possible to make use of the historic environment. A free catalogue of publications is available. For England and Wales the series of videos *Teaching on Site* have now been compiled on a single video for purchase or free loan, and it provides an excellent in-service or initial teacher training guidance based on the various subjects of the National Curriculum. It is up to individuals to tease out the cross-curricular approach. As we write there are plans to 'privatize' a number of the sites under the care of English Heritage. This could lead to a less effective guidance service for school parties who may need to deal with several agencies rather than one. Unfortunately, therefore, some of this information may be overtaken by events. Nevertheless the two guides we mentioned earlier will update the situation.

Private properties abound, most of them members of the Historic Houses Association. Although many are world famous, Blenheim Palace, for example, which has excellent educational facilities, others are less well known and smaller in size. Often they are unable to provide professional education officers but this may well be replaced by the personal attention of the owner(s). It is well worth building a school– property relationship with sites relatively near to the school base. At best such a relationship, built on trust established over several years, may lead to a freedom of access to the estate or building which allows any visits to be totally integrated into the curriculum, as and when it is convenient to both parties.

Churches, religious orders, cathedrals, mosques and other similar institutions are anxious to help schools. Some of our most prestigious cathedrals, Canterbury and York for example, have full-time education departments. Role-play scenarios have been developed at many of them and though it may be invidious to pick out any for special mention the programme at St Albans is hard to better. All does not have to be bustle and frantic activity – for a group of children to sit in silence in the echoing vastness of a mighty building with the sunlight streaming through stained glass to light up the interior with a range of colour is something which we have found to have a most impressive effect on young and old alike. Unfortunately enthusiastic guides sometimes overwhelm school parties with historical dates and facts. It is essential that teachers make a preliminary visit to any field study site, in order to plan and assess any special needs or hazards.

One word of warning to the inexperienced – nationally famous heritage sites are overcrowded in the summer season yet schools still concentrate their visits in June or July as well. Earlier or later in the year improves the chances of unimpeded access and personal attention.

British Leisure Publications
Windsor Court
East Grinstead House
East Grinstead
West Sussex RH19 1XA

Publications:
Historic Houses, Castles and Gardens
Museums and Galleries

Historic Houses Association
PO Box 21
Unit 7
Campus 5
The Business Park
Letchworth SG6 2JF

English Heritage Education Service,
Keysign House,
429 Oxford Street,
London W1R 2HD

Publications:
Teaching on Site
Remnants
Catalogue of Publications

Heritage Education Trust
University College of Ripon &
   York St John
College Road
Ripon HG4 2QX

The National Trust

All territories of the United Kingdom have their National Trust. Not only do they conserve an important part of our national heritage, historic buildings, gardens, wild areas and create imaginative preservation schemes such as the coastal path, but they are very important providers of environmental education facilities. Many of their properties have been singled out for recognition with a Sandford Award and others have equally worthwhile educational programmes. The best advice to any progressive school is to take out corporate membership of the appropriate Trust and so gain a remarkably inexpensive way to freedom of access to properties. Lucky are the schools with a NT institution in their neighbourhood. Most large properties have education officers and most have special facilities for school parties. Although the Trusts are organized regionally, information and help is available from the NT education officer at each headquarters. The Trusts publish much useful resource material as well as a news magazine aimed at the young.

For those who have not been involved do try to participate in the performances of the National Trust Youth Theatre where historic events are recreated at various properties around the country with the children costumed and taking part. After one such performance a little girl was heard to remark 'I forgot it was now but thought it was then'. The current programme is available from NT headquarters – but you need to book early.

The National Trust
(for England, Wales & Northern Ireland)
36 Queen Anne's Gate
London SW1H 9AS

National Trust for Scotland
5 Charlotte Square
Edinburgh EH2 4DU

Field Studies Council

The FSC has nine residential and two day centres in England and Wales located in areas of high environmental interest. They are staffed by experts who are skilled in field study teaching as well as in specific aspects of science. The residential centres not only provide field work facilities with a whole range of equipment, laboratories and reference material, but the social side of a group stay is not neglected. Both groups and individuals are catered for so that any school unable to provide the time or skilled teaching for a particular aspect of advanced study can rest assured that students will be in responsible care. Schools can either use the centre staff for teaching, use their own staff or (most frequently) combine the two. One great advantage of FSC centres is that access to study sites has been negotiated with landowners so that the potential hazards are known to centre staff. Farmers will be aware of the dangers inherent for young visitors and act accordingly to prevent accidents occurring.

Most centres are well equipped with computers generally compatible with those of visiting schools so that work done at the centre can be followed up at school. Software has been developed by the FSC specifically for the range of investigations carried out at the centres. Although each centre specializes, all are able to provide the usual needs of school curricula, and are particularly geared up to help primary schools with project work. Out of season day visits or an ongoing programme can easily be arranged with a local centre.

All this has to be paid for; low season prices are cheaper than those for the busier time of the year. Early March to late September is the high season and the rest the low. In the low time of the year staff with the school party pay nothing, not even for board and lodging, and individual charges are reduced. Proper quotations must be obtained from the centre to be used. Special travel terms have been negotiated with School Rail.

In addition to direct field work for schools the FSC arranges in-service training courses – to discuss the possibility of setting up a special local course, contact the Director of Studies at an individual centre. The FSC has been working to establish field study centres in parts of Eastern Europe following the break-up of the USSR and its satellites. It is worth contacting the FSC to discover if environmental study is planned for that area. 1993 sees the 50th birthday of the FSC – congratulations on a job well done.

Central Services, Field Studies Council,
Preston Montford, Montford Bridge, Shrewsbury SY4 1HW

Field Studies Council Study Centres

Dale Fort Field Centre
Dale
Haverfordwest
Dyfed SA62 3RD
Dale Fort is situated on the clifftop at the tip of a narrow peninsula at the approach to Milford Haven, South Wales. Magnificent folded and faulted rocks exposed in cliff sections. Variety of coastal habitats and marine biology. The centre operates an ex-RNLI lifeboat so that access is available to the offshore islands.

Flatford Mill Field Centre
East Bergholt
Colchester
Essex CO7 6UL
Flatford Mill comprises the historic mill, Willy Lott's cottage, and Valley Farm. A most historic setting in 'Constable Country' . A variety of natural and created habitats. A rich agricultural area. Local villages provide interesting architecture. An area full of historic interest.

Juniper Hall Field Centre
Dorking
Surrey RH5 6DA
Juniper Hall is a large country house in a dry valley of the North Downs near Box Hill. Chalk scenery and other landscapes. A suitable base for studying the effects of the urban sprawl, new towns (Crawley) and transport problems.

Leonard Wills Field Centre
Nettlecombe Court
Williton
Taunton
Somerset TA4 4HT
The Leonard Wills Centre is a country mansion on the eastern edge of Exmoor about half an hour from Taunton. Close by are marine and freshwater habitats as well as heather moorland. Porlock Bay and the Bristol Channel are nearby.

Preston Montford Field Centre
Montford Bridge
Shrewsbury SY4 1DX
Preston Montford is a country house set in 12 hectares of grassland bordering the River Severn. It encompasses its own stream and two large ponds. The hills of the Welsh borderlands are close by including the Longmynd with its Carding Mill Valley. Shrewsbury and other historic towns are close to hand as are Ironbridge Industrial Museum and the Acton Scott Farm Museum.

Orielton Field Centre
Pembroke
Dyfed
South Wales SA71 5EZ
Orielton is a Georgian mansion set in 60 hectares of woodland. Similar field study area to Dale Fort.

Slapton Ley Field Centre
Slapton
Kingsbridge
Devon TQ7 2QP
Slapton Ley has purpose built accommodation on the Devon coast near Totnes. Sea shore studies are the centre's speciality within the Slapton Ley Nature Reserve. Dartmoor is near to the centre.

Epping Forest Conservation Centre
High Beach
Loughton
Essex IG10 4AF
Epping Forest Centre is a day centre managed by the FSC. As the crow flies it is only 12 miles from St Paul's Cathedral in London. Woodland and urban studies with the intense agriculture of the Lea and Roding valleys. Harlow New Town is close by.

The Drapers' Field Centre
Rhyd-y-creuau
Betwys-y-coed
Gwynedd LL24 0HB
Drapers' Field Centre is situated in the Conwy Valley on the eastern edge of

Snowdonia. All of the spectacular landscapes of North Wales are within the environs of Rhyd-y-creuau. Anglesey and the North Wales coast are accessible to the centre. The area is full of historical interest.

Malham Tarn Field Centre
Settle
North Yorkshire BD24 9PU
The centre lies on the north shore of Malham Tarn, part of the limestone plateau of the Yorkshire Dales National Park. Glaciated scenery and features of Karst landscape are its particular speciality. Hill sheep farming and tourism are important local activities.

Fort Popton Field Centre
Angle Bay
Pembroke SA71 3BD
This centre is a research station directed towards studies of oil pollution. Although it does put on specialist courses it is not intended for school use. It is close to Orielton and Dale Fort if schools wish to visit the area.

National Parks

There are 11 national parks in England and Wales, directed by the Countryside Commission. There are a variety of day visit centres, residential centres, study bases, lecture rooms and information centres although not all parks have the full range. Most parks produce education leaflets promoting their services for schools. Losehill Hall (Peak District) and Plas-Tan-y-Bwlch (Snowdonia) are worthy of particular mention for they provide not only a full range of tutored courses but also conference facilities.

Scotland has no designated national parks although it has an impressive list of nature reserves, some of which can be visited. Similarly there are nature reserves in England and Wales.

Countryside Commission
John Dower House
Crescent Place
Cheltenham GL50 3RA

English Nature
Northminster House
Peterborough PE1 1UA

Scottish Natural
  Heritage
12 Hope Terrace
Edinburgh EH9 2AS

The National Parks of England and Wales

Brecon Beacons National Park
7 Glamorgan Street
Brecon
Powys LD3 7DP
Danywenalt residential centre at Talybont on Usk. Day centres at the mountain centre near Brecon and at Craig-y-nos Country Park in the Upper Swansea Valley.

The Broads Authority
Thomas Harvey House
18 Colegate
Norwich
It was only in 1989 that The Broads was established as an area similarly protected as the other national parks. There are several information centres. Facilities for schools are being developed.

Dartmoor National Park
Parke
Haytor Road
Bovey Tracey
Devon TQ13 9JQ
There is a schools guided walks
service.

Exmoor National Park
Exmoor House
Dulverton
Somerset TA22 9HL
There is a lecture room at Exmoor
House, several field centres which can
be used for day visits and some camp
sites.

Lake District National Park
National Park Visitor Centre
Brockhole
Windermere
Cumbria LA23 1LJ
Residential facilities at Blencathra
Centre, Threkeld with day visit bases
at Brockhole, Windermere and
Seatoller, Borrowdale.

Northumberland National Park
Eastburn
South Park
Hexham
Northumberland NE46 1BS
Study bases are to be found at the
information centres. Guided walks
and field work available.

North York Moors National Park
The Moors Centre
Danby
Whitby
North Yorkshire YO21 2NB
Activities based at the educational
visits centre at Danby.

Peak District National Park
Losehill Hall
Castleton
Derbyshire S30 2WB
Residential centre at Losehill Hall,
Castleton with day visit bases at
Bakewell, Ham and Edale.

Pembrokeshire Coast National Park
County Offices
Haverfordwest
Pembrokeshire
Dyfed SA61 1QZ
Residential or day visits at Broad
Haven. Day visits at Kilgetty.

Snowdonia National Park
Penrhyndeudraeth
Gwynedd LL48 6LS
Residential centre at Plas Tan y Bwlch,
Maentwrog.

Yorkshire Dales National Park
Colvend
Hebden Road
Grassington
Skipton BD23 5LB
Day or residential bases at Malham,
Clapham and Whernside.

Farms and city farms

Unfortunately the Association of Agriculture no longer has an education
service. The organization had a long and distinguished history of providing schools with details of school visits. The establishment of the
Food and Farming Information Service has done something to fill the
gap. Several local authorities have their own school visit farms as with
the Money Lane Farm for infants and the Chapmans Hills Farm for
juniors run by the Birmingham LEA. In our comments on IT we mention
the provision made by Staffordshire, a leader in farm visiting and
education for agriculture. The National Farmers' Union is most helpful
and personal approaches to farmers can be extremely rewarding. Both of
us have had experience of creating a school–farm link which not only

involved farm visits but school visits by the farmer. A word of serious warning: FARMS ARE DANGEROUS PLACES and with the best will in the world farmers tend to leave equipment in odd places – and animals are never anything but unpredictable – a horse's hoof on an unwary foot can cause severe damage and pain!

One interesting development of recent years has been that of the creation of city farms. Each of these farms is unique as their size, facilities and services vary considerably as do the range of animals housed. Opinion as to the value and ethical status of such artificial institutions varies considerably. But they exist with many of them affiliated to the National Federation of City Farms. As far as we know all welcome school parties but approaches will need to be made direct. It is absolutely essential for a teacher to see what there is on site before taking children on a visit. The following list of establishments has been provided by the NFCF who warn that opening times are flexible and individual contact must be made to avoid a wasted journey.

Many local authorities have farm liaison officers, not always a member of the education department. Agricultural colleges can be helpful to schools and will receive young visitors. Obviously they are useful for career guidance. The Royal Show Ground at Stoneleigh in Warwickshire also provides help and advice to schools as does the Welsh equivalent at Builth Wells. Most large shows have days particularly geared towards children. As a member of the public it is worth finding out which days they are – for obvious reasons!

Food and Farming Information
   Service
Euro Business Centre
462 Fulham Road
London SW6 1BY

National Farmers' Union
Agriculture House
Knightsbridge
London SW1X 7NJ

National Federation of City Farms
AMF House
93 Whitby Road
Brislington
Bristol BS4 3QF

Royal Agricultural Society of England
National Agricultural Centre
Stoneleigh Park
Warwickshire CV8 2LZ

City Farms

Belfast
Farset City Farm
77 Springmartin Road
Belfast BT12 3PL

Birmingham/West Midlands
Birmingham Wheels Park
Alderly Road South
Saltley
Birmingham B8 1AD

Hawbush Urban Farm Assoc.
Bull Street
Brierley Hill
West Midlands

Holy Trinity Urban Farm
Holy Trinity School
Oakley Road
Small Heath
Birmingham B10 0AX

Malvern Street Farm
Malvern Street
Balsall Heath
Birmingham B12 8NJ

South Aston Comm. Project
Upper Sutton Street
Aston
Birmingham B6 5ND

Woodgate Valley Urban Farm
Clapgate Lane
Bartley Green
Birmingham

Bradford
Bradford City Farm
Illingworth Fields
Walker Drive
Bradford BD8 9ES

Bristol
Hartcliffe Comm. Park Farm
Lampton Avenue
Hartcliffe
Bristol BS13 0QH

Lawrence Weston Comm. Farm
Saltmarsh Drive
Lawrence Weston
Bristol

St Werburghs City Farm
Watercress Road
St Werburghs
Bristol BS2 9YJ

Windmill Hill City Farm
Philip Street
Bedminster
Bristol BS3 4DU

Cardiff
Cardiff City Farm
Sloper Road
Grangetown
Cardiff CF2 8AB

Coventry
Coventry City Farm
1 Clarence Street
Hillfields
Coventry CV1 4SS

Edinburgh
Gorgie City Farm
51 Gorgie Road
Edinburgh EH11 2LA

Gateshead
Bill Quay Comm. Farm Assoc.
Hainingwood Terrace
Bill Quay
Gateshead NE10 0TL

Glasgow Area
Inverclyde Community Farm
off Papermill Road
near Overton
Greenock PA15

Knowetop Community Farm
113 Castlehill Road
Castlehill
Dumbarton G82 5AT

Lamont Farm Project
Barrhill Road
Erskine PA8 6BX

Huddersfield
Huddersfield Comm. Farm
Peace Pit Lane
off Leeds Road
Deighton
Huddersfield HD2 1JE

Leeds
Meanwood Valley Urban Farm
Sugarwell Road
Meanwood
Leeds LS7 2QG

Leicester
Gorse Hill City Farm
Anstey Lane
Beaumont Leys
Leicester LE4 0FL

New Park Adv. Playground
Glenfield Road
Leicester

Wycliffe Farm
Hamelin Road
Braunstone
Leicester LE5 1JN

Liverpool/Merseyside
Acorn Venture Farm
Depot Road
Kirkby L33 3AR

Liverpool 8 Garden Farm
15/19 Back Canning Street
Liverpool L8 7PB

Rice Lane City Farm
Walton Park Cemetery
off Rawcliffe Road
Liverpool L9 1AW

Tam O'Shanter Urban Farm
Boundary Road
Wirral
Birkenhead L43 7PD

London Area
Brooks Farm
Skeltons Lane
Leyton
London E10

Coram's Fields
93 Guilford Street
London WC1N 1DN

Deen City Farm
1 Batsworth Road
off Church Road
Mitcham CR4 3BX

Elm Farm
Gladstone Terrace
Lockington Road
Battersea
London SW8 3BA

Freightliners Farm
Paradise Park
Sheringham Road
London N7 8PF

Hackney City Farm
1a Goldsmiths Row
London E2 8QA

Hounslow Urban Farm
Faggs Road
Feltham TW14 0LZ

Kentish Town City Farm
1 Cressfield Close
London NW5 4BN

Mudchute Community Farm
Pier Street
Isle of Dogs
London E14

Newham City Farm
King George Avenue
Custom House
London E16 3HR

Spelthorne Farm Project
6 Burrows Hill Close
Heathrow Airport
Hounslow TW6 2ND

Spitalfields Farm
Thomas Buxton School
Weaver Street
London E1 6HJ

Stepping Stones Farm
Stepney Way
Stepney
London E1 3DG

Surrey Docks Farm
South Wharf
Rotherhithe Street
Rotherhithe
London SE16

Thameside Park Association
40 Thames Road
Barking IG11 0HH

Vauxhall City Farm
24 St Oswald's Place
London SE11 5LD

Wellgate Community Farm
Collier Row Road
Romford RM5 3NP

Manchester
Clayton Community Farm
Turner Street
Clayton
Manchester M11 4WH

Wythenshawe Comm. Farm
Altrincham Road
Sharston
Manchester M22 4NZ

Middlesbrough
Clarences Community Farm
Port Clarence Comm. Centre
Holly Terrace
High Clarence
Middlesbrough

Newcastle-upon-Tyne Area
City Farm Byker
Stepney Bank
Newcastle-upon-Tyne NE1 2PW

Milldene Town Farm
Simonside View
Primrose
Jarrow
Tyne & Wear NE32 5TS

Nottingham
Stonebridge City Farm
Stonebridge Road
St Ann's
Nottingham NG3 2FR

Oxford
Blackbird Leys City Farm
Windale Avenue
Blackbird Leys
Oxford

Peterborough
New Ark Adventure Playground
   and City Farm
Hill Close
Reeves Way
Peterborough PE1 5LZ

Rotherham
Dearne Urban Farm
1 Barnburgh Lane
Goldthorpe
Rotherham S63 9PS

Sheffield
Darnall Community Farm
Acres Hill Lane
Darnall
Sheffield S9 4LR

Heeley City Farm
Richards Road
Heeley
Sheffield S2 3ET

Southampton
Southampton City Farm
Millbrook School
Green Lane
Millbrook
Southampton

Sunderland
Southwick Village Farm
217–273 Southwick Road
Sunderland SR5 2AB

Wakefield
Wakefield City Farm
off Breton Lane
Crigglestone
Nr Wakefield
Yorkshire

Warrington
Heybrook Farm
Lowton
Warrington
Cheshire WA3 1BZ

Development Education Centres

Development education is so much concerned with environmental education that we take the view that it is another aspect of our curriculum area alongside urban studies, nature studies, demography, environmental science, outdoor education, ecology and many more. However there is a strong development education movement which tends to see itself as separate from, even if parallel to, environmental education. We are not prepared to argue semantics here but do feel it would be extremely remiss not to comment on the wealth of environmental resources and expertise to be found in development centres and development publications. The National Association of Development Education Centres provides information and sells publications. In September 1993 the Development Education Association was set up from an amalgamation of the NADEC and the Inter-Agency Committee for Development Education (which represents Oxfam, Christian Aid, etc.). Most individual centres have resource centres and shops at which educational materials can be hired or purchased. In our experience the DEC based in Birmingham provides a very good service to schools and its catalogue of curriculum development projects, which have all involved teachers in their production, is particularly worth obtaining. Their photopacks are good sources of secondary material for classroom-based activities. The addresses listed below have been supplied by the NADEC.

Development Education Association (DEA),
3rd floor, 29–31 Cowper Street, London EC2A 4AP

Aberdeen
Third World Centre
c/o Kirk of St Nicholas
Back Wynd
Aberdeen AB1 1JZ

Ambleside
Cumbria Development Education
    Centre
Kelsick Annexe
Charlotte Mason College
Ambleside
Cumbria LA22 9BB

Aylesbury
Development Education Centre
Methodist Church
Buckingham Street
Aylesbury
Bucks HP20 2NQ

Bangor
World Education Project
School of Education
UCNW
Deiniol Road
Bangor
Gwynedd LL57 2UW

Bath
Bath Development Education Centre
12a Westgate Street
Bath
Avon BA1 1EQ

Belfast
One World Centre (NI)
4 Lower Crescent
Belfast B17 1NR

Birmingham
Development Education Centre
Gillett Centre
998 Bristol Road
Selly Oak
Birmingham B29 6LE

Brighton
Development Education Centre,
    Worldwise
Brighthelm Centre
North Road
Brighton
East Sussex BN1 3LA

Bristol
BREAD
84 Colston Street
Bristol BS1 5BB

Cambridge
Harambee Centre for Environment
    and Development Studies
110 Regent Street
Cambridge CB2 1DP

Canterbury
World Development Education Group
The Canterbury Centre
St Alphege Lane, off Palace Street
Canterbury CT1 2EB

Cheltenham
Rendezvous
16 Portland Street
Cheltenham
Glos GL52 2PB

Cleveland
Cleveland Development Education
  Centre
Brackenhow School
Middlesborough
Cleveland TS4 3RY

Cork
Development Education Network
University College
Cork
Eire

Derby
Rainbow Centre for Environment and
  Development
88 Abbey Street
Derby DE3 3SQ

Derry
Development Education Centre
15 Pump Street
Derry
N. Ireland BT48 6JG

Dorking
One World Link
20 St Paul's Road West
Dorking
Surrey RH4 2UH

Dorset
Development Education in East
  Dorset (DEED)
East Dorset Professional Education
  Centre
Lowther Road
Bournemouth
Dorset BH8 8NR

Dudley
Dudley One World
Dudley Teacher's Centre
Laburnum Road
Kingswinford
Dudley
West Midlands DY6 8EH

Dundee
One World Centre
5 Victoria Street
Dundee DD4 EG6

Edinburgh
Scottish DEC
Old Playhouse Close
Moray House Institute of Education
Holyrood Road
Edinburgh EH8 8AQ

Exmouth
Centre for International Studies
Meadow Lea House
86 Littleham Road
Exmouth
Devon EX8 2QT

Glasgow
Centrepeace
143 Stockwell Street
Glasgow G1 4LR

Hull
Development Education Centre
c/o David Lister School
Rustenberg Street
Hull HU9 2PR

Leamington Spa
Warwickshire World Studies Centre
Manor Hall
Sandy Lane
Leamington Spa CV32 6RD

Leeds
Development Education Centre
151–153 Cardigan Road
Leeds LS6 1LJ

Leicester
Leicester World Development Centre
10a Bishop Street
Leicester LE1 6AF

Llanelli
Gwandraeth Development Education
  Centre
The Old School
Llannon Road
Pontyberem
Llanelli
Dyfed SA15 5PU

Llanidloes
Powys Environment and
   Development Education Centre
12 Great Oak Street
Llanidloes
Powys SY18 6BU

London (Africa Centre)
38 King Street
Covent Garden
London WC2 8JT

London (North West)
LONDEC
205–217 Instrument House
Kings Cross Road
London WC1X 9DB

Malvern
Third World Centre
22 Church Street
Malvern
Worcestershire WR14 2AY

Manchester
Development Education Project
c/o Manchester Polytechnic
801 Wilmslow Road
Didsbury
Manchester M20 8RG

Marlborough
Marlborough Brandt Group
Third World Education Centre
St John's Lower School
Savernake Building
Chopping Knife Lane
Marlborough
Wilts SN8 2AU

Milton Keynes
World Development Education
   Centre
Stantonbury Campus
Milton Keynes MK14 6BM

North Staffordshire
Development Education Centre
Newcastle Under Lyme College
Liverpool Road
Newcastle
Staffs ST5 2DF

Norwich
Norfolk Education and Action for
   Development (NEAD)
38–40 Exchange Street
Norwich
Norfolk NR2 1AX

Nottingham
Mundi
St George's Centre
91 Victoria Road
Netherfield
Nottingham

Oxford
Development Education Centre
East Oxford Community Centre
Prince's Street
Oxford OX4 1DD

Pendle
Just Dust Ltd
Pendle Centre for Development and
   Peace
Shackleton Hall
32 Church Street
Colne BB8 0LG

Preston
Lancashire Development Education
   Group
Global Education Centre
37 St Peter's Square
Preston
Lancs PR1 7BX

Reading
Reading International Support Centre
103 London Street
Reading RG1 4QA

Sheffield
Development Education Centre
   (South Yorkshire)
Woodthorpe School
Woodthorpe Road
Sheffield S13 8DD

Southampton
Tools for Self Reliance (TFSR)
Netley Marsh
Southampton SO4 2GY

Stevenage & North Herts
Development Education Centre
c/o Stevenage Urban Studies Centre
Pin Green School Site
Lonsdale Road
Stevenage
Herts SG1 5DQ

Winchester
Hampshire Development Education
  Centre
Divisional Professional Centre
Elm Road
Winchester
Hampshire SO22 5AG

Youth Hostels Associations in the UK and Eire

The Youth Hostel movement was founded by Robert Schirrmann, a German school teacher using schools in holiday times as venues for parties of school children. His idea was to give young people experience of the countryside. Later separate hostels were provided. The idea spread throughout Europe; the British Isles has the YHA (England and Wales), the Scottish YHA, the Irish YHA (An Oige), and the YHA of Northern Ireland. There are now 61 YHAs throughout the world and an International Youth Hostel Federation coordinates their activities.

All hostels provide a centre for environmental education based on field work with some of the hostels specially equipped with workrooms and other study facilities. The new International Centre in Bristol, England, has been developed from a former dockside warehouse and provides all that is needed for urban study in particular. It has conference facilities and points the way to future developments across the British Isles and elsewhere.

Scottish YHA (7 Glebe Crescent, Stirling FK8 2JA)

The following hostels provide for group residential stays and have workrooms:

Aberdeen YH
The King George VI Memorial Hostel
8 Queen's Road
Aberdeen AB1 6YT

Ayr YH
Craigweil Road
Ayr KA7 2XJ

Cannich YH
Cannich
Beauly
Inverness-shire IV4 7LT

Carbisdale Castle YH
Culrain
Ardgay
Sutherland IV24 3DP

Coldringham YH
The Mount
Coldringham
Eyemouth
Berwickshire TD14 5PA

Garramore YH
Morar
Inverness-shire PH40 4PD

Glendevon YH
Glendevon
Dollar
Clackmannanshire FK14 7JY

Glendoll YH
Clova
Kirriemuir
Angus DD8 4RD

Islay YH and Field Centre
Main Street
Port Charlotte
Islay PA48 7TX

Kirkwall YH
Old Scapa Road
Kirkwall
Orkney KW15 1BB

Kyleakin YH
Kyleakin
Isle of Skye IV41 8PL

Loch Ard YH
Kinlochard
Stirling FK8 3TL

Loch Lomond YH
Arden
Alexandria
Dunbartonshire G83 8RB

Lochranza YH
Lochranza
Isle of Arran KA27 8HL

Melrose YH
Priorwood
Melrose
Roxburghshire TD6 9EF

Oban YH
Esplanade
Oban
Argyllshire PA34 5AF

Perth YH
107 Glasgow Road
Perth PH2 0NS

Rowardennan YH
Rowardennan
by Drymen
Glasgow G63 0AR

Stirling YH
Argyll Lodging
Castle Wynd
Stirling FK8 1EG

Strathpeffer YH
Strathpeffer
Ross-shire IV14 9BT

Torridon YH
Torridon
Achnasheen
Ross-shire IV22 2EZ

Youth Hostels Association of Northern Ireland (YHA of Northern Ireland, 56 Bradbury Place, Belfast BT7 1RU)

Several hostels in Northern Ireland provide group accommodation but two in particular are directed towards environmental education:

Castle Archdale YH
Castle Archdale Country Park
Irvinestown
Enniskillen
Co. Fermanagh BT94 1PP

This hostel has a classroom, lecture theatre and laboratories.

Cushendall YH
Layde Road
Cushendall
Co. Antrim BT44 0NQ

There are extensive gardens suitable for conservation exercises and, as well as the normal room provision, a new field study centre should now be open.

Irish Youth Hostels Association (Irish YHA – An Oige, 39 Mountjoy Square, Dublin)

Details can be obtained from the Irish YHA.

YHA, England and Wales (Trevelyan House, St Stephen's Hill, St Albans, Hertfordshire SG1 5DQ)

A data pack for Group Leaders details the facilities available at all hostels. Hostels with field study centres are:

Bristol
International Centre
Hayman House
64 Prince Street
Bristol BS1 4HU

Cornwall
Golant YH
Penquite House
Fowey PL23 1LA

Cumbria
Hawkshead YH
Esthwaite Lodge
Hawkshead
Ambleside LA22 0QD

High Close YH
Loughrigg
Ambleside LA22 0EU

Derbyshire
Eyam YH
The Edge
Eyam S30 1QP

Hartington YH
Hartington
Buxton SK17 0AT

Ilam Hall YH
Nr Ashbourne DE6 2AZ

Devon
Instow YH
Worlington House
Instow
Bideford EX39 4LW

Dorset
Swanage YH
Cluny
Cluny Crescent
Swanage BH19 2BS

Gloucester
Duntisbourne Abbots YH
Cirencester GL7 7JN

Slimbridge YH
Shepherd's Patch
Slimbridge GL2 7BP

Lancashire
Arnside YH
Oakfield Lodge
Redhills Road
Arnside
Carnforth LA5 0AT

Norfolk
Sheringham YH
1 Cremers Drift
Sheringham NR26 8HX

Northumberland
Rock Hall YH
Alnwick NE66 3SB

Oxford
Charlbury YH
The Laurels
The Slade
Charlbury OX7 3SJ

Shropshire
Ironbridge Gorge YH
Coalbrookdale Institute
Paradise
Coalbrookdale
Telford

Wilderhope Manor YH
Easthope
Much Wenlock TF13 6EG

Somerset
Crowcombe Heathfield YH
Denzel House
Crowcombe Heathfield
Taunton TA4 4BT

Suffolk
Blaxhall YH
Heath Walk
Blaxhall
Woodbridge IP12 2EA

Teesside
Saltburn YH
Victoria Road
Saltburn by Sea
Cleveland TS12 1JD

Yorkshire
Boggle Hole YH
Whitby
North Yorks YO22 4UQ

Grinton Lodge
Grinton
Richmond DL11 6HS

North Wales
Bryn Gwynant
Caernafon LL55 4NP

Llangollen YH
Tyndwr Hall
Tyndwr Road
Llangollen LL20 8AR

Hostels with classrooms:

Cumbria
Eskdale YH
Boot
Holmrock CA19 1TH

Derbyshire
Edale YH
Rowland Cote
Nether Booth
Edale
Sheffield S30 2ZH

Ravenstor YH
Miller's Dale
Buxton SK17 8SS

Devon
Exeter YH
47 Countess Wear Road
Exeter EX2 6LR

Essex
Castle Hedlingham YH
7 Falcon Square
Halstead CO9 3BU

Kent
Kemsing YH
Cleves
Pilgrim's Way
Kemsing
Sevenoaks TN15 6LT

Lledr Valley YH
Lledr House
Pont-y-Pant
Dolwwyddelan LL25 0DQ

South Wales
Borth YH
Morlais
Borth SY24 5JS

Broad Haven YH
Haverfordwest
Dyfed SA62 3JH

Llwynypia YH
Glyncornel
Llwynypia
Mid Glamorgan CF40 2JF

Norfolk
Norwich YH
112 Turner Road
Norwich NR2 4HB

Oxford
Ridgeway YH
Court Hill
Wantage

Suffolk
Brandon YH
Heath House
Bury Road
Brandon IP27 0BU

Colchester YH
East Bay House
18 East Bay
Colchester CO1 2UE

Yorkshire
Osmotherley YH
Northallerton
N. Yorks DL6 3AH

North Wales
Bala YH
Plas Rhiwaedog
Rhos y Gwaliau
Bala LL23 7EU

South Wales
Chepstow YH
Mounton Road
Chepstow NP6 6AA

Many other hostels will allow the use of the dining room as a classroom at times when it is free. Further details of hostels can be obtained from the national headquarters. It is advisable to book early in the spring and summer months.

Young Men's Christian Association

The YMCA provides three school residential centres where field study can be undertaken: Otterburn Hall, Northumberland; Weardale House, North Pennines; and Tavool House, Isle of Mull.

Urban Study Centres

As with development education we see urban study as an important part of environmental education and regret that those promoting urban study often seem to wish to plough a lone furrow while, at the same time, protesting that much of environmental education is too natural-world based. Xanthoria, the yellow lichen, growing on the wall of a school in an inner-city site, not only indicates that the urban clean-air policy locally has been most successful, but that a study of the environment must be a fully integrated look at both worlds, built and natural. People, buildings and nature are not to be placed in separate departments, as the best of the urban centres show. Recent developments in urban studies have given rise to the National Association for Urban Studies (NAUS) which publishes *Streetwise*, a magazine replacing the *Bulletin for Environmental Education* (BEE) which collapsed along with its parent body *Streetwork*. The list of urban study centres which follows has been supplied by *Streetwise*. As with all study centres in these difficult economic times some of them are struggling to survive and deserve all the support which schools can give them.

Bath
Huntingdon Centre
Countess of Huntingdon's Chapel
The Vineyards
The Paragon
Bath BAI 5NA

Brighton
Lewis Cohen Urban Studies Centre
Brighton Polytechnic
68 Grand Parade
Brighton BN2 2JY

Bristol
Bristol Urban Studies Centre
1 All Saints Court
Bristol BSI IJN

Bristol Youth Hostel Association
International Centre
Hayman House
64 Prince Slreet
Bristol BS1 4HU

Canterbury
Canterbury Urban Studies Centre
82 Alphege Lane
Canterbury
Kent CT1 2EB

Chester
St Mary's Centre
St Mary's Hill
Chester CH1 2DW

Edinburgh
Environment Centre
Drummond High School
Cochran Terrace
Edinburgh EH7 4QP

Gillingham
Gillingham Urban Heritage Centre
Byron CP School
Byron Road
Gillingham
Kent

Glasgow
Bellarmine Environmental Resource
    Centre
Bellarmine Secondary School
42 Cowglen Road
Pollok
Glasgow

Harlow
Harlow Study & Visitors' Centre
Nettleswellbury Farm
Harlow
Essex

London
Bromley Urban Studies Centre
Kent House Road
Penge
London SE20

Hammersmith & Fulham Urban
    Studies Centre
1–15 King Street
London W6 9HR

Holy Trinily Urban Centre
Carlisle Road
London SE1 7LG

Nottingdale Urban Studies Centre
189 Freston Road
London W10 6TH

The Urban Studies Centre
Tower Hamlets and Newham
Hayward House

55–58 East India Dock Road
Limehouse
Poplar
London E14 6JE

Willowbrook Urban Studies Centre
48 Willowbrook Road
London SW15 6BW

Manchester
Manchester Urban Studies Centre
328–330 Deansgate
Manchester M3 4FN

Milton Keynes
City Discovery Centre
106 Tanners Drive
Blakelands
Milton Keynes MK14 5BP

Newcastle-upon-Tyne
Newcastle Architectural Workshop
6 Higham Place
Newcastle-upon-Tyne NE1 8AF

Rhondda
Glyncornel Environmental Centre
Nant-y-Gwyddon Road
Llwynypia
Rhondda CF40 2JF

Stevenage
Stevenage Urban Studies Centre
Lonsdale Road
Stevenage
Hertfordshire SG1 5DQ

Swindon
Swindon Urban Studies Centre
North Wilts Centre for the
    Curriculum
Drove Road
Swindon SN1 3QQ

Warrington
North Cheshire Urban Studies Centre
New Town House
Buttermarket Street
Warrington WA1 2LF

Royal Society for the Protection of Birds

The RSPB is the charity that takes action for wild birds and the environment. Where schools are concerned it brings matters ornithological to the attention of students and teachers through its three termly publications *Early Birds* directed at infants, *Focus on Birds*, the original RSPB newsletter for teachers, and *Sixth Sense* for upper school students. All provide information and activity suggestions for bird study. The material provided can be used for its own sake or built into cross-curricular environmental education. For example the summer term 1992 *Early Birds* concentrates on the migration of the swallow. If 'journeys' is taken as the centre of interest for an infants class it would be possible, it suggests, to compare journeys (daily to school, shopping with mother, holiday) they make with those of the swallow. Preparation, food, method of travel, time, distance, locations, maps – all can come into the learning. The RSPB provides coloured illustrations of swallows, information and, in this case, even a game to be played which will establish some basic locational geography. All material supplied may be photocopied copyright free. The society has many nature reserves some of which (see below) have countryside classrooms where teaching facilities are available for school groups. These facilities are open to the general public at weekends and can be used by young people's groups other than those from schools. Sometimes temporary visiting schemes at times of peak interest are established at certain reserves and other wildlife areas. Teacher training is another aspect of the work of the RSPB through its education service. Calls on its resources for in-service days are always received sympathetically. The Young Ornithologists Club is another educational activity for children, an attractive opportunity for extra-mural involvement.

Visiting parties to the nature reserves are taught by trained teacher-naturalists. There is normally a charge for visits and arrangements must be made in advance.

RSPB
The Lodge
Sandy
Bedfordshire SG19 2DL

RSPB Wales
Bryn Aderyn
The Bank
Newtown
Powys SY16 2AB

RSPB Scotland
17 Regent Street
Edinburgh EH7 5BN

RSPB Northern Ireland
Belvoir Park Forest
Belfast BT8 4QT

RSPB Nature Reserves

Scotland
Loch of Strathbeg
Starnafin Farmhouse
Crimond
Fraserburgh
Aberdeenshire AB4 4YN

Loch of Kinnordy
The Flat
Home Farm
Kinnordy Estate
Kindemuir
Angus DD8 5FH

Vane Farm
RSPB Nature Centre
Vane Farm Nature Centre
By Loch Leven
Kinross KY13 7LX

Lochwinnoch
RSPB Nature Centre
Largs Road
Lochwinnoch
Strathclyde

Baronshaugh
9 Wisteria Lane
Carluke
Strathclyde ML8 5TB

England
Marsden Rock
RSPB North of England Office
E Floor, Milburn House
Dean Street
Newcastle-upon-Tyne NE1 1LE

Bolam Lake
RSPB North of England Office

Hodbarrow
29 Mainsgate Road
Millom
Cumbria LA18 4JZ

Bempton Cliffs
RSPB East Midlands Office
The Lawn
Union Road
Lincoln LN1 3BU

Cleethorpes
RSPB East Midlands Office

Eastwood
RSPB North West England Office
Brookfoot House
Brookfoot Mills
Elland Road
Brighouse
West Yorks HD6 2RW

Fairburn Ings
2 Springholm
Caudle Hill
Fairburn
Knottingley
Yorks WF11 9JQ

Leighton Moss
Myers Farm
Silverdale
Carnforth
Lancs LA5 0SW

Coombes Valley
Six Oaks Farm
Bradnop
Leek
Staffordshire ST13 7EU

Ellesmere
Ranger Service
Shropshire County Council

Coombe Abbey
Country Park

Symonds Yat
RSPB Midlands Office
44 Friar Street
Droitwich Spa
Droitwich
Worcestershire WR9 8ED

Nagshead
RSPB Midlands Office

Highnam Woods
RSPB Midlands Office

Fowlmere
19 Whitecroft Road
Meldreth
Nr Royston
Hertfordshire SG8 6ND

Sandwell Valley
RSPB Nature Centre
20 Tan House Avenue
Great Barr
Birmingham B43 5AG

Titchwell Marsh
Three Horseshoes Cottage
Titchwell
King's Lynn
Norwich PE31 8BB

Strumpshaw Fen
Staithe Cottage
Low Road
Strumpshaw
Norfolk NR13 4HS

Minsmere
Minsmere Reserve
Westleton
Saxmundham
Suffolk IP17 2BY

Stour Wood
24 Orchard Close
Great Oakley
Harwich
Essex CO12 5AX

Rye House Marsh
Toad Cottage
4 Cecil Road
Rye Park
Hoddesdon
Hertfordshire EN11 0JA

Dungeness
Boulderwall Farm
Dungeness Road
Lydd
Kent TN29 9PN

Pulborough Brooks
RSPB South East England Office
8 Church Street
Shoreham-by-Sea
West Sussex BN43 5DQ

Radipole Lake
Radipole RSPB Nature Centre
The Swannery Car Park
Weymouth
Dorset DT4 7TZ

Arne
Syldata
Arne
Wareham
Dorset BH20 5BJ

Aylesbeare Common
Mount Pleasant
Stoneyford
Colaton Raleigh
Sidmouth
Devon EX10 0HZ

Northern Ireland
Greenmount College
RSPB Northern Ireland Office
Belvoir Park Forest
Belfast
Northern Ireland BT8 4QT

Wales
South Stack
Swn-y-Mor
South Stack
Holyhead
Anglesey
Gwynedd

Ynys-hir
Cae'r Berllan
Eglwysfach
Machynlleth
Powys SY20 8TA

Lake Vyrnwy
Bryn Awel Llanwddyn
Oswestry
Salop

Cwm Clydach
2 Ty'n y Berllan
Craig Cern Parc
Clydach
West Glamorgan

Environmental Study Centres on the sites of the electricity industry

Electricity generating, transmission and distribution sites often occupy areas of land beside rivers or lakes or near to the sea. It is now quite common for part of this land, safely clear of any dangerous installations, to be made available for field work by schools with suitable buildings and staffed by professional educators. In many cases the physical items are supplied by the electricity company and the education staff by the local education authority or by a consortium of authorities. The site nearest to a school may be directly controlled by the school's local education department so that the facility is available only to schools in that jurisdiction; others may be open to all and access is made through the company.

Nuclear Electric plc
Barnett Way
Barnwood
Gloucester GL4 7RS

Powergen
Haslucks Green Road
Shirley
Solihull
West Midlands B90 4PD

National Grid
National Grid House
Sumner Street
London SE1 9JU

National Power
Sudbury House
15 Newgate Street
London EC1A 7AU

Scottish Hydro-Electric
16 Rothesay Terrace
Edinburgh
Scotland EH3 7SE

S S E B
Scottish Power
Cathcart House
Spean Street
Glasgow G44 4BE

The following are 'electricity' sites with study facilities as supplied by the companies themselves:

Powergen Centres

Kingsnorth Power Station
Hoo, St Werburgh
Rochester
Kent ME3 9NQ
A wildlife reserve

Drakelow Field Study Centre
Drakelow Power Station
Near Burton on Trent
Staffordshire DE15 9TZ
Small classroom; 5 hectares of woodland

Hams Hall E S Centre
Hams Hall Power Station
Lea Marston
Sutton Coldfield
West Midlands
Full centre complex, woodland; ponds; 17th century farm labourer's cottage

Rheidol Centre
Rheidol Power Station
Capel Bangor
Aberystwyth
Dyfed SY2 3NB
Field study classroom; 2½ mile trail around reservoir

National Grid

Amersham FS Centre
Mop End
Amersham
Buckinghamshire
arrangements to
County Adviser for Middle Years
Bucks CC
County Hall
Aylesbury HP20 1UX
Centre and trail in 30 hectares of woodland

Bishops Wood Educational Study
  Area
Stourport on Severn
Worcestershire
arrangements to
Arden Transmission Office
202 Waterloo Road
Yardley
Birmingham B25 8LD
Fully equipped field classroom; woodland

Bramley Frith Wood Trail
Sub station
Bramley
Basingstoke
arrangements to
District Manager
Thames District
617 London Road
Reading RG6 1AX
33 hectares of woodland

Ninfield Study Centre
Potman's Lane
Ninfield
Sussex
arrangements to
ES Adviser
East Sussex CC
PO Box 4
County Hall
St Annes Crescent
Lewes B77 1SG
Centre in 22 hectares of woods and meadows

Canterbury FS Centre
Ex Broadoak Substation
Broadoak Road
Canterbury
Kent
Study centre in 10 hectares of old gravel workings

Pelham FS Centre
Pelham Substation
Stocking Pelham
Buntingford
Hertfordshire
Study centre on 20 hectare site of ponds, spinneys and hedges

Penwortham FS Centre
Penwortham Substation
Preston
arrangements to
c/o Hothersall Lodge
Longridge
Preston
Wood, pond and fields beside study centre

National Power

Didcot Power Station
Oxfordshire
arrangements to
Headteacher
Sutton Courtenay Primary School
Didcot
Oxfordshire
Centre in 18 hectares of regenerated land

Rugeley ES Centre
Rugeley Power Station
Armitage Road
Rugeley
Staffordshire WS15 1PR
Classroom beside lake; woodland; butterfly garden

Thorpe Marsh Nature Reserve
Thorpe Marsh Power Station
arrangements to
Yorkshire Wildlife Trust
43 Princes Street
Doncaster
South Yorkshire
25 hectares of nature reserve

Environmental Study Centres at the power stations of Nuclear Electric

Berkeley Technology Centre
Berkeley
Gloucestershire GL13 9PB

Breakheart Quarry Field Centre
Nr Dursley
Gloucestershire
Small field centre, limited numbers, education pack, nature trail, geology projects

Dungeness Nature Trail
Power Station Visitor Centre
Romney Marsh
Kent TN29 9PL
Nature trail, education pack

Heysham Field Centre
Power Station Visitor Centre
PO Box 17
Heysham
Lancashire LA3 2YB
Fully staffed classroom in 10 hectare nature reserve

Hinkley Point Nature Trail
Power Station Visitor Centre
Nr. Bridgwater
Somerset TA5 1UD
Woods, scrub, ponds, beach

Oldbury Nature Trail
Power Station Visitor Centre
Oldbury Naite
Thornbury
Avon B12 1RQ
Classroom, education pack. Ponds, orchard, silt lagoon

Sizewell Wildlife Area
Power Station Visitor Centre
Nr Leiston
Suffolk IP16 4UR
Classroom, education pack. Pond, woodland

Teesmouth Field Centre
Hartlepool Power Station
Tees Road
Hartlepool
Cleveland TS25 2BZ
Fully staffed classroom. Salt marshes, dunes

Trawsfynydd Nature Trail
Power Station Visitor Centre
Blaenau Ffestiniog
Gwynedd LL41 4DT

Classroom, several nature trails, education pack

Wylfa Nature Trail
Power Station Visitor Centre
Cemaes Bay
Anglesey
Gwynedd LL67 ODH
Classroom, education pack

British Trust for Conservation Volunteers

The BTCV is Britain's largest practical conservation charity. It caters for people of all ages, from all sections of the community, who wish to take action in caring for the natural and urban environments. The activities include:

- Weekday and weekend conservation projects
- Conservation training courses
- Working holidays
- Supporting local and community groups

It provides labour for school projects, aspects of which are beyond the strength and skill of young people – erecting fences, creating steps, digging tree holes, etc. It can give teachers specialist training and is able to dispense advice and provide materials for most conservation projects.

BTCV, 36 St Mary's Street,
Wallingford, Oxfordshire OX10 0EU

INFORMATION TECHNOLOGY

As with education as a whole the use of computers and other forms of modern technology is playing an increasing part in the presentation of environmental education. Our purpose here is to make readers aware of this but not to present a comprehensive overview of these new approaches. We have explained elsewhere that the acquisition of the skills needed to examine, protect and improve the environment is an important goal for environmental education. Information technology in all of its forms is becoming increasingly important in this process as well as the dissemination of information both nationally and globally. Many of these skills can be gained using basic computer applications. IT supports well such skills as collecting data, measuring and recording, organizing and classifying information, analysing and evaluating such data and information, making predictions based on evidence, communicating information and various viewpoints in a fair and rational way and devising methods of presenting facts in a visually stimulating fashion. Teachers and pupils need access to IT if they are to face up to the realities of environmental education in a modern world.

Basically technology can provide up-to-date information for use as secondary sources for teacher or pupil use or it can be used as a direct learning tool.

Three examples of the former range from a local computerized information system to direct access to environmental information from a government source or indirect access to the wealth of information available both nationally and internationally.

A local service to schools – the Staffordshire Farm Link

Schools in Staffordshire use their computer systems to access the Farm Link which provides information on the milk records and farm operations of the Brewood Farm Centre. This county facility is built around an Ayrshire herd of cattle, sheep, pigs and poultry and is available for normal field study visits. The figures for milk yields provide a cross-curricular resource which is used in many subjects of the National Curriculum and which together achieve viable environmental education. In the opposite direction schools can feed information into the

Staffordshire Woodlands Scheme, a computer recording technique designed to promote and sustain the planting and curriculum integration of tree planting on school sites. This database and electronic magazine is seen as an area of rapid expansion. Increasing use is being made in the county of the local authority's central computer using Whittle 'Viewdata' software and a Linnet modem on similar compatible materials via a telephone link.

Weather information from the Met. Office

Any serious study of the weather requires daily information. Hopefully most schools will have their own weather station of varying complexity. The MetFAX Education system of the UK's Met. Office provides schools with 12 different options of weather information to augment that gathered locally. Synoptic charts, weather reports, shipping forecasts, general news and facts together with guidance on how to interpret them are available with the charts updated eight times a day to give the school the exciting possibility of following weather patterns as they develop and to see if an individual's forecast for the day is proven to be true or false. MetFAX is an innovation in classroom teaching and a breakthrough in fax technology – the first educational dial-up fax service. It enables any school with a fax machine to access up-to-the-minute weather information immediately and automatically at the press of a button, as each chart has its own dedicated telephone number.

GreenNet – a global computer communications network for the environment

GreenNet is an example of an international computerized network which can provide schools with a wealth of information on environment and development. In addition it can link schools to an extensive international database of useful contacts. Its use for classroom and project work, along with other online services, is as wide as the individual school can manage and is limited only by the information technology available to the institution and the expertise of the operator.

GreenNet,
23 Bevenden Street, London N1 6BH, UK

IT as a direct learning tool

The second use for IT in environmental education is by the use of prepared programs. More and more of these are coming onto the market with many schools producing their own software. A school in Uttoxeter has taken full advantage of these to back up environmental education in the environmental science course leading to GCSE and 'A' level. For the record the school uses Laser ROM and CD-ROM in addition to RM word processors. Typical of the software in use are the two programs 'Microsoft Bookshelf' and 'Earthquest explores Ecology'. Commercial interactive discs, such as 'Countryside' and 'Eco-disc', give opportunities for problem solving and decision making with a wide range of options.

It is obvious that venturing into the realms of IT is not something to be taken casually. Fortunately local and central back-up for the use of computers in education is well established with advice and financial help readily available. Membership of local and national environmental groups is one way to keep abreast of opportunities in environmental technology. *The Eco Directory of Environmental Databases* (1992) gives information on 300 environmental databases in the UK.

Eco Trust,
10–12 Picton Street, Bristol BS6 5QA

OTHER USEFUL PUBLICATIONS

Association of County Councils (1990) *County Councils and the Environment*, Luton.

British Leisure Publications (annual) *Historic Houses, Castles and Gardens* and *Museums and Galleries*, East Grinstead, BLP.

Carson, S. McB. (1978) *Environmental Education – Principles and Practice*, London, Edward Arnold.

Council for Environmental Education (1991) *Environmental Education Across the Curriculum*, Reading, CEE.

Council for Environmental Education (1992) *INSET for Environmental Education 5–16: Introductory Activities*, Reading, CEE.

Council for Environmental Education (1992) *Planning and Evaluation of Environmental Education 11–16*, Reading, CEE.

Council for Environmental Education (1992) *Reviewing and Evaluating Provision for Environmental Education 5–11*, Reading, CEE.

Council for Environmental Education *Annual Review of Environmental Education*, Reading, CEE.

Department of Education and Science (1981) *Environmental Education – A Review*, London, DES.

Faculty of Education, University of Malta (1991) *Incorporating Environmental Education into the Primary School Curriculum*, Valetta.

Lancashire County Council (1992) *Environmental Education Guidelines 4–16*, Lancaster, LCC.

Lewis, Bob (1991) *Education for the 1990s: The Wildwood Idea*, Aspen, CO, Aspen Center for Environmental Studies.

Mays, Pamela (1985) *Teaching Children Through the Environment*, London, Hodder & Stoughton.

Morrison, Keith and Ridley, Ken (1988) *Curriculum Planning in the Primary School*, London, Paul Chapman Publishing Company

Neal, P. and Palmer, J. (1990) *Environmental Education in the Primary School*, Oxford, Basil Blackwell.

Palmer, J. (1992) *Blueprints, Environmental Education Key Stage 1 and Key Stage 2*, Cheltenham, Stanley Thornes.
Robottom, I. (1987) *Environmental Education: Practice and Possibility*, Deakin, Australia, Deakin University Press.
RSPB (1991) *Environmental Education: The Vital Link*, Sandy, RSPB.
Scottish Environmental Education Council, Annual publication (untitled), Stirling, SEEC.
Scottish Office (1993) *Learning for Life. A report of the working group for environmental education to the Secretary of State for Scotland*, Edinburgh.
Scottish Office Education Department (1991) *Environmental Studies 5–14*, Working Paper 13, Edinburgh, SOED.
Shropshire County Council (1992) *A Guide to Developing Environmental Education in Shropshire Schools*, Shrewsbury.
Taylor, (1980) *Towards a School Policy in Environmental Education*, Paisley, Scottish Committee for Environmental Education.
UNEP/UK (1992) *Good Earthkeeping*, London.
UNESCO/UNEP (1985) P. Bennett, *Evaluating Environmental Education in Schools*, EE series 12, New York.
UNESCO/UNEP (1990) 'Planning environmental education at the national level', *Connect*, EE newsletter XV (3).
UNICEF and DEC (South Yorkshire) (1992) *It's our World Too*, Sheffield.
Victoria Environmental Education Council (1991) *Educating for Our Environment*, Melbourne, Australia.

Conference reports

Consultation Conference Report 1992, Secretary of State for Scotland's Working Group on Environmental Education, Stirling.
Know Your Surroundings, Environmental Education Conference Report 1986, School of Environmental Studies, Gloscat, Oxtalls Lane, Gloucester GL2 9HW.
Policies for Environmental Education and Training, 1992 and Beyond, Conference Report 1992, English Nature, Nature Conservancy Council for Scotland, Department of the Environment (N. Ireland), Countryside Council for Wales.

National Association for Environmental Education: selected publications

All published by the NAEE, Walsall

Practical guides

1 Incubator in the Classroom
2 Organisation of Outdoor Studies and Visits
4 Using the School Greenhouse
5 An Aviary in School
6 An Aquarium in School
7 Heritage Education
8 Using Maps 5–16
9 Traffic Study and Surveys
10 Amphibians and Reptiles

11 Developing a School Nature Reserve
12 Creating and Maintaining a Garden to Attract Butterflies
14 Using Invertebrates in the Classroom

Occasional Papers

 9 Planners and Environmental Education
11 Planning and Implementing Environmental Initiatives Curriculum in England and Wales
12 Assessing Skills Progression in Environmental Studies Curricula
13 The National Curriculum – The Location of Environmental Education as a Cross-Curricular Issue
14 Towards a School Policy for Environmental Education: An Environmental Audit
15 Coming of Age – A Short History of Environmental Education to 1989
16 Positive Action – Ideas for enhancing the environmental performance of your school

Other publications

Environmental Education, the termly journal of the NAEE
Using the Environment in Early Education (booklet)

USEFUL ADDRESSES

UK

Association for the Conservation of
  Energy
9 Sherlock Mews
London W1M 3RH

British Coal
Hobart House
40 Grosvenor Place
London SW1X 7AE

British Ecological Society
Burlington House
Piccadilly
London W1V 0LQ

British Gas PLC
Education Liaison Officer
Marketing Division
326 High Holborn
London WC1V 7PT

British Naturalists Association
48 Russell Way
Higham Ferrers
Northamptonshire NN9 8EJ

British Petroleum Company
Britannic House
Moor Lane
London EC2Y 9BU

British Rail Board
PO Box 100
24 Eversholt Street
London NW1 1DZ

British Trust for Conservation
  Volunteers
36 St Mary's Street
Wallingford
Oxford OX10 0EU

British Waterways
Willow Grange
Church Road
Watford
Herts WD1 3QA

British Wind Energy Association
4 Hamilton Place
London W1V 0BQ

Butterfly Conservation
PO Box 222
Dedham
Essex CO9 6EY

Centre for Alternative Technology
Llwyngwern Quarry
Machynlleth
Powys SY20 9AZ

Centre for Environmental
  Interpretation
Manchester Polytechnic
Bellhouse Building
Lower Chatham Street
Manchester M15 6BY

Centre for Global Education
University of York
Department of Education
Heslington
York YO1 5DD

Civic Trust
17 Carlton House Terrace
London SW1Y 5AW

CLEAR (Campaign for Lead Free Air)
3 Endsleigh Street
London WC1H 0DD

Common Ground
45 Shelton Street
London WC1H 9HJ

Commonwealth Institute
Kensington High Street
London W8 6NQ

Community Service Volunteers
237 Pentonville Road
London N1 9NJ

Concord Films Council Ltd
201 Felixtowe Road
Ipswich
Suffolk IP3 9BJ

Conservation Foundation
1 Kensington Gore
London SW7 2AR

Council for Education in World
  Citizenship (CEWC)
Seymour Mews House
Seymour Mews
London W1H 9PE

Council for Environmental Education
Faculty of Education and Community
  Studies
University of Reading
London Road
Reading RG1 5AQ

Council for National Parks
246 Lavender Hill
London SW11 1LN

Council for the Protection of Rural
  England
Warwick House
25 Buckingham Palace Road
London SW1W 0PP

Council for the Protection of Rural
  Wales
Ty Gwyn
31 High Street
Welshpool
Powys SY21 7JP

Country Houses Association
41 Kingsway
London WC2B 6UB

Country Landowners Association
16 Belgrave Square
London SW1X 8PQ

Countryside Commission
John Dower House
Crescent Place
Cheltenham
Gloucestershire GL50 3RA

Countryside Commission for Scotland
Battleby
Redgorton
Perth
Scotland PH1 3EW

Department of the Environment
2 Marsham Street
London SW1P 3EB

Development Education Association
3rd Floor
29–31 Cowper Street
London EC2A 4AP

Earth Resources Research Ltd
258 Pentonville Road
London N1 9JY

Electricity Council
30 Millbank
London SW1P 4RD

English Heritage
Fortress House
23 Savile Row
London W1X 2HE

English Nature
Northminster House
Peterborough
PE1 1UA

Environment Council
London Ecology Centre
80 York Way
London N1 9AG

Environmental Forum
12a Ennis Road
Finsbury Park
London N4 3HD

Esso UK
Esso House
Victoria Street
London SW1E 5JW

Farming and Wildlife Advisory
   Group
National Agricultural Centre
Stoneleigh
Warwickshire CV8 2RX

Fauna and Flora Preservation Society
1 Kensington Gore
London SW7 2AR

Field Studies Council
Preston Montford
Montford Bridge
Shrewsbury
Shropshire SY4 1HW

Forestry Commission
231 Corstorphine Road
Edinburgh EH12 7AT

Forestry Trust for Conservation &
   Education
The Old Estate Office
Englefield Road
Theale
Reading
Berkshire RG7 5DZ

Friends of the Earth
26–28 Underwood Street
London N1 7JQ

Friends of the Earth (Scotland)
15 Windsor Street
Edinburgh EH7 5LA

The Game Conservancy Trust
Burgate Manor
Fordingbridge
Hampshire SP6 1EF

Geographical Association
343 Fulwood Road
Sheffield S10 3BP

The Geologists' Association
Dept of Geology
University College London
Gower Street
London WC1E 6BT

Greenpeace
Canonbury Villas
London N1 2PN

Groundwork Foundation
Bennetts Court
Bennetts Hill
Birmingham B2 5ST

Gulf Oil GB Ltd
The Quadrangle
Imperial Square
Cheltenham GL50 1TH

Heritage Education Trust
University College of Ripon and
   York St John
College Road
Ripon HG4 2QX

Historical Association
59a Kennington Park Road
London SE11 4JH

Historic Houses Association
2 Chester Street
London SW1X 7BB

Inland Waterways Association
114 Regents Park Road
London NW1 8UQ

Institute of Biology
20 Queensbury Place
London SW7 2DZ

Institute of British Geographers
1 Kensington Gore
London SW7 2AP

Institute for Earth Education
PO Box 14
Mortimer
Reading RG7 3YA

Institution of Environmental Sciences
14 Princes Gate
Hyde Park
London SW7 1PU

Intermediate Technology
 Development Group (ITDG)
103–105 Southampton Row
London WC1B 4HH

International Broadcasting Trust (IBT)
2 Ferdinand Place
London NW1 8EE

International Centre for Conservation
 Education
Greenfield House
Guiting Power
Gloucestershire GL54 5TZ

International Solar Energy Society
Campden Hill Road
Kensington
London W8 7AH

International Union for Conservation
 of Nature and Natural Resources
 (IUCN)
c/o World Conservation Monitoring
 Centre
219c Huntingdon Road
Cambridge CB3 0DL
(ICUN Head Office
Avenue de Mont Blanc
CH–1196 Gland
Switzerland)

Ironbridge Gorge Museum Trust
Ironbridge
Telford
Shropshire

Keep Scotland Beautiful
Old Country Chambers
Cathedral Square
Dunblane
Perthshire PK1 0AQ

Learning Through Landscapes
3rd Floor
Southside Offices
The Law Courts
Winchester
Hampshire SO23 9DL

London Wildlife Trust
80 York Way
London N1 9AG

The Mammal Society
Dept of Zoology
University of Bristol
Woodland Road
Bristol BS8 1UG

Marine Conservation Society
9 Gloucester Road
Ross on Wye
Herefordshire HR9 5BU

Mobil Oil Company Ltd
Mobil House
24–60 Victoria Street
London SW1E 6QB

The Museums' Association
34 Bloomsbury Way
London WC1A 2SF

National Association of Development
 Centres (NADEC)
6 Endsleigh Street
London WC1H 0DX

National Association for
 Environmental Education (NAEE)
Wolverhampton University
Walsall Campus
Gorway
Walsall
West Midlands WS1 3BD

National Association of Field Studies
 Officers (NAFSO)
c/o Stouhall Environmental Education
 Centre
Reynoldston
Swansea SA3 1AP

National Association for Outdoor
 Education
251 Woodlands Road
Woodlands
Southampton SO4 2GJ

National Association for Urban
   Studies
68 Grand Parade
Brighton N2 2JY

National Environment Research
   Council
Polaris House
North Star Avenue
Swindon
Wiltshire SN2 1EU

National Farmers Union
Agriculture House
Knightsbridge
London SW1X 7NJ

National Federation of City Farms
Avon Environmental Centre
Junction Road
Brislington
Bristol BS4 3JP

National Grid
National Grid House
Sumner Street
London SE1 9JU

National Power
Sudbury House
15 Newgate Street
London EC1A 7AU

National Society for Clean Air and
   Environmental Protection
136 North Street
Brighton BN1 1RG

National Trust
36 Queen Anne's Gate
London SW1H 9AS

National Trust for Scotland
5 Charlotte Square
Edinburgh EH2 4DU

Natural History Museum
Cromwell Road
London SW7 5BD

Nuclear Electric plc
Barnett Way
Barnwood
Gloucester GL4 7RS

Nuclear Industry Radioactive Waste
   Executive (NIREX)
Curie Avenue
Harwell OX11 0RA

Overseas Development
   Administration (ODA)
94 Victoria Street
London SW1E 5JL

Peak National Park Study Centre
Losehill Hall
Castleton
Derbyshire S30 2WB

Population Concern
231 Tottenham Court Road
London W1P 9AE

Powergen
Haslucks Green Road
Shirley
Solihull
West Midlands B90 4PD

Prince of Wales Committee
Room 11
Burrows Chambers
East Burrows Road
Swansea SA1 1RF

Ramblers' Association
1–5 Wandsworth Road
London SW8 2XX

Rare Breeds Survival Trust
National Agricultural Centre
Stoneleigh
Kenilworth
Warwickshire CV8 2RX

Royal Agricultural Society of England
National Agricultural Centre
Stoneleigh
Kenilworth
Warwickshire CV8 2RX

Royal Botanic Gardens
Kew
Richmond
Surrey TW9 3AB

Royal Commission on Environmental
   Pollution
Church House
Great Smith Street
London SW1P 3BL

Royal Entomological Society
41 Queen's Gate
London SW7 5HU

Royal Forestry Society
102 High Street
Tring
Herts HP23 4AH

Royal Geographical Society
1 Kensington Gore
London SW7 2AR

Royal Institute of British Architects
   (RIBA)
66 Portland Place
London W1N 4AD

Royal Society of Arts
8 John Adam Street
London WC2N 6EZ

Royal Society for Nature
   Conservation (RSNC)
The Green
Witham Park
Waterside South
Lincoln LN5 2JR

Royal Society for the Prevention of
   Cruelty to Animals (RSPCA)
Causeway
Horsham
West Sussex RH12 1HG

Royal Society for the Protection of
   Birds (RSPB)
The Lodge
Sandy
Bedfordshire SG19 2BL

Royal Town Planning Institute
26 Portland Place
London W1N 4BE

Schools Partnership Worldwide
1 Catton Street
London WC1R 4AB

Scottish Civic Trust
24 George Square
Glasgow G2 1EF

Scottish Conservation Projects
Balallan House
21 Allan Park
Stirling FK8 2QG

Scottish Education & Action for
   Development (SEAD)
29 Nicolson Square
Edinburgh EH8 9BX

Scottish Environmental Education
   Council
Dept of Environmental Science
University of Stirling
Stirling FK9 4LA

Scottish Field Studies Association
Kindrogan Field Centre
Enochdhu
Blairgowrie
Perthshire PH10 7PG

Scottish Hydro-Electric
16 Rothesay Terrace
Edinburgh
Scotland EH3 7SE

Scottish Wildlife Trust
25 Johnstone Terrace
Edinburgh EH1 2NH

Shell Better Britain Campaign
Red House
Hill Lane
Great Barr
Birmingham B43 6LZ

Society for the Interpretation of
   Britain's Heritage
31 Deansgate Lane
Formby
Merseyside L37 3LE

The Soil Association
86–88 Colston Street
Bristol
Avon BS1 5BB

SSEB
Scottish Power
Cathcart House
Spean Street
Glasgow G44 4BE

Think Green
Premier House
43–48 New Street
Birmingham B2 4LJ

Tidy Britain Group
The Pier
Wigan
Greater Manchester WN3 4EX

Tourism Concern
Froebel College
Roehampton Lane
London SW15 5PU

Town and Country Planning
  Association
17 Carlton House Terrace
London SW1Y 5AS

Transport 2000
3rd Floor
Walkden House
10 Melton Street
London NW1 2EJ

Tree Council
35 Belgrave Square
London SW1X 8QN

UK Atomic Energy Authority
  Technology
11 Charles II Street
London SW1Y 4QP

UK Centre for Economic and
  Environmental Development
  (UK CEED)
Suite E
3 Kings Parade
Cambridge CB2 1SJ

UK 2000
Unit 101
Butlers Wharf Business Centre
45 Curlew Street
London SE1 2ND

Ulster Society for the Preservation of
  the Countryside
West Winds
Carney Hill
Holywood
County Down BT18 0JR

Ulster Wildlife Trust
Barnett's Cottage
Barnett Demesne
Malone Road
Belfast B19 5PB

UNICEF
55–56 Lincoln's Inn Fields
London WC1A 3NB

United Nations Information Centre
20 Buckingham Gate
London SW1E 6LB

Universities Federation for Animal
  Welfare
8 Hamilton Close
South Mimms
Potters Bar
Hertfordshire EN6 3QD

Urban Wildlife Trust
Unit 213
Jubilee Trades Centre
130 Pershore Street
Birmingham B5 6ND

Voluntary Service Overseas (VSO)
317–325 Putney Bridge Road
London SW15 2PN

Waste Watch
68 Grafton Way
London W1P 5LE

Watch
The Green
Witham Park
Waterside South
Lincoln LN5 7JR

Water Services Association
1 Queen Anne's Gate
London SW1H 9BT

Welsh Centre for International Affairs
Temple of Peace
Cathays Park
Cardiff CF1 3AP

The Wildfowl & Wetlands Trust
Slimbridge
Gloucestershire GL2 7BT

Wind Energy Trust
345 Ruislip Road
Southall
Middlesex

Woodcraft Folk
13 Ritherdon Road
London SW17 8QE

The Woodland Trust
Autumn Park
Dysart Road
Grantham
Lincs NG31 6LL

World Development Movement
  (WDM)
25 Beehive Place
London SW9 7QR

World Society for the Protection of
  Animals
Park Place
10 Lawn Lane
London SW8 1UD

World Wide Fund for Nature (UK)
Panda House
Weyside Park
Godalming
Surrey GU7 1XR

YMCA National Centre
Lakeside
Ulverston
Cumbria LA12 8BD

Young Ornithologists' Club
RSPB Youth Unit
The Lodge
Sandy
Bedfordshire SG19 2DL

Young People's Trust for the
  Environment and Nature
95 Woodbridge Road
Guildford
Surrey GU1 4PY

Youth Hostel Association (England &
  Wales) (YHA)
Trevelyan House
8 St Stephen's Hill
St Albans
Hertfordshire AL1 2DY

Youth Hostels Association of
  Northern Ireland
56 Bradbury Place
Belfast B17 1RU
Northern Ireland

The Zoological Society of London
Regent's Park
London NW1 4RY

Australia

Alternative Technology Association
Address as Environment Centre

Australian Association for
  Environmental Education (AAEE)
PO Box 12003
Elizabeth Street
Brisbane
QLD 4002

Australian Forestry Council
GPO Box 858
Canberra ACT 2601

Australian Trust for Conservation
  Volunteers
13 Duke Street
South Caulfield 3162
16 Victoria Street
Ballarat 3350

Bird Observers Club of Australia
183 Springvale Road
Nunawading 3131

Built Environment Education
  Network
Education Division
Royal Australian Institute of
  Architects
PO Box 373
Manuka ACT 2603

Centre for Education and Research in
  Environmental Strategies
8 Lee Street
Brunswick East 3057

Commissioner for the Environment
1st Floor
477 Collins Street
Melbourne 3000

Department of the Arts, Sport, the
  Environment, Tourism &
  Territories
Environment Education &
  Information Unit
GPO Box 787
Canberra ACT 2601
Price Waterhouse Building
19–23 Moore Street
Turner
Canberra 2601

Department of Conservation &
  Environment
Information Centre
240 Victoria Parade
East Melbourne 3002

Energy Information Centre
139 Flinders Street
Melbourne 3000

Environment Centre (Victoria)
1st Floor
Ross House
247 Flinders Lane
Melbourne 3000

Environment Protection Authority
6th Floor
477 Collins Street
Melbourne 3000

Environmental Choice
4th Floor
477 Collins Street
Melbourne 3000

Field Naturalists Club of Victoria
National Herbarium
1 Birdwood Avenue
South Yarra 3141

Friends of the Earth
222 Brunswick Street
(PO Box 222)
Fitzroy 3065

Geography Teachers Association of
  Victoria
503 Burke Road
Camberwell South 3134

Greenhouse Unit
Office of the Environment
4th Floor
477 Collins Street
Melbourne 3000

Greening Australia Vic. Education
  Program
National Herbarium
1 Birdwood Avenue
South Yarra 3141

Greenpeace Australia
389 Lonsdale Street
Melbourne 3000

Health Department Victoria
Information Centre
Ground Floor
555 Collins Street
Melbourne 3000

Institute for Earth Education,
  Australia
GPO Box 124A
Melbourne 3001

Marine Studies Centre
PO Box 138
Queenscliff 3225

National Trust of Australia (Victoria)
Tasma Terrace
Parliament Place
East Melbourne 3002

Rainforest Action Group
PO Box 3217GG
Melbourne 3001

Royal Society for the Prevention of
  Cruelty to Animals (Vic.)
3 Burwood Highway
Burwood East 3151

Science Teachers Association of
  Victoria
191 Royal Parade
Parkville 3052

Victorian Association for
  Environmental Education
Address as Environment Centre

Victorian Conservation Trust
49 Spring Street
Melbourne 3000

Victorian Environmental Education
  Council
Level 22
Rialto Towers South
525 Collins Street
Melbourne 3000

World Wide Fund for Nature
Address as Environment Centre

Worldwide Home Environmentalists
  Network
PO Box 186
Carnegie 3163

United States of America

The Acid Rain Foundation, Inc.
1410 Varsity Dr.
Raleigh, NC 27606

Alliance for Environmental Education
10751 Ambassador Dr.
Suite 201
Manassas, VA 22110

American Forestry Association
PO Box 2000
Washington, DC 20013

American Geographical Society
156 Fifth Ave
Suite 600
New York, NY 10010–7002

Animal Protection Institute of
   America
2831 Fruitridge Rd
Sacramento, CA 95822

Center for Environmental Information
46 Prince St
Rochester, NY 14607

Center for Marine Conservation
1725 DeSales St NW
Suite 500
Washington, DC 20036

Conservation International
1051 18th St NW
Suite 1000
Washington, DC 20036

The Cousteau Society, Inc.
930 W 21st St
Norfolk, VA 23517

Defenders of Wildlife
1244 19th St NW
Washington, DC 20036

Earthwatch
PO Box 403
680 Mt Auburn St
Watertown, MA 02172

Environmental Action &
   Environmental Action Foundation
6930 Carroll Ave
Suite 600
Takoma Park, MD 20912

Environmental Data Research
   Institute
797 Elmwood Ave
Rochester, NY 14620

Friends of the Earth
218 D St SE
Washington, DC 20003

Greenpeace USA
1436 U St NW
Washington, DC 20009

Inform
381 Park Ave S
New York, NY 10016

Institute for Conservation Leadership
2000 P St NW
Suite 413
Washington, DC 20036

Institute for Earth Education
PO Box 288
Warrenville, IL 60555

International Fund for Animal
   Welfare
411 Main St
Yarmouth Port, MA 02675

Kids for a Clean Environment (Kids
   FACE)
PO Box 158254
Nashville, TN 37215

National Association of Biology
   Teachers
11250 Roger Bacon Dr. 19
Reston, VA 22090

National Audubon Society
950 Third Ave
New York, NY 10022

National Wildflower Research Center
2600 FM 973 N
Austin, TX 78725-4201

National Wildlife Federation
1400 16th St NW
Washington, DC 20036

The Nature Conservancy
1815 N Lynn St
Arlington, VA 22209

North American Association for
  Environmental Education
PO Box 400
Troy, OH 45373

Rainforest Action Network
301 Broadway
Suite A
San Francisco, CA 94133

Sierra Club
730 Polk St
San Francisco, CA 94109

United Nations Environment
  Programme
2 United Nations Plaza
Room DC2–303
New York, NY 10017

The Wilderness Society
900 17th St NW
Washington, DC 20006

Wildlife Conservation International
Bronx Zoo
Bronx, NY 10460

World Resources Institute
1709 New York Ave NW
Suite 700
Seventh Floor
Washington, DC 20006

World Society for the Protection of
  Animals
PO Box 190
Boston, MA 02130

World Wildlife Fund
1250 24th St NW
Suite 400
Washington, DC 20037

Canada

Environment Canada
Information Directorate
Ottawa
Ontario, KIA 0H3

North American Association for
  Environmental Education (*see* USA)

Council of Outdoor Educators of
  Ontario
Forest Valley Outdoor Education
  Centre
60 Blue Forest Drive
Downsview
Ontario, M3H 4W5

Canadian Association of UNESCO
  Clubs
22 Kew Beach Avenue
Toronto
Ontario, M4L 1B7

Project Wild
Leslie Frost Centre
Dorset
Ontario, P0A 1E0

Energy Educators of Ontario
517 College Street
Suite 406
Toronto
Ontario, M6G 4A2

Canadian Camping Association
1806 Avenue Road
Toronto
Ontario, M5M 3Z1

Canadian Forestry Association
65 Rue Brunswick St
Fredericton
New Brunswick, E3B 1G5

Space does not permit full addresses
of other helpful organizations.
Environment Canada will provide details of the following:

Ontario Association of Geography
  and Environmental Educators
UN Association of Canada
Organisations connected with the
  natural world
Canadian branches of international
  organisations

New Zealand

New Zealand Natural Heritage
  Foundation
Massey University
Palmerston North

Global Rivers EE Programme
'GREEN' network
NZ Natural Heritage Foundation
Massey University
Palmerston North

Global Issues School Links
Freyberg High School
Palmerston North

United Nations Association
Wakefield Street
Wellington

Eco-School Network
Ashurst Primary School
Palmerston North
or
Eco-School Network
NZ Natural Heritage Foundation
Massey University
Palmerston North

The NZ Natural Heritage Foundation will provide details of the following organizations of help to environmental education:

Civic Trust
Historic Places Trust
Royal NZ Forest and Bird Protection
   Society
Maruia Society
Native Forest Restoration Trust
Auckland Botanical Society
NZ branches of International
   organizations

Appendices

Agenda 21, Earth Summit

For environmental educators, Section IV, Chapter 4 of UNCED's Agenda 21 – on 'education, public awareness and training' – is of primordial interest. 'The Declaration and recommendations of the Tbilisi Conference on Environmental Education', the pertinent chapter states, 'organized by UNESCO and UNEP and held in 1977, have provided the fundamental principles for the proposals' of UNCED.

The programme areas described are: (1) reorienting education towards sustainable development; (2) increasing public awareness; and (3) promoting training. The first programme area includes as its objectives: (a) to endorse recommendations of the World Conference on Education for All (Jomtien, Thailand, 1990), which included environmental literacy; (b) to achieve environmental and developmental awareness in all sectors of society on a worldwide scale as soon as possible; (c) to strive to achieve the accessibility of environmental and development education, linked to social education, from primary school age through adulthood to all groups of people; and (d) to promote integration of environment and development concepts, including demography, in all educational programmes, in particular the analysis of the causes of major environment and development issues in a local context, drawing on the best available scientific evidence and other appropriate sources of knowledge, and giving special emphasis to the further training of decision makers at all levels.

The activities proposed for the first programme area include, in turn:

(a) *Governments should strive to update or prepare strategies aimed at integrating environment and development as a cross-cutting issue into education at all levels within the next three years. A thorough review of curricula should be undertaken to ensure a multidisciplinary approach, with environment and development issues and their socio-cultural and demographic aspects and linkages.*

(b) Countries are encouraged to set up advisory national environmental education coordinating bodies or round tables of representatives of various environmental, developmental, educational, gender and other interests, including non-governmental organizations, to help mobilize and facilitate different population groups and communities to assess their own needs and to develop the necessary skills to create and implement their own environment and development initiatives.

(c) Educational authorities, with the appropriate assistance from community groups of non-governmental organizations, are recommended to assist or set up pre-service and in-service training programmes for all teachers, administrators, and educational planners, as well as non-formal educators in all sectors, addressing the nature and methods of environmental and development education.

(d) Relevant authorities should ensure that every school is assisted in designing environmental activity work plans, with the participation of students and staff.

(e) Educational authorities should promote proven educational methods and the development of innovative teaching methods for educational settings. They should also recognize appropriate traditional education systems in local communities.

(f) Within two years, the UN system should undertake a comprehensive review of its educational programmes, encompassing training and public awareness, to reassess priorities and reallocate resources. The UNESCO/UNEP International Environmental Education Programme [IEEP] should, in cooperation with the appropriate bodies of the United Nations system, governments, non-governmental organizations and others, establish a programme within two years to integrate the decisions of the Conference into the existing UN framework adapted to the needs of educators at different levels and circumstances.

(g) There is a need to strengthen, within five years, information exchange by enhancing technologies and capacities necessary to promote environmental and developmental education and public awareness.

(h) Countries could support university and other tertiary activities and networks for environmental and developmental education. Cross-disciplinary courses could be made available to all students. Existing regional networks and activities and national university actions which promote research and common teaching approaches on sustainable development should be built upon, and new partnerships and bridges created with the business and other independent sectors, as well as with all countries for technology, know-how, and knowledge exchange.

(i) Countries, assisted by international organizations, non-governmental organizations and other sectors, could strengthen or establish national or regional centres of excellence in interdisciplinary research and education in environmental and developmental sciences, law and the management of specific environmental problems.

(j) Countries should facilitate and promote non-formal education activities at the local, regional and national levels by cooperating with and supporting the efforts of non-formal educators and other community-based organization. The appropriate bodies of the United Nations system in cooperation with non-governmental organizations should encourage the development of an international network for the achievement of global educational aims. At the national and local levels, public and scholastic forums should discuss environmental and development issues, and suggest sustainable alternatives to policy makers.

(k) Educational authorities, with appropriate assistance of non-governmental organizations, including women's and indigenous people's organizations, should promote all kinds of adult education programmes for continuing education in environment and development, basing activities around elementary/secondary schools and local problems. These authorities and industry should encourage business, industrial and agricultural schools to include such topics in their curricula.

As for the means of implementation:

More support for education, training and public awareness activities related to environmental and development could be provided by: (a) giving higher priority to those sectors in budget allocations, protecting them from structural cutting requirements; (b) shifting allocations within existing education budgets in favour of primary education, with focus on environment and development; (c) promoting conditions where a larger share of the cost is borne by local communities, with rich communities assisting poorer ones; (d) obtaining additional funds from private donors concentrating on the poorest countries, and those with rates of literacy below 40 per cent; (e) encouraging debt for education swaps; (f) lifting restrictions on private schooling and increasing the flow of funds from and to non-governmental organizations, including small-scale grass-roots organizations; (g) promoting the effective use of existing facilities, for example multiple school shifts, fuller development of open universities and other long-distance teaching; (h) facilitating low-cost or no-cost use of mass media for education purposes; and (i) encouraging twinning of universities in developed and developing countries.

UNICEF, UNESCO, UNDP and non-governmental organizations should develop support programmes to involve young people and children in environment and development issues.

Actually environmental education, training and information do not end with the special section devoted to them in Agenda 21. They recur consistently as components of almost all thirty-nine chapters of UNCED's programme of action from now until the 21st century, falling under 'capacity building' primarily, but also under 'human resources development' and similar subsections.

Indeed, 'capacity-building', or the strengthening and building of a nation's capacity for environmentally sound, sustainable development, is viewed as a key factor, that is, the capacity of both a country's people and its institutions. 'A fundamental goal of capacity-building', it is further stated, 'is to enhance [their] ability to evaluate and address the crucial questions related to policy choices and modes of implementation among development options' with an informed understanding of both the potentials and limits of the environment, a need shared by all nations.

Building this capacity, Agenda 21 stresses, means not only a country's own efforts, but also a partnership with the international community in the improvement of the level of environmental and development skills, knowledge and technical know-how on the part of individuals, groups and institutions. People participation and responsibility are an essential part of environmental protection and sustainable development. Education, training and public awareness are essential factors. So is strengthening the roles of women, youth, indigenous peoples, farmers, local officials, trade unions, business and industry, and the scientific community.

Governments are to encourage the emergence of an informed consumer public by providing information on the consequences of consumption choices and behaviour in terms of environmental impact and one's own health. In this connection, more emphasis should be placed on including the subject of environmental health in the curricula of secondary schools and universities and on generally educating the public.

Governments should ensure adequately educated people to undertake and participate in the harmonization of environmental concerns and development at all stages of the decision-making and implementation process. To do this, they should improve education by including interdisciplinary approaches in technical, vocational and university curricula. They should also undertake systematic training of government personnel, planners and managers on a regular basis, giving priority to integrative approaches and planning and management techniques.

Source: *Connect*, UNESCO-UNEP environmental newsletter, Vol. XVII, no. 2, June 1992

Appendix B

Environmental education in Scotland

The Scottish education system is entirely different from that in England, Wales and Northern Ireland. The Scottish Office Education Department under the Secretary of State for Scotland oversees all matters of formal education in Scotland. A review of the curriculum, 5–14 has been carried out over the past four years. The Scottish Consultative Council on the Curriculum was served with the task of reviewing the curriculum. It was divided into six curriculum areas:

1 Language
2 Mathematics
3 Environmental studies
4 Expressive arts
5 Moral and religious studies
6 Cross-curricular areas.

Review and Development Groups (they may be considered as the equivalent of the Task Groups of the English National Curriculum Council) were set up for each. As a result of their reports, published by the Scottish Office Education Department for consultation, guidelines for (1) and (2) have been produced. For (4), (5) and (6) work is still in progress; for (3), which includes our area of interest, a consultation process has now been undertaken.

In April 1993 the report by the working group on environmental education produced *Learning for Life: A National (Scotland) Strategy for Environmental Education in Scotland*.[1] This was distributed to all interested parties by the Secretary of State for Scotland for comment. The report of some 100 pages rehearses all the arguments for environmental education such as have been contained in documents over the years and which we have mentioned earlier in this book. Firm decisions about the role of environmental education in the curriculum of Scottish schools still seem to be a long way off. If the national strategy for environmental education outlined in the report is implemented our curriculum area will be well set in Scottish schools. The consultation process continues.

Environmental studies includes all science, geography, modern studies, technology, economics, domestic studies, history and health. It is interesting to note that a certain measure of integration is implied by the subject grouping under the curriculum area of environmental studies. With regard to the sixth group looking at cross-curricular areas it is likely that their report will be published in due course as teaching and learning support material. Environmental education will probably be one of the themes. There are other aspects of the Scottish system beyond this review which include environmental education, as with sixth form studies. It is to be noted that the Secretary of State for Scotland produced a report on Environmental Education.

The Scottish Environmental Education Council was established in 1977. It has broadly similar aims to the Council for Environmental Education, with whom it works closely on UK matters. It is based at the Department of Environmental Science, University of Stirling, Stirling FK9 4LA.

NOTE

1 The Scottish Office (1983) *Learning for Life* from:

The Scottish Office Library
Room 2/64
New St Andrew's House
Edinburgh EH1 3TG

Environmental education in the Welsh school 5–16 curriculum

The main components of the Curriculum Cymreig Wales are the eight aspects of learning, one of which is *social and environmental*. The principal features of this aspect are:

- Developing a sense of place, space and environment, time and context.
- Developing understanding of:
    the physical environment and human influences on it
    the past and its influence on the present
    the human environment and the interrelatedness of individuals, groups and societies
    the operation of institutions in society
    the nature, causes and effects of economic and industrial activity.

It is recognized that statutory subjects which make major contributions to the social and environmental aspect of learning are geography, history, science, English/Welsh, religious education, and modern foreign languages. Environmental education is recognized as a theme of all the remaining aspects of learning. The principal features of these which apply to environmental education in each are:

Expressive and aesthetic
Developing emotional and intellectual response to sensory experience.

Linguistic and literary
Developing:
    effective communication in speaking and listening, reading and writing
    enjoyment and fascination in the use of language.

Mathematical
Developing:
    ability to think logically and analytically
    positive personal qualities and attitudes
    appreciation of the wonder and excitement of mathematics.

Physical and recreational
Developing personal qualities related to perseverance and the pursuit of excellence; coping with success and failure and cooperating with others in individual and team activities.

Scientific
Developing:
    ability to use scientific methods of enquiry in an imaginative and disciplined way
    understanding of physical, biological and social phenomena in terms of scientific concepts and theories
    balanced appreciation of the power and limitations of science as a human activity
    positive personal qualities and attitudes.

Spiritual and moral
Developing:
    feeling and convictions about the significance of human life and the world as a whole
    a sense of fairness and justice.
Developing understanding of:
    moral and ethical issues
    codes of human behaviour.

Technological
Developing:
    ability to apply knowledge and skills to practical tasks, operating within a range of constraints
    ability to think and act imaginatively and creatively
    critical awareness of the role and effects of technology in cultures and societies
    positive personal qualities and attitudes.

Statutory subjects which make major contributions

Art	Mathematics
English	Science
Welsh	Technology
Music	Religious education
PE	Geography
Modern foreign languages	History

Other subjects and activities

Classics
Other languages
Economics/business studies
Social science

Preparing an environmental education policy: the use of matrices

The following is taken from Shropshire's environmental education guide.

There are two matrices here – one for knowledge and understanding and one for skills, attitudes and values. These can be used for both raising awareness and attempting to discover where environmental education is currently taking place – that is the process of 'recognition'. These are best used as the basis for a discussion with subject specialists. The coordinator should find time to go through the matrices with them in order to develop understanding and raise awareness of environmental education.

It might be useful to weigh the responses so that emphasis and import-ance can be estimated. One way of doing this is to use a 1 to 3 scoring system, with 1 being given to an item that is given some attention or coverage to 3 which indicates that an item has been covered or dealt with in some depth.

When the survey has been completed it would be useful to transfer all the information onto a 'master sheet'. This should be a very large piece of paper so that all results can be included. When this has been completed, gaps in the school's environmental education provision can be seen in addition to showing those items that are covered by a number of subjects. It can also provide an indication of where action and further work should take place.

An extract from part of the attitudes and values survey sheet is reproduced below.

Attitudes and values	Year				
	1	2	3	4	5
1 A willingness to adopt and demonstrate a critical stance to information					
2 A willingness to give reasons for particular views or acts relating to the environment					
3 A respect and understanding of other people's reasoning for particular acts or views					
4 A respect for evidence on forming and holding views about human/ environment interaction					
5 Willingness to change attitudes and values in the light of evidence					
6 Value fairness and care as criteria for decision making about the environment					
7 Value freedom to choose between particular environmental actions					
8 Toleration of a diversity of ideas, beliefs, values and interests					
9 Value the opportunity for a personal interest in and response to environmental issues					

Source: From *A Guide to Developing Environmental Education in Shropshire Secondary Schools*, Shropshire County Council, 1992

An environmental audit as a stimulus to the construction and implementation of a school policy for environmental education

SUBJECT-BASED APPROACH

Various aspects of the audit are introduced into the work scheme for individual subjects as follows.

Physics and/or technology

- the insulation properties of different materials, e.g. glass, wool, fabric, bricks (single wall), bricks (double wall with and without insulation material in cavity), wood, plaster board, compressed paper board, compressed chipboard, slate, tile, thatch, roofing felt
- heat losses through different thicknesses of glass fibre, polystyrene beans, polystyrene sheeting, other loft materials
- infra red survey of external walls and roof of school. Relating survey pictures to real situation
- noise surveys
- energy supplies
- alternative energy

Environmental issues: global warming, energy conservation, noise pollution

Chemistry

- effects of sunlight on different materials
- the effect of the passage of rays through various materials
- the creation of ozone by photochemical processes
- analysis of exhaust fumes from vehicles, heating system, kitchen extractors, laboratory extractors
- pH measurement of water supplies and other water areas
- CFC gases

Environmental issues: acid rain, air pollution, ozone creation and destruction

Biology

- photosynthesis – estimation of CO_2 extraction of plants and trees on or near school estate
- survey of animal and insect life in and around school
- encouraging wildlife

Environmental issues: global warming, species diversity

Geography

- waste disposal locally
- mapping of scientific data
- local water supplies
- council services

Environmental issue: waste disposal

History

- study of local records to ascertain covenants or restrictions on developments such as erection of wind turbine on roof of school

Mathematics and/or information technology

- presentation of scientific data
- reading and study of electric, gas and other service meters
- examination and interpretation of service accounts

English

- business letter writing
- preparing questionnaires
- interviewing local experts
- summarizing reports
- production of a 'green' newsletter

Physical education

- play areas
- safety aspects around the school

Religious education

- local community groups
- caring for the neighbourhood

The National Curriculum for New Zealand

Environmental education will provide a focus for learning experiences and outcomes in all the essential learning areas identified in the National Curriculum for New Zealand. Figure F gives quotations from that curriculum document and indicates some of the connections between environmental education and the essential learning areas.

The following are extracts from the New Zealand consultation document on Essential Learning Areas.

THE ESSENTIAL LEARNING AREAS

The National Curriculum spells out the broad knowledge, understanding, skills, and qualities which students should develop. These are organized under the Essential Learning Areas and the Essential Skills. They provide the basis for the development of the more specific National Curriculum Objectives, which make clear to parents, students, and teachers what should be taught and learned in schools.

The National Curriculum specifies seven Essential Learning Areas which describe in broad terms the knowledge and understanding required by all students. This does not mean that schools must divide the curriculum into seven learning areas. Schools may achieve a coherent and balanced curriculum in many ways. Whatever plan is adopted, schools will be required to ensure that all students undertake study in each of the Learning Areas during their years of compulsory schooling, and, in the case of English, mathematics, science, and technology, to the end of F5.

The Essential Learning Areas are broad categories of knowledge and understanding. They take into account the common curriculum experience of schooling today, both in New Zealand and overseas. This broad classification has the following advantages:

- It is designed to provide flexibility for schools to devise programmes

The Essential Learning Areas:

the essential categories of knowledge and understanding to be developed by all students.

   Language
   Mathematics
   Science and environment
   Technology
   Social sciences
   The arts
   Physical and personal development

MATHEMATICS
'Students will be enabled to solve a range of problems using the skills and tools which mathematics provides.' Environmental issues provide a focus for mathematics

LANGUAGE
'The ability to listen, speak, read, write and express oneself with confidence and skill' will be promoted as students develop awareness of their environments

SCIENCE AND ENVIRONMENT
The curriculum should give students an opportunity to explore environmental issues important to their communities, to New Zealand, to the Pacific, and the wider world

SOCIAL SCIENCE
'Students will understand the relationship between their rights and responsibilities as citizens in a democratic society. They will also be challenged to think clearly and critically about human behaviour and values in order to make reasoned choices.' Environmental issues are central to citizenship education

EDUCATION ABOUT, IN, AND FOR THE ENVIRONMENT

TECHNOLOGY
A technology programme should enable students to examine the impact of technology on people, the environment, and the workplace. It should also help them to make appropriate decisions about the use of technology in relation to the environment, the economy, and society

PHYSICAL AND PERSONAL DEVELOPMENT
'Education which develops students' ability to build responsible and satisfying relationships with a range of people at school, at home, and in the wider community.' Appreciation of people and personal relationships as part of the environment

THE ARTS
'The creative arts will encourage students to investigate their own values and those of others, including aesthetic and spiritual dimensions. Through the arts, their knowledge and understanding of the cultural heritages (and environments) of New Zealand and other countries will be developed. They will be given opportunities to develop satisfying leisure interests.'

Figure F Environmental education in the essential learning areas

Source: Environmental Education for Aotearoa/New Zealand, Booklet One, *Overview for the Curriculum*, New Zealand Natural Heritage Foundation, Massey University, Palmerston North, New Zealand

appropriate to the needs of their particular students. Schools may decide how their curriculum is to be organized and taught. They might prefer approaches other than the subject-based curriculum (such as integrated learning, topic, thematic, or modular approaches, or a combination of these).

- It suggests a more integrated view of learning.
- It allows the curriculum to respond more easily to changes in society and the economy.
- It is consistent with recent measures devolving decision making to school communities.
- It should prevent premature specialization and create a wider base from which students can make training and employment decisions later in their school life.

Relationship of the Essential Learning Areas to subjects and school courses

Traditionally, New Zealand schools have approached the curriculum through subjects. While subject syllabuses will continue to be developed to provide guidance to teachers, the aim in future is to ensure that the curriculum offered by each school covers all the Essential Learning Areas. The Essential Learning Areas are broad categories which are cross-curricular in nature and which enable the grouping of subjects similar in kind.

Science and environment

The curriculum should provide for learning which develops students' experience and understanding of the physical, biological, and technological world, their understanding of how people interact with their environment, and their ability and confidence to solve problems in scientific ways.

Science is fundamental to understanding our world. It helps people to investigate phenomena systematically, to clarify ideas, to ask questions, to test explanations through measurement and observation, and to use their findings to establish the worth of an idea.

Through this area of learning, students will be enabled to develop a clearer understanding of aspects of the world around them: living things, the environment, matter, energy, and industrial and technological processes. Science education should enable students to develop their understanding of the changing nature of science and its influence on people's lives.

Environmental education enables students to understand how people modify, respond to, and conserve their environment. The curriculum should give students the opportunity to explore environmental issues important to their community, to New Zealand, to the Pacific, and to the wider world; and it should give them the knowledge and skills to make appropriate decisions about the use of resources and of the environment.

Teacher training exercise

Aims

- To initiate a debate on environmental education as a cross-curricular theme to stimulate the environmental awareness of each subject department
- To encourage cooperation between subject departments
- To establish the role of the coordinator for environmental education

Objectives

- To contribute to the preparation of a school environmental education curricular policy
- To explore the ways in which each subject department could contribute to the student's understanding of a global environmental issue
- To introduce staff to a major global issue and its relevance to the school curriculum
- To establish the concept of an environmental audit

Basically there are major global environmental problems all interconnected but for convenience established as:

World population problems
Greenhouse effect
Ground level ozone and ozone layer depletion
Acid rain
Waste
Antarctica
Bio-diversity

Few of them, if any, are tackled in any holistic way in schools. At the same time, little attention is being given to environmental education as a cross-curricular theme of the National Curriculum for England and Wales or as a curricular area in other regions. Even fewer schools have established an environmental policy. Initial teacher training exercises on in-service training days should, on occasions, be used to tackle these matters in a comprehensive way. An example of an exercise which has been successful in achieving some or all of these aims and objectives is detailed here.

The problem is to determine the contributions which the major subject departments can make to tackle the environmental problem of ground level ozone and ozone layer depletion. Nine individual aspects of contribution are identified:

Curriculum content
Practical work in/out classroom
Lunch/after school/club activities
School grounds/buildings/displays
Special timetable activities
Special events (school or subject)
Assemblies
Contribution to environmental audit
Support from other subjects

For each individual aspect every subject department is asked to detail the various items it can contribute to the aspect in question. It is recognized that detailed knowledge of the ozone problem may be sketchy so that it is essential that a briefing paper (Figure G) is presented by the coordinator giving broad details. The exercise requires the coordinator to organize the completed work sheets into a coherent whole and eventually to incorporate the findings into the environmental education policy and curriculum document. What follows details the results of one such exercise without any attempt to 'polish' the documents into an acceptable school policy.

ENVIRONMENTAL EDUCATION CROSS-CURRICULAR EXERCISE

ENVIRONMENTAL ISSUE: Ground level ozone and ozone layer depletion

Curriculum content

History

11–13

History of medicine – environmental health
Discoveries of ozone. CFC
Industrial Revolution

OZONE

$$O_2 = O + O \quad O_2 + O = O_3 \quad O_3 = O + O_2 \qquad \text{equilibrium}$$

←——————— sunlight ———————→   photochemical
reaction

Ozone layer

Dr Jekyll
Blocks UV B & C
Spectrum, rainbow
Skin cancer
CFC (1930—Midgley)
CFCs destroy O_3
   (1973 Molina & Rowland)
   Cl destroys O_3
Aerosols, foam, freezing,
   cleaning, insulation
Antarctic hole
Vortex, Roaring 40s
S. hemisphere spring
Greenhouse gas
Catalytic converter
Lean Burn engine
Electric cars
Alternative fuel
Alternative power
Public transport
Energy conservation
Halons (fire precautions)
Value of research

Ground level ozone

Mr Hyde
Nitrogen oxides, hydrocarbons
Vehicle exhaust
Industrial air pollution
Domestic air pollution
Smog
Nausea, throat, lungs
Secondary pollutant
1956 Clean Air Act

London
Los Angeles, Athens
Temperature inversion
UV B affects plants/animals
WATCH O_3 survey
Nicotine plants
Countermeasures
Montreal Protocol 1987
London O_3 conference 1989
Earth Summit 1992
O_3 friendly products
Sun Smart campaign
Sun protection factor

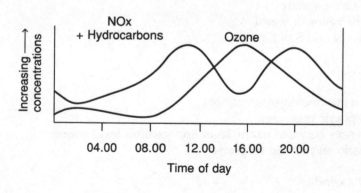

Figure G Briefing paper for participants giving main considerations for teaching a project on ozone. This was expanded upon verbally

Inventions – electricity, etc., motor car, petrol
Hiroshima
London pea soups
Clean Air Act 1956
Historical volcanic eruptions

14–16

Atom bomb testing, etc.
Hiroshima
Oil crisis of 1973

17/18

Do the above in greater depth, allow for development of ideas. (NB – limited in this as have to fit to requirements of the NC.)

Geography

11–13

What is the ozone layer?
What are its benefits?
Why do we need it?
Ozone layer destruction – where is it worse?
What can we do to help?
What is being done in other parts of the world?
Volcanoes
Earth's atmosphere
Climatic zones of world
Seasons N and S of Equator

14–16

Bring it into meteorology classes
Atmospheric processes
Differences between ozone layer and ground level ozone
International/political response
CFCs
World's winds
Polar vortex
Weather station – NO_2 diffuser

17/18

Chemistry of ozone
Ozone layer depletion
Global equality of ozone destruction

Science

11–13

Ozone – where it comes from and its effects on plants and animals, how
  to reduce it
Energy conservation
Alternative energy/power
Biology of skin
Light spectrum
Chemistry of CFC
Use of CFCs – aerosols, fridges, etc.
UV light – the rays of the sun – wavelength
Extinguishing fire-halons
Greenhouse effect/the effect on weather (affected by)
Respiratory disorders (e.g. caused by smog)
Studies of greenhouse effect on Venus (as related to Earth)
Leaded and unleaded petrol
Effect of sun on the skin (protection against sunburn)
What is ozone? Advantages and disadvantages depending where
  located

14–16

Engines, chemistry $O_2 - O_3$ at ground level
Effects on breathing, smog
Asthma
Catalytic converter
Lean Burn engine – electric cars
How refrigeration works, how aerosols work – alternatives and the
  safety of alternatives
Epidemiology – Australia – UV
How ozone stops UV, what is UV?
Teaching about environmental groups and their work
Alternative energy sources
Use of hydrocarbons as an alternative to CFCs – chemistry of hydro-
  carbons topic

17/18

Car fume chemistry
Halides. Various forms of UV
Cancers, emphasizing skin cancers
Complicated chemical reactions of ozone breakdown
Build up and movement of ozone in the atmosphere/temperature inversion
Detailed effects of UV radiation
Origin of atmosphere and ozone layer

Maths

11–13

Grow trees and plants – measure how much they grow
Noise pollution – basic statistics, bar charts, etc.
Collection of own data

14–16

More advanced statistics – pie charts, graphs
'Best buy' problems on ozone friendly products
Graphical display of ozone depletion

17/18

Statistical investigation about ozone
Applied maths – how economical electrical cars would be
School survey of methods of transport
Mathematical modelling

English

11–13

Where the Wind Blows – Raymond Briggs
Newspaper reports
TV news
'Green' poetry anthologies
Compose ozone friendly slogans

14–16

Dr Jekyll and Mr Hyde – Robert Louis Stephenson
Examine newspaper reports of ozone matters
TV news
'Green' poetry anthologies
Discursive essays
TV drama, e.g. *Grange Hill* covering issues
Campaign programme for anti-cancer campaign

17/18

Frankenstein – Mary Shelley
Newspaper reports
TV news
'Green' poetry anthologies
Discursive essays

Practical work in/out classroom

History

11–13

Questionnaires, e.g. leaded/unleaded petrol among staff or students'
    families' cars.

Geography

11–13

Survey of CFC sources in school
Survey of ozone sources in school
Survey of pollution levels around school site

14–16

Survey of CFC sources in the local community
Survey of ozone sources in the local community
Local government response to ozone/CFC issue
Private/commercial response
Survey of pollution levels around community

Science

11-13

Spotting of nicotine plant leaves (watch ozone survey)
Posters of dangers of ozone
Survey of members of staff using unleaded petrol
Tree planting

14–16

Epidermal work on industrial disasters
Investigate CFCs in aerosols
Survey measuring exhaust gases
Measure the amount of ozone in air (machine)
Tree planting and care of previously planted trees
Posters
Presentations, radio interview, video
Graphs

17/18

Data analysis of ozone hole and greenhouse, i.e. evaluating the
    evidence
Monitor exhaust emissions, rural areas, industrial regions
Infra red photography

Maths

11–13

Growing plants measuring their growth
Traffic surveys

14–16

Measure how much ground the school is in, how many trees hence how
    many trees per square foot
Calculate classroom and corridor space, how much cleaning agent is
    needed

17/18

Collecting data on noise pollution in town
Calculating how many trees can be planted within a certain area and
    how much CO_2 they will recycle.

English

11–13

In class – read appropriate novels – *Dr Jekyll and Mr Hyde, Frankenstein,*
stories where characters mess with chemicals (see curriculum content)
Talk about ozone
Frieze – work on walls
Visit a newspaper

14–16

Letters to council about traffic pollution/noise, etc.
In class – discursive writing – arguments for/against
Ozone's effects – cancer?
Look at newspaper articles
Publicity campaign?
Role-play
Drama
Debates
} Factual work (part of GCSE requirement)

17/18

Get students to produce pamphlet for younger children (tell them to
make it interesting)

Lunch/after school/club activities

History

Trips to museums of historical and/or natural scientific nature
Trips to World Development Centre, to investigate ozone problem
worldwide

Geography

Initiate club/group at lunch (including guest speakers) and/or after
school
Arrange visits to local companies especially those involved in packaging
Visit library for sources of information – could be done voluntarily by
pupils in own time
Watch TV programmes if relevant
Read newspapers and collect any articles on the issue

Finding out at home how their family are using and causing ozone and how they could prevent it. Perhaps survey/questionnaire asking family and neighbours what CFC products they have and what alternatives they are using

Visit supermarkets to see what ozone friendly items are on offer

Science

Weather Club – data information
Science Club
School newspaper
Tree planting
Environment Club – bringing items of interest, get outside speakers
Recycling of cans, paper and plastics
Cycling proficiency

Maths

Set up 'Maths Environment Club' concentrating on data collection, etc. that can lead to presentations and displays
Set up 'Modern Languages Environment Club' that can concentrate on pollution in Europe, etc.
Environmentally friendly detentions! Where children pick up litter
'Astronomy Club' that can investigate Venus's massive global warming as a warning to us all!
'Think Green' displays and presentation afternoons (evenings for parents and the public to attend)

English

Environment Club
Fund raising activities
Video shows
Films
Articles in school magazine, or *English in the Environment* magazine
Drama Club – script and perform a play or a group presentation
Lobbying local industry – apply to companies' PROs to find out what they are doing about the environment
Organizing petitions
Lobbying parliament
School visits to parliament
Interviewing local MPs, journalists
Debating Society

School grounds/buildings/displays

History

Recycling scheme: newspapers, crushed cans, plastic, bottles
Energy and heating in school – oil heating
Double/triple glazing
Grow your own vegetables: potatoes, tomatoes, cucumbers, cauli-
flowers, etc.
Environmental displays on fuel consumption, air pollution, etc., smog
Farm on school site: chickens, cows, sheep, goats
Use manure to fertilize soil
Compost heap – all vegetable peel and natural foodstuffs ploughed back
into soil
Plant as many trees and plants as possible and show responsibilities of
looking after them

Geography

Competition for posters to encourage use of CFC free products
School greenhouse
Pond for students – ecology/conservation
Encourage growth of plants/posters
Develop a school recycling campaign
Mural in corridor to illustrate ozone both at ground level and in upper
air

Science

Posters
Promotions for parents' evenings and open days (parental awareness)
Nicotine plants – spots on leaves (direct indication)
Posters from pressure groups
Posters from pupils – fridges, aerosols, skin cancer, catalytic converters,
etc.
Tree planting
Recycling of cans, paper, plastic, glass
Encourage use of bicycles
Encourage cycling proficiency
Fuels used for lighting and heating
Create air quality display with weather information

Maths

Litter collection – tally chart of cans, paper, etc.
Vegetable patch – calculate most efficient usage of land
Calculating how much paint required to paint room
Calculate whether it would be cheaper to use environmentally friendly
   light bulbs although more expensive to buy
Statistical displays on walls, pie charts, etc.
Anti-smoking display with mathematical statistics

English

Frieze – built round work they have done
Displays of writing they have done or posters – what words and designs
   would be the most effective
Outdoor pageant – role-plays/publicity campaigns
From the audit work, write reports to display about measures they could
   take to protect environment; display them next to library/resources
   rooms, etc.
Examining the environment of the school – writing a report for the
   governors/newspaper/council about its good/bad state. Writing poetry
   about what they see, focusing on a particular area/item

Special timetable activities

Geography

11–13

Collecting aerosols
Plant some trees
Identifying CFC products
Growing nicotine plants
Pond hour – construction and maintenance
Start recycling scheme at school – glass, paper, plastics
Weather station – possible satellite link-up in computer rooms

14–16

Visiting local industries
Questionnaires on community awareness
Greenhouse hour
Producing a video (role-play on news items)

Guest speakers on certain subjects
Field trip

17/18

Writing to industries: electricity, coal, oil, gas, to ask what they are
doing for their environment (ozone); to car industry on catalytic
converter installation; to ask local people at a garage if their car uses
unleaded petrol
Write to local MPs on government issues – possible guest speaker

Science

11–13

Tree planting trips
Assemblies
Tutorial work
Environmental activity week
Bicycle instruction

14–16

Monitoring air pollution: car exhausts, ozone, over period of weeks to
see how it changes
Environmental audit

Maths

11–13

Listen to presentation from 14–16 and then follow up work

14–16

Survey of how people travel to/from work/school for statistical analysis.
For presentation to lower school at a level they would understand

17/18

Deeper survey of transport analysis of wider sample group, taking
information from scientific magazines and other relevant literature.
For presentation to whole school

English

11–13

Produce practical guide to recycling, etc.

14–16

'Page to Stage' – drama
Hinckley Times – local newspaper – their policies? – writing articles
Work experience in electricity industry

17/18

Newspaper/magazines – for younger children!

Special events (school or subject)

History

11–13

Recycling – collections by students
Visit recycling plant (if possible)
Perform play – discussing implications for health of smog and air
    pollution, e.g. Dickens
Visit to transport science museum – look at advent of industrial machin-
    ery, cars, burning fuels, etc.

14–16

Sponsored activities to raise money for FOE
Visit to FOE resources centre, look at posters and information packs
    which deal with the depletion of the ozone layer
Alternative fuel – visit to BNFL information centres
Visits by speaker – FOE, BNFL

17/18

Debates – conflicting viewpoints regarding use of energy and wastage

Geography

11–13

Recycling – bottles, newspaper
Newspaper/letter (on recycled paper) – talking about green issues

Sponsored event for skin cancer research
Eminent guest speakers
Ozzy the Ozone club to be set up

14–16

Weathering station (measuring ozone, nitrogen dioxide, sulphur dioxide)

Science

11–13

Traffic survey, measuring pollution
Trip to the Centre for Alternative Technology – wind, power, etc. (whole-school activity)
School WATCH group – nicotine plant survey in school grounds/homes
Activity week – investigations into ozone matters
Visit to dump – assess scheme for disposal of fridges
Thought for the day/week, etc. aim to go through given period without using aerosol, without using car. Can involve staff as well as pupils

14–16

Whole-school Environment Fayre (organized by pupils)
Ozone layer effect of environment week return to natural means (walking, cycling) of getting anywhere
Sun Smart campaign (Australia)
Visit to research establishment looking at ozone problems – weather centre?
Visit car factory – developing Lean Burn engine
Visit production of electric vehicles (electric trains, car development) – catalytic converter production
Work experience – garage – engine tuning for efficiency

17/18

Part of 'A' level project work or work experience placement in garage – emission control – MOT test
Visit to Public Health Department

Maths

11–13

Maths afternoon – green – measuring pollutant levels of different cars
Competition – design a poster for sun protection/sensible sun
   precautions

14–16

Maths booklets – energy efficient houses and heat loss (EMEB)
Topic on this
Growing plant competition – what makes it grow better

17/18

Design – small electric car prototype – design

English

Organize campaigns. Perhaps write leaflets and posters for special days,
   e.g. can collecting
Visit exhibitions plus write up later
Plays covering issues
Visit local National Trust property

Assemblies

History

Industrial Revolution: working in a textile mill, accident down a pit,
   blundering about in a London smog
Talk on CFCs, etc. – when invented, when their harmfulness was
   discovered
Outside speakers – from environmental groups

Geography

Drama and simulations to explain practically any benefits and draw-
   backs ozone may have, involving the children at all levels to increase
   their awareness – personally, locally, nationally, and perhaps most
   important, internationally/globally
Argument/debate – developed world v. less developed world – role-play
   exercises

Science

Pupils could carry out various role-plays on the issues of:
- CFCs in hairsprays and other aerosol cans
- unleaded petrol v. leaded petrol
- getting rid of old fridges safely

Any other issue which directly affects them and where they can do something to alter the situation
Anything in the local/daily press could be incorporated

Maths

Maths is an international language; by supplying statistics can again make the youngsters more aware of the problems of ozone depletion
Class presentation of their own data collections where practical

English

Dramatic re-presentations of traditional stories (Frankenstein, Jekyll and Hyde) along theme of humankind interfering with nature
Readings of creative responses to environmental issues
Students' own dramatic pieces
Biblical and other religious attitudes to the sun. Sun gods, sun worship

Contribution to environmental audit

History

1 Audit of methods of transport to school – foot, car, shared car, school bus, public transport by pupils and teachers
   Changes in recent times
2 School heating – coal and coal mining, oil and North Sea oil
3 Hygiene and history
   Environmental (cleaning buildings) – school
   Personal (deodorants, hairsprays, asthma) – pupils
4 Discovery of tobacco – local pollution and personal choice – cancer, etc. – entitlement to clean air/'no risk breathing'
5 History of Australia – shipping criminals from smog-bound London to pollution-free Australia – Australia and London now – northern hemisphere blame for southern hemisphere problems
   Could be history of LA/Athens
6 History of the car, problems with cars – the 'greening' process of cars to date – a long way to go
   Pedestrianization in inner cities and clean air

Geography

Saving money within the school
Minimize transport costs
Cleaning materials to be pump action, reusable to cut down on aerosol
    use
School fridges to be non-CFC
Packaging to be non-CFC
Recycling schemes, i.e. bottle banks, waste paper, plastics
Alternative energy sources. Solar panels, etc.

Science

Check not to use CFCs or aerosols
Check cleaning agents
Photocopiers and ozone production
Polystyrene cups – what materials does the café use (dining area)?
Promoting – catalytic converters
School minibus – staff cars – exhaust levels
Use of spray cans (CFCs)
Feedback to/from other schools and education authority re policy
Heating/lighting – fuel source?
Insulation – how much makes how much difference
Whole-school information
• simplified/classified scientific basis
• produced information re audit itself
• how to present results to whole school
• what action can be taken

Maths

Assess heat conservation policies in maths department – monitor num-
    ber of days lights left on/external doors open in department. Check
    usage of paper – recycled paper, for scrap, etc. Some plants in the
    rooms
Disinfectants – cleaning materials – environmentally friendly?
Put items from press onto walls of classrooms

English

Abolish Banda in favour of other technology – check spirit used
Recycling drive – aluminium cans, newspapers
Photocopier awareness – cut down on non-essential use
Waste paper and rough paper collection

Recycle obsolete books
Recover old books to make them more attractive
Fundraising for the school through surplus books
Ensure all writing material recyclable

Support from other subjects

History requires from:

Science

Industrial projects – link with Industrial Revolution
Nuclear testing debates, etc.
Medicine – environmental hazards of 18th and 19th centuries
Iron production

Geography

Ozone layer, etc.

English

Industrial Revolution – Dickens, *Hard Times*; Gaskell, *North and South*;
  Disraeli, *The Two Nations*

Geography requires from:

Science

Atmosphere/weather/climate
Catalytic converter
Alternative energy
Conservation of energy
Test quality of air
Quality of exhausts

History

Industrial Revolution
Second World War – scientific development, i.e. nuclear
Consumer society
Politics/internal affairs
Clean Air Act

Maths

Collect data
Graphs
Figures, i.e. CO_2 and NO_2 levels
Computers

English

Creative writing
Reports/advertising literature

Science requires from:

Geography

Weather studies
Pollution levels in various countries
Motion of ozone within atmosphere
Vortex and holes at poles

English

Multicultural studies of areas under threat by environmental pollution
TV/media study of reporting ozone problems
Use of language and politics in public information from government/
    pressure groups/scientists
Role-playing in drama
Play
Poems
Produce a newspaper

History

Cultural history of environmentally aware races
History of Industrial Revolution, with associated pollution

Art

Project on displays increasing environmental awareness of public
Posters

RE

Moral attitudes/responsibilities to care of environment

Maths

Analysis of data relating to ozone depletion/greenhouse effect

Politics

Government policies of environmental issues (i.e. green papers). Work of other countries/governments to reduce pollution and ozone depletion

Economics

Cost effectiveness of ozone friendly industries, catalytic converters, production of lead free petrol

Music

Writing and performing songs or a musical on the subject

IT

Databases

Maths requires from:

Geography

Data/use of databases for statistical work

Physics

Information about how electric cars, etc. work so that mathematical models can be made

Chemistry

Use of equations

Biology

For data on skin cancer for statistical analysis

IT

Use of computers for simulation of ozone problems, also presentation of statistical findings by graphical means

Economics

Information on how marketing products is done so that mathematical problems concerning 'best buys' can be worked out

English requires from:

Art

Make recycled books more attractive

Science

Recommend suitable books on subject of ozone for pupils

All subjects

Read aloud and discuss topics

PE

Generate human power by use of physical exertion of some kind?

A school review of environmental education

Richard Moseley, Secretary of the Environmental Education Advisers' Association and County Adviser for Environmental Education in Cornwall, has suggested that a fairly simple assessment basis for a school review of environmental education can be set up using Table H set out below.

Notes to Table H

The so-called features would fall into three distinct categories.

1 Facts, which could easily be established beyond dispute (e.g. a written policy or a record of a visit)
2 *Tangible evidence*, to which a personal or professional judgement could be applied (e.g. displays, children's work, resource material and development) and
3 *Impressions* made on professional judgements (e.g. commitment shown by pupils, staff dedication and planning, or a continual and persistent involvement by pupils in environmental matters leading to positive attitudes).

The development of such 'features' for a cross-curricular theme can, if one is not careful, become very complex and involved, thus rendering the review exercise impossible. A fairly simple approach has to be adopted if the cross-curricular themes are to have a hope of falling within the review process.

Table H Features suggesting success for environmental education from 5 to 16

	ASSESSMENT BASIS		
Concise description of the features	Facts	Tangible	Impressions
There is a collaboration between most subject areas and a forum for planning to ensure the delivery of programmes and their review	Coordinator appointed	Minutes of meetings. Details of planned meetings	The awareness of a large number of teachers. Lack of repetition for children
There is a planned approach to ensure that all children have a basic understanding of the ecological principles on which all life depends	Documents outlining planned approaches	Children's work. School displays	
A wide range of environments are used, visited and enjoyed to give relevance and reality to learning across a wide range of core and foundation subjects	List of school visits, local and distant environments	Reports of school visits. Relevance noted for different subject areas	Enthusiasm in children and staff for out of school activities
Children are encouraged to debate real environmental issues, both local and global with an approach that is balanced and well informed		Visual displays. Children's work, demonstrating issues-based learning. Report on projects with local community	Open discussions on issues

Concise description of the features	Facts	Tangible	Impressions
Children have the opportunity to come into contact with, to take responsibility for, and develop attitudes towards living things	School nature reserve or ecological garden. Animals and plants kept and reared in school	Children's work. Reports of farm visits. Ecological reports	General interest in living things
The school campus and immediate environment are developed as an educational resource for use on the day-to-day curriculum	Educational developments in school grounds	Children's work. Diaries. Displays	A wide range of subject areas using the school grounds
The school life and organization reflect responsible attitudes to environmental issues	School management plan reflects environmental concern	Reports of environmental projects in school. Existence of groups and clubs with an environmental concern	Concern for waste management, conservation, recycling, etc.
There is a policy statement referring to environmental education as a cross-curricular theme	Policy statement		

Source: Environmental Education, NAEE journal, Vol. 37, summer 1991

Appendix J

Environmental education in the United States

John J. Kirk

On November 16, 1989, President Bush signed into law the National
Environmental Education Act of 1990. This legislation was passed over-
whelmingly in both houses of the Congress and called for the establishment of an Office of Environmental Education within the structure of
the Environmental Protection Agency of the United States. The wording
of the Act states rather bluntly that efforts on the part of the Federal
Government to inform and educate the public concerning the problems
with the natural and built environment was not adequate. The legislation further states that the existing support for development and
training of professionals in environmental fields was insufficient.

This new law calls upon the Federal Government acting through the
Offices of the Environmental Protection Agency (E.P.A.) to work with
local education institutions, State Departments of Education, environmental organizations, non-profit educational groups and private sector
interests in efforts to support the development of curriculum materials,
special projects and other activities, to increase the understanding of the
general public about the natural and built environment and to improve
their awareness of environmental problems that threaten life on the
planet. The Act further states that the E.P.A., through the new Office
of Environmental Education should develop programs to provide
increased financial resources for the purpose of attracting students into
environment professions.

In the Legislation, there was some difficulty defining environmental
education and finally within the framework of the Act passed and
signed by the President, the following language is included:

> Environmental education and environmental education and training,
> mean educational activities and training activities involving elemen-
> tary, secondary and post secondary students, as such terms are
> defined in the state in which they reside.

Obviously this rather broad and loose definition does not specifically
identify the content that should be included in an environmental edu-

cation curriculum. It does, however, indicate the audiences at whom such programs should be directed.

The new law also creates a Federal Task Force on Environmental Education which will be chaired by a representative of the E.P.A. and this Task Force includes government personnel from the Departments of Education, Interior, Agriculture, the National Oceanic and Atmospheric Administration, the Council on Environmental Quality, the Tennessee Valley Authority and the National Science Foundation. The new law also establishes an eleven member Advisory Council on Environmental Education.

Funding for the new Act has been authorized by the Congress.

To supplement federal appropriations, the new law also creates the National Environmental Education and Training Foundation, as a non-profit charitable corporation. The purpose of this Foundation, will be to seek private contributions to supplement government funding provided for E.P.A's environmental education programs. Contributions may not be accepted by this Foundation if they are contingent upon reflecting a particular point of view favoring certain economic interests. Further-more, no contributions may be accepted if they contain an explicit or implied requirement which in any way could benefit the donor and which appears to be inconsistent with the environmental and education goals proposed within the framework of the law.

In addition to activities at the Federal level, several states now have Legislation requiring in varying degrees, environmental education in the schools and teacher training colleges. The oldest such program in the United States, exists in the State of Wisconsin and it is the model that other states hope to some day match. In the late 1980's, the Commonwealth of Pennsylvania also passed a law requiring environ-mental education in the schools and teacher training colleges, which has been well received and well administered within their Department of Education. Since that time, the states of Arizona and Minnesota have passed laws establishing a Master Plan for environmental education within their jurisdiction. In the State of New Jersey, the Governor has established a State Commission on Environmental Education to explore the development of a Master Plan.

Dr John J. Kirk is the Director and Professor of Environmental Studies at the New Jersey School of Conservation, Montclair State College, New Jersey, USA.

Source: *Environmental Education*, NAEE journal,
Vol. 41, winter 1992

Environmental education information system in Kent

Krysia Baczala

Each term every school in Kent receives a big, green, recycled envelope, packed full of information relating to environmental education. Formally known as the 'Environmental Education Information System', the nickname 'Big Green Envelopes' or 'BGE' seems to have become commonly adopted.

The system is funded by Kent County Council's (KCC) Environmental Programme and distribution is possible thanks to the generous sponsorship of the Woolwich Building Society. The envelopes are packaged and prepared by the County Coordinator for environmental education with the frequent help of members of the Environmental Forum.

There are a number of significant features of the BGE that are worthy of note. A fundamental one has to be that the Kent County Council Environment Programme pays for all of its 800 schools to be members of the National Association for Environmental Education, making Kent the largest membership group in the NAEE and as such, the largest 'local organization'. The termly journal of the NAEE is an important element of the contents of the BGE. Similarly, Kent subscribes to the Council for Environmental Education (CEE) and Learning Through Landscapes, and the news-sheets from these organizations are also included.

Contents of the BGE, usually over 20 items, are generally grouped to begin with local information from KCC about courses, Environmental Teachers' Support Groups (ETSG), school grounds developments, recycling opportunities and so on, followed by national information from NAEE, CEE, etc. Also included is regular information from the Kent Trust for Nature Conservation, Kent's Field Centres and a host of other organizations such as the Canterbury Urban Studies Centre or Whitbread Hop Farm. There are often special features, for example Cooperative Retail Services recently sponsored a poetry festival on the theme of 'Environmental Care' and this was coordinated in Kent through the BGE.

Communication with schools is a two-way process. Through the BGE, schools are invited to register for courses and conferences, ask for advisory support, or make suggestions as to themes for ETSG meetings or contents they would like to see in the BGE.

Sponsorship and support for the BGE have been assured for at least three years. The next step will be to find a way that, with the changes taking place in the school system, grant maintained and other schools will in the future be able to buy into the Environmental Education System.

Source: Krysia Baczala in *Environmental Education*,
NAEE journal, vol. 40, summer 1992

References

Agenda 21 (1992), United Nations Conference on Environment and Development (The Earth Summit).

Bennett, S.N. (1976) *Teaching Styles and Pupil Progress*, Wells Open Books.

Bloom, B.S. (ed.) (1956) *Taxonomy of Educational Objectives*, London, Longman.

Carson, R. (1962) *Silent Spring*, London, Penguin.

CEE (Council for Environmental Education) (1987) *Introducing Environmental Education. Book 2, Schools: Educating for Life*, Reading, CEE.

Cooper, D.E. and Palmer, J.A. (eds) (1992) *The Environment in Question*, London, Routledge.

Cooper, G. and Sterling, S. (1992) *In Touch: Environmental Education for Europe*, Godalming, World Wide Fund for Nature.

The Conservation and Development Programme for the UK (a response to the World Conservation Strategy) (1983), London, Kogan Page, ISBN O 85038 746 9.

Council of the European Community (1988) *Environmental Education*, Resolution of the Council and the Ministers of Education Meeting within the Council, 88/C177/03, 24 May.

DES (Department of Education and Science) (1967) *Children and their Primary Schools* (The Plowden Report), London, HMSO.

DES (1986) *The Curriculum from 5–16, Curriculum Matters 2*, London, HMSO.

DES (1989) *Environmental Education 5–16, Curriculum Matters 13*, London, HMSO.

DES (1991a) *Geography in the National Curriculum (England)*, London, HMSO.

DES (1991b) *History in the National Curriculum, Programme of Study for Key Stage 3*, London, HMSO.

DES and the Welsh Office (1991) *Science in the National Curriculum, Programme of Study for Key Stage 3*, London, HMSO.

Dewey, J. (1934) *Art As Experience*, New York, Minton, Balch.

Disinger, J. (1983) 'Environmental education's definitional problem', *ERIC Information Bulletin No. 2*, Ohio, ERIC.

Eisner, E.W. (1979) *The Educational Imagination*, New York, Macmillan.

Eisner, E.W. (1982) *Cognition and Curriculum*, New York, Longman.

Eisner, E.W. (1985) *The Art of Educational Evaluation*, Lewes, The Falmer Press.

Eisner, E.W. (1991) *The Enlightened Eye: Qualitative Inquiry and the Enhancement of Educational Practice*, New York, Macmillan.

Engel, R. and Engel, J. (1990) *Ethics of Environment and Development*, Belhaven Press.

Etobicoke Board of Education (1992) *West Humber Collegiate – An Environmentally Focused Secondary School*, Information Pack.

The Geographical Association (1992) *A Case for Fieldwork*, leaflet, Sheffield.

ICC (International Chamber of Commerce) (1989) *Environmental Auditing*, London, ICC Publishing.

IUCN (International Union for Conservation of Nature and Natural Resources) (1970) *International Working Meeting on Environmental Education in the School Curriculum, Final Report*, September, IUCN USA.

IUCN (1980) *The World Conservation Strategy*, IUCN/WWF/UNEP.

Kent County Council (1988) *An Education for Life. Kent Curriculum Statement: Children aged 5–16*, consultation document, Maidstone, Kent County Council.

Malcolm, S. (1990) *Local Action for a Better Environment*, published by the author, PO Box 452, Ringwood 3134, Victoria, Australia.

NAEE (National Association for Environmental Education) (1975, revised and reprinted 1982, 1992) *A Statement of Aims*, Walsall, NAEE.

NAEE (1987) *Traffic Study and Surveys*, Walsall, NAEE.

NAEE (1992) *Towards a School Policy for Environmental Education: An Environmental Audit*, Walsall, NAEE.

NAFSO (National Association for Field Study Officers) (1992) *The Value of Field Centres*, leaflet, Swansea, NAFSO.

NCC (National Curriculum Council) (1990a) *Curriculum Guidance 3: The Whole Curriculum*, York, NCC.

NCC (1990b) *Curriculum Guidance 7: Environmental Education*, York, NCC.

Neal, P. (1975) *Continuity in Education (Junior to Secondary)*, EDC Project Five, available from City of Birmingham Education Department.

New South Wales Department of Education (1989) *Environmental Education Guidelines*, Sydney, NSWDE.

New Zealand Natural Heritage Foundation (1991) *Environmental Education for Aotearoa/New Zealand. Booklet One. Overview for the Curriculum*, NZNHF.

Palmer, J.A. (1992) 'Life experiences of environmental educators: first report on autobiographical research data', *Environmental Education* 41, NAEE.

Schools Council (1974) *Project Environment*, Harlow, Longman.

Scottish Education Department (1974) *Environmental Education: Inspectors of Schools (Scotland)*, Edinburgh, HMSO Scotland.

SEEC (Scottish Environmental Education Council) (1987) *Curriculum Guidelines for Environmental Education*, Paisley, SSEC.

Sterling, S. (1990) 'Environment, development, education – towards an holistic view', in J. Abraham, C. Lacey and R. Williams (eds) *Deception, Demonstration and Debate*, London, WWF/Kogan Page.

Sterling, S. (1992) 'Mapping environmental education', in W.D.S. Leal Filho and J.A. Palmer (eds) *Key Issues in Environmental Education*, University of Bradford/ UNESCO.

Stodolsky, S.S. (ed.) (1988) *The Subject Matters*, Chicago, The University of Chicago Press.

UNESCO (1975) 'Trends in environmental education', based on working documents for the Belgrade Conference.

UNESCO (1977) *Final Report*, First Intergovernmental Conference on Environmental Education, Tbilisi, Paris, UNESCO.

UNESCO (1987) 'Environmental education in the light of the Tbilisi Conference, Education on the Move', Paris, UNESCO.

Wiltshire County Council (1989) *Wiltshire Curriculum Policy 5–16* (revision), Salisbury, WCC.

Wolverhampton Environmental Awareness Unit (1984) minutes, quoted by B. Milton in *Bulletin for Environmental Education* 163, December.

World Commission on Environment and Development (1987) *Our Common Future*, Milton Keynes, OUP Gland.

Index